PEARL HARBOR TO TOKYO BAY

PACIFIC WAR COMBAT MISSIONS

PEARL HARBOR TO TOKYO BAY

PACIFIC WAR COMBAT MISSIONS

FIRST-HAND ACCOUNTS OF AIR, LAND, AND SEA OPS IN THE PTO

CHRIS McNAB

METRO BOOKS
NEW YORK

METRO BOOKS
New York

An Imprint of Sterling Publishing Co., Inc.
1166 Avenue of the Americas
New Tork, NY 10036

© 2016 by Elephant Book Company Limited

ISBN: 978-1-4351-6057-6

For information about custom editions, special sales, and
premium and corporate purchases, please contact
Sterling Special Sales at 800-805-5489
or specialsales@sterlingpublishing.com

Manufactured in China

2 4 6 8 10 9 7 5 3 1

www.sterlingpublishing.com

Editorial Director: Will Steeds
Project Manager/Author: Chris McNab
Designer: Philip Clucas MSIAD
Front cover illustration: "Uncommon Valor" by Roy Grinnell
Photographer: Patrick Bunce
Color reproduction: Pixel Colour Imaging Ltd., London

Roy Grinnell, Official Artist of the American Fighter Aces
Association and the American Combat Airman Hall of Fame
(Commemorative Air Force), was an honors graduate of the
Art Center School in Los Angeles. He has received many honors
and awards including the R.G. Smith Award for Excellence in
Naval Aviation Art, becoming an Honorary Ace of the AFAA,
and most recently the opening of the Roy Grinnell Gallery in
the American Airpower Heritage Museum (CAF) in Midland,
TX. He is also well known for his Western and Native American
art. Grinnell's oil paintings have been displayed throughout the
world in museums and private collections. His work also
features on the covers of *B-24 Combat Missions* and *Spitfire:
Life of the Legend*. (Website: www.roygrinnell.com)

The author would like to thank Mike Lebens, Curator of
Collections at the National Pacific War Museum, Texas, for his
assistance in sourcing textual materials and memorabilia images,
and for the museum's general support behind this publication.
Thanks also go to Patrick Bunce for the original photography,
Ted Cody for supplying archive images, and to Phil Clucas for his
always excellent work on the design and layout. Final thanks are
due to Chad Daniels, Director, Mississippi Armed Forces Museum,
for doing a thorough expert read of this title, and to Will Steeds
and Laura Ward of Elephant Books for their support throughout
this project.

Contents

Introduction

The Pacific War has always had a special hold over my historical imagination. What must it have been like, I have asked myself, to be a young man of, say, nineteen years old, born and brought up in the pleasant continuity of 1920s and 1930s suburban America? Equally, what must it have been like for that same young man to be uprooted and transported from a generally temperate, largely predictable world, into a tropical, violent, and war-torn region thousands of miles from home?

The shock of being thrust into uniform in the first place would probably have been significant in itself. Whether volunteer or conscript, the young man would have to mature rapidly as he donned a uniform and underwent rigorous physical and tactical training, forcing his body to strengthen and his mind to adopt the discipline and resilience of a soldier. If he passed all training satisfactorily, and was accepted into the ranks, then came deployment. About 5.4 million American soldiers served overseas in World War II. The majority of these—more than 3 million—went to the European Theater of Operations (ETO). While the experience of combat there could be just as traumatic as it could be in the Pacific Theater of Operations (PTO), there was much about Europe that would be familiar to the Americans soldier, not least the fairly benign climate and landscape. For some 1.3 million US servicemen who went to the Pacific, however, the contrast between their home lives and their service lives could be absolute. Most of these young men had to adjust to the scorching heat and oppressive humidity of the tropics, plus the vast oceanic distances and claustrophobic jungle landscapes that were utterly alien to their pre-war experience. In such terrain, many would have to fight in the most brutal conditions imaginable.

This book, drawing extensively on the archives of the National Museum of the Pacific War, collects the first-hand accounts of dozens of such men. It reveals their experiences from the daily grind of boredom and heat, through to the intensive life-or-death struggles in far-flung corners of the Pacific and East Asia against a implacably fanatical enemy. Of course, this is not solely an American story. On December 7, 1941, the Japanese unleashed their infamous attack on the US Pacific Fleet at Pearl Harbor, transforming what had been a European, Middle Eastern, and North African conflict into a truly global war. With this act, the strategic isolationism that had run strong throughout American politics crumbled, and the United States had to plunge into a major multi-theater conflict. At the same time, imperial powers such as the French, British, and Dutch saw their Eastern colonies steadily stripped from their possession by a seemingly unstoppable Japanese offensive. Thus the Pacific War drew in soldiers, sailors, airmen, and marines from across the globe, such as the sizable British deployment to the China–Burma–India (CBI) Theater, and the commitment of Australians and New Zealanders to New Guinea. Some of their stories are also given here.

Yet it remains the fact that the Pacific War was a conflict dominated by two ideological and military opponents—the United States and Japan. The Japanese government and its armed forces, imbued with militaristic nationalism and the desire for empire, planned on a short and decisive campaign, cutting off the head of the Pacific Fleet at Pearl Harbor and rapidly conquering a huge swathe of Pacific and East Asian territory. Its offensive strategy was certainly, initially, successful. By mid 1942, the Japanese domain stretched from northern China down to near the coast of Australia, and from Burma to the mid Pacific. Through this huge territorial acquisition, the Japanese authorities hoped that not only would the country be able to obtain all the raw materials it desperately desired for the country's continuing hegemony, but it would also create a huge defensible perimeter against which the United States would batter itself to a negotiated defeat.

As events subsequently transpired, this plan did not produce the conflict that the Japanese desired. The United States, scalded into action by the nefarious attack on Pearl Harbor, transformed itself rapidly into the greatest military power the world had ever seen. The economy was reconfigured dramatically for the exigencies of war. In the process, the United States truly became the "arsenal of democracy," producing volumes of weapons, vehicles, ships, aircraft, and other materiel in volumes far greater than anything either Germany or Japan could match. To give just one example of this disparity, between 1939 and 1945 Japan produced 76,320 military aircraft. The United States manufactured 324,750. Thus by 1944, the United States had built up an unassailable physical strength and firepower in the Pacific, qualities that were channeled by excellent military training, prodigious logistical efficiency, and the growing confidence in the ability to win. Japan, by contrast, was locked in a war of attrition that it simply could not sustain over the long term.

What Japan could do, however, was fight with the ferocity of a nation imbued with renewed warrior traditions and a deep-seated fear of ignominious defeat. One key characteristic of fighting in the Pacific Theater was its almost absolute lack of mercy, with the Japanese troops fighting with a suicidal disregard for life, often for seemingly irrelevant and tiny scraps of land dotted around a vast ocean. The island of Tarawa, for example, was just 2 miles (3km) long and, at its widest point, 800yds (732m) wide. Yet despite the humble nature of its geography, Tarawa saw 4,690 Japanese soldiers and Korean construction laborers fight to the death. Of the 3,636 actual soldiers on Tarawa, only seventeen surrendered. Taking the island cost the US Marine Corps and US Navy 1,696 killed and 2,101 wounded.

This theme, of terrible cost for minor territorial gain, continued throughout the Pacific War, and burned names such as Peleliu, Saipan, Iwo Jima, and Okinawa into historical memory. But the Pacific War was not just a conflict of small island amphibious battles, although these were critical to the eventual victory. In fact, the Pacific conflict was a struggle of diverse forms. It included some of the longest campaigns of the war, such as the British and American fight in Burma, and the US struggle to secure the Solomons. It ranged from harrowing guerrilla-warfare-like struggles in the Burmese jungle through to major urban battles in the Philippines. Nor was the combat just expressed in tropical zones; soldiers in the Aleutians fought in near arctic conditions. New types and instruments of warfare emerged. In the naval domain, the aircraft carrier truly came of age, emerging as one of the primary instruments of strategic decision. The tactics, techniques, and logistics of amphibious warfare were honed to perfection by the United States. Conversely, the US Navy had to face one of the most alarming acts of martial desperation—the kamikaze aircraft that unleashed suicidal destruction on the Allied forces off the Philippines, Okinawa, and other locations.

Ultimately, the Pacific War was brought to a conclusion by the most terrifying revolution in warfare—the atomic bomb—two of which were dropped on Japan in August 1945. Yet the mushroom clouds of these weapons should not obscure the sacrifice and endurance of hundreds of thousands of individual Allied servicemen and women, and the part that they each played in the destruction of the brutal Japanese empire. Through the collection of stories gathered here, and the history retold, this book remains an imperfect tribute to their memory.

Dr. Chris McNab
Author/Historian

PART 1
The Road to War

Origins of a Widening War

"Yesterday, December 7, 1941—a date which will live in infamy—the United States of America was suddenly and deliberately attacked by naval and air forces of the Empire of Japan. . . . With confidence in our armed forces—with the unbounded determination of our people—we will gain the inevitable triumph—so help us God."

—President Roosevelt to the US Congress, December 8, 1941

Although there are parallels between Germany's descent into war-hungry fascism, and Japan's equally precipitous slide into militaristic nationalism, in many ways Japan's road to the Pacific War is more nuanced. After all, Germany ended World War I in catastrophic defeat, the financial and political ignominy of which sowed the seeds of Adolf Hitler's subsequent rise to power. Japan, by contrast, fought on the Allied side in that conflict, however, and seemed to enter the 1920s as an internationally accepted and politically liberal-leaning nation. In the long term, however, such outward appearances were to be deceptive.

Prior to the 1920s, Japan had many reasons for self-confidence. It had built up for itself a powerful and respected military, which had defeated Russia in the Russo-Japanese War of 1904–05 and had become the most potent force in East Asia. Militaristic expansion did appear ingrained in Japanese thinking, as illustrated by its annexation of Korea in 1910 and its bullying occupations of north-east China from 1915. (The island of Formosa, modern-day Taiwan, had been occupied back in 1895.) Yet there were also moderating influences within Japanese society and government. By the end of 1918, Japan had a modern multi-party government and a liberal Prime Minister, Takashi Hara. Western cultural influences were shaking loose some of the social and political rigidities of the past, aided by a rising prosperity and a flourishing consumer goods industry. Even militarism appeared to be tempered, particularly

Left: A recruitment poster for the Japanese Army's Tank School, reflecting the vigorous militarism that gripped Japan during the 1930s.

through postwar reductions in the size of the army and limitations on the size of the Imperial Japanese Navy (IJN) in relation to the navies of the United States and Great Britain, as agreed at the Washington Disarmament Conference in 1921–22. Thus while the Western nations occasionally raised their concerns over aggressive Japanese attitudes toward China, where the United States had long-standing religious and economic interests, in general Japan offered little indication of the threat to the global order it would pose by the early 1940s.

The faultlines were there, however. Pushing back against the liberalization and Westernization of Japanese culture was a strong nationalist undercurrent, centered particularly on certain groups within the Japanese military leadership and around extremist right-wing organizations such as the *Ketsumeidan* (League of Blood) and *Kokusuikia* (National Purity Society). These groups wanted a firm rejection of Western culture, returning to the purity of a past embedded in warrior virtues. Furthermore, they believed, in a manner reminiscent of Hitler's belief in the German need for *Lebensraum* ("growing room"), that Japan's future lay in territorial conquest and expansion.

There was a certain twisted logic to this last belief, one that is an essential ingredient in the story of Japan's road to war. Japan's

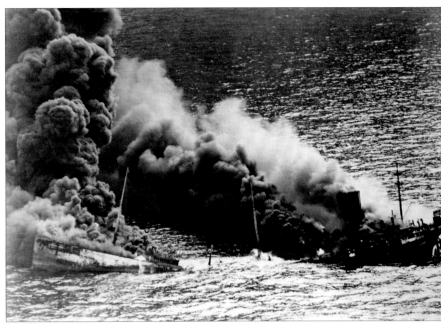

leadership and armed forces were acutely aware that Japan had significantly limited access to raw materials within its own borders. The country's industrial and military expansion, and its ability to feed a swelling population, was largely dependent upon importation of vital materials such as coal, iron, oil, bauxite, rubber, and rice. Rather than seeing this dependence as an opportunity to develop expanding international trade, the hardened nationalists saw the situation in terms of humiliation and vulnerability, which could be rectified by taking what they did not own.

The extremist influences in Japan kept pushing their way to the surface, often brutally, such as in the murder of Hara in 1921. But as in Nazi Germany, it was economic hardship that truly opened the door for the warmakers. In the late 1920s, Japan was plunged into the global depression, resulting in financial collapse (thirty-six major banks were closed in 1929 alone), destitution for many, especially in the already improverished rural areas, and the increasing power of the nationalist radicals. Many in the military leadership advocated the return to a non-democratic military-style government, under the supreme authority of the Emperor (Emperor Hirohito from 1926). At the same time, they pushed for military options to end Japan's material dependence, while also steadily bullying political and economic opponents into submission. The militarists were keen to break loose from Western armament limitations, seen most visibly in their virulent resistance to the disarmament terms of the London Naval Treaty in 1930.

The late 1920s and the 1930s in Japan have been labeled the "Dark Valley," on account of the brutal nationalism into which the country descended. The phrase is apt. Levels of political repression against

Above left: A column of Japanese troops moves through the Chinese landscape during the largely victorious Japanese operations of 1938.

Above right: The German sinking of British and even American shipping in the Atlantic put a severe pressure on US isolationism in 1940–41.

Above: British children sit outside the wreckage of bombed-out homes in London, 1940. By December 1941, Britain was weakened by two years of war.

ideological opponents increased, particularly against those of either a Marxist or very liberal persuasion. The murder of politicians became commonplace, such as the killing of the Prime Minister Yuko Hamaguchi in August 1931 and that of Prime Minister Tsuyoshi Unukai in May 1932. Other moderating figures were driven from office and public life.

Japan's government was also steadily losing control of its military forces. In the late summer of 1931, the Japanese Kwantung Army, stationed in the Kwantung region of Manchuria to protect Japanese commercial interests there, unilaterally invaded the rest of the country, following a staged Chinese bombing on a Japanese-owned rail line. Despite both Emperor Hirohito and his Foreign Minister, Kijuro Shidehara, being vociferously opposed to the action, they were thwarted by the regional commanders and by the Japanese War Minister, General Jiro Minami.

The expansion continued throughout Manchuria, northern China, and into Mongolia. The brakes also came off military expenditure. In 1931, the total military expenditure was 29.4 percent of the overall government budget; by 1935 it was nearly 47 percent; by 1938 it would reach an astonishing 75.4 percent. From the assassination of Prime Minister Unukai in 1932, the military was effectively in control of the

Left: Isoroku Yamamoto was the commander-in-chief of the Japanese Combined Fleet from the beginning of the Pacific War until his death in April 1943.

government (although an attempted outright military coup in 1936 was put down), so such diversions of investment were straightforward. The power of the army was illustrated when it, not the Japanese Foreign Ministry, negotiated the Anti-Comintern Pact with Nazi Germany in 1936, establishing an alliance that would eventually make the Axis a global entity.

In 1937, again after the engineering of an contrived "incident," Japan's armed forces launched a full-scale invasion of China, beginning a war that would last until 1945. The invasion included atrocities that still haunt the world to this day, such as the "Rape of Nanking," in which up to 300,000 civilians were murdered following the Japanese occupation of the city. In 1940–41, Japan also moved into and occupied French Indochina; by this point France had been conquered by Germany, so

Below: A unit of Chiang Kai-shek's Chinese Nationalist Army conducts a drill in 1940. Although the Nationalist forces were combat experienced, they generally lacked good leadership, and morale and fighting efficiency were typically poor.

Above: *The British Prime Minister Winston Churchill fires a .30-cal. carbine during a visit to the US 2nd Armored Division on the UK, March 23, 1944. Churchill worked hard in 1939–40 to bring the United States into the conflict as an Allied partner.*

Far right: *A newspaper seller broadcasts the new reality for the United States on December 8, 1941—the country was now at war with Japan.*

country's strategic reach, particularly in terms of the naval shipbuilding program. Yet several key events began to galvanize Roosevelt, and slowly the US government, to take firmer action against Japan. The first was the Japanese invasion of China, and the second was the unfolding war in Europe in 1939–40. America was at this time largely isolationist in outlook, not eager to become embroiled in another of Europe's conflicts. Roosevelt pushed back against this sentiment, as suggested by this excerpt from one of his speeches, delivered on December 29, 1940: "At this moment the forces of the States that are leagued against all peoples who live in freedom are being held away from our shores. The Germans and the Italians are being blocked on the other side of the Atlantic by the British and by the Greeks, and by thousands of soldiers and sailors who were able to escape from subjugated countries. In Asia the Japanese are being engaged by the Chinese nation in another great defense. In the Pacific Ocean is our fleet. Some of our people like to believe that wars in Europe and in Asia are of no concern to us. But it is a matter of most vital concern to us that European and Asiatic war-makers should not gain control of the oceans which lead to this hemisphere."

Roosevelt's sense of threat is acute, seeing the distance between the United States and the foreign wars as no cast-iron guarantee of American safety in the future. Certainly, the overseas conflicts began to intrude more and more into American consciousness. On December 12, 1937, the American gunboat USS *Panay* was on patrol along the Yangtze River in China, part of the US Asiatic Fleet attempting to protect American citizens and interests in China. Despite being painted in American flags, the *Panay* came under air attack from Japanese aircraft, resulting in the ship's sinking plus the

death of three crew members and the wounding of forty-three others. Three Standard Oil tankers were also attacked in the same incident. The sinking of the *Panay* sharpened US hostility towards Japan, and Japan's shallow protestations that the bombing was an accident was largely not bought into by the American press and public.

America's isolationism was challenged further during the war years of 1939 to 1940, especially once the Atlantic became a battleground that directly endangered American shipping. In March 1941 Roosevelt signed the Lend-Lease Act, a bill that enabled the United States to

was in no position to resist the move. Japan also cemented its associations with the Axis by signing up to the Tripartite Pact with Germany and Italy in September 1940.

So where was the international community, and particularly the United States, while Japan was developing its ambitions? Naturally, Japan's actions were alienating it from much of the rest of the world. Following Japan's 1931 invasion of Manchuria, the League of Nations had ineffectively tried to enforce a Japanese withdrawal, the outcome of which was that Japan simply pulled out of the organization. Generally, however, Japan was able to steer its course enduring little but censure.

In some ways, matters began to change in the 1933, when the United States received a new President, Franklin Delano Roosevelt. From the outset of his presidency, Roosevelt was aware of the possibility of a future war with Japan, and began a limited boost of the

Right: Hitler and Mussolini were European partners in the Tripartite Agreement between Germany, Italy, and Japan.
Below: A German antitank crew in action in the Soviet Union in 1941. By the time of the Pearl Harbor attack, most of Europe was under Axis control.

organizing powers to give you the strength to regain and maintain a free world. We shall send you in ever-increasing numbers, ships, planes, tanks, guns. That is our purpose and our pledge.'"

The primary focus of the Lend-Lease program was sustaining Britain against the Germans, but China was also a beneficiary. By this time the United States had already increased the commercial credits extended to China, enabling them to purchase more weapons and equipment, and the Chinese Lend-Lease investment would total $846 million, on top of $643 million in other credits.

The Japanese armed forces, under the leadership of General Hideki Tojo (War Minister 1940–41, then Prime Minister from 1941 to 1944), would have been painfully aware of the implications of the industrial backing of China by the United States, especially when compared with its own difficulties in acquiring raw materials. Access to strategic goods was becoming more pressing, and the breakdown of commercial treaties between the United States and Japan meant that Roosevelt was beginning to put the squeeze on the importation of materials into Japan. By this time, a planned military solution was already taking shape. The intention was simple. What industrial and raw material resources Japan lacked within its borders, it could acquire through direct conquest. Take Burma, Malaya, the Dutch East Indies, and the Philippines, plus a range of other Pacific and East Asian territories (including larger swathes of China), and Japan would reach a position of self-sufficiency that could sustain its military growth and regional hegemony.

provide war materiel to Britain and China, essentially free of charge until the war was over. In a speech delivered the preceding January, Roosevelt justified this move to the nation: "I do not recommend that we make them a loan of dollars with which to pay for these weapons— a loan to be repaid in dollars. I recommend that we make it possible for those nations to continue to obtain war materials in the United States, fitting their orders into our own program. And nearly all of their material would, if the time ever came, be useful in our own defense. Taking counsel of expert military and naval authorities, considering what is best for our own security, we are free to decide how much should be kept here and how much should be sent abroad to our friends who, by their determined and heroic resistance, are giving us time in which to make ready our own defense. For what we send abroad we shall be repaid, repaid within a reasonable time following the close of hostilities, repaid in similar materials, or at our option in other goods of many kinds which they can produce and which we need. Let us say to the democracies: 'We Americans are vitally concerned in your defense of freedom. We are putting forth our energies, our resources, and our

Of course, the Japanese government attempted to give this imperialism a veneer of respectability. Japan offered itself as the head of what would be known as the "Greater East Asia Co-Prosperity Sphere." In theory, this was an offer for all the colonized nations of East Asia to throw off the shackles of European colonial rule and American influence, and embrace independence plus profitable regional trade relations, free from Western dominance. The rhetoric of the proposal was very much that of "Asia for the Asians," but as the war itself would later show, there was no feeling of solidarity between the Japanese nationalists and the wider Pacific and Asian peoples. In reality, Tojo and his cabinet looked at the region as little more than a cornucopia of material wealth, which Japan could tap into by military conquest and the violent crushing of any resistance.

The Japanese takeover of Indochina raised the threat of war even higher. It was now clear to the West that Japan was pursuing a methodical campaign of expansion, and it responded with the economic sanctions it knew would sting the Japanese most. On July 26, 1941,

Roosevelt announced that his government would now take measures to freeze all Japanese assets within the United States, and would also sever all trading relations with Japan. This last point was crucial, as it meant that Japan would receive no more of the American oil on which its militarization and industrialization depended. Nor could it look easily elsewhere to fill the gaps. Both the UK and the Netherlands implemented similar measures to those of the Americans, cutting off oil, minerals, and food supplies from the European colonies in Asia.

The Japanese government now faced a stark choice. Either it went to war to take the natural resources it lacked, or it faced a form of economic starvation as the embargoes took hold. Of course, it could comply with the American demands that Japan withdraw from China and Indochina, but for the military leadership the loss of face and power left this option untenable. On September 6, 1941, the Japanese held an imperial conference, which came to the conclusion that Japan would have to execute its plans for war if an agreement with the United States could not be reached by early October. Attempts to establish talks failed, and on November 16 Prime Minister Konoe fell from power, replaced by the more belligerent Tojo.

The United States, thanks to the insight provided by its MAGIC intelligence, was fully aware of the Japanese preparations for war. What they didn't know was the specific war plan, designed by IJN commander-in-chief Admiral Isoroku Yamamoto. Yamamoto was not a fan of the idea of war against the United States, having spent time there, where he became aware of the vast industrial potential of the nation. Yamamoto believed that if Japan was to have any chance of victory, the key was to expand the perimeter of conquest as widely and as quickly as possible, then hold onto this perimeter from a strong negotiating position. There were two threads to his plan. First, he would launch an audacious carrier strike against the US Pacific Fleet at Pearl Harbor, intending to destroy America's capacity to respond to events further east. Second, as the Pearl Harbor strike was going in, Japanese forces would begin a lightning offensive throughout East Asia and the Pacific, aiming to conquer Burma, Malaya, Singapore, Hong Kong, the Philippines, the Solomon Islands, the Dutch East Indies, and a host of other islands and territories. Once conquered, these places could be turned into fortresses against which any counteroffensive would be broken.

The plan was high risk, and Yamamoto had to push it through against some resistance. Yet it was ratified, and as talks between Japan and Washington pushed on fruitlessly through November, Japanese forces began concrete preparations for action. The US government remained largely committed to avoiding war, but pushed back against ultimatums from Tokyo on November 20. On November 26, with arguments still rattling backward and forward, the Japanese High Fleet sailed for Pearl Harbor.

Left: Hideki Tojo, the militaristic ruler of Japan, was Prime Minister from 1941 to 1944.

Below: An aerial view of Pearl Harbor. The orderly arrangement of the shipping in the harbor made target acquisition easier for the Japanese attack aircraft.

The Rival Forces

"You marched about two weeks without a rifle and learned
how to close-order drill. Then they issue you with the M1 rifle. . . .
You get the rifle issued to you, the serial number is recorded, and
you immediately learn that serial number and it stays with you. . . .
My first rifle that I ever had. I never wrote it down or anything."

—US Marine Wayburn Hall

The Pacific War, when it broke out in December 1941, brought three disparate armed forces into conflict. On the one hand were the aggressors, the Japanese, a rigorously martial and freshly militarized country, well-trained and equipped for a continental war. Against them were, principally, Great Britain and its empire allies, and the United States. Britain had already been locked in war for more than two years in Europe, the Balkans, and North Africa, conflicts that had honed its war skills while also wearing down its forces through attrition and exhaustion, leaving it ill-placed to fight a fresh conflict in Asia. The United States' armed services, by contrast, were fresh and largely inexperienced and undermanned, but with the enormous potential for industrialized growth looming high in the background. It was such armed forces that would decide the fate of nearly half the earth's surface and its peoples.

Looking first at the United States, America was defended my four major organizations: the US Army, the US Army Air Forces (USAAF), US Navy, and the US Marine Corps (USMC). Technically, the USAAF—which administratively replaced the US Army Air Corps (USAAC) in June 1941—was part of the US Army, but its growth and status demanded a more autonomous stature, and in March 1942 the US Army was divided into three administrative organizations with equal status: the USAAF; the Army Ground Forces; and the Services of Supply (later called Army Service Forces). Similarly, the USMC belonged under the umbrella of the Department of the Navy, but while it certainly had

Left: A US Army recruitment poster encourages young men to join the services. The age range on the poster indicates the youthfulness of the average GI.

a lot of unilateral authority, it did not have a representation on the Joint Chiefs of Staff (JCS) until after the war, unlike the USAAF.

The US Army was the largest of the US armed services, but it had to undergo a dramatic transformation to fight a global conflict. At the beginning of the war in Europe in 1939, it had a regular army of about 190,000 troops, 200,000 part-time National Guardsmen, plus a body of men assigned to the Organized Reserve (composed of the Officers Reserve Corps and Enlisted Reserve Corps). With war in one theater or another appearing likely, Roosevelt initiated conscription through the Selective Service Act in 1940, and the Army began a period of inexorable growth. By the end of December 1941, with the Pacific War just weeks old, the US Army's ground arms and special services (engineers, signals, medical etc.) numbered 1.3 million. One year later that figure had risen to 3.8 million, and by March 1945 it was at a staggering 5.5 million.

Of course, not all of these men were destined to fight in the Pacific. In fact, the majority of the US Army served in the European and Mediterranean Theaters. If we look at the percentages of Army combat troops deployed in late April 1945, 69.7 percent were in the European and Mediterranean Theaters combined, while just 22.2 percent were in

the Southwest Pacific, Pacific Ocean, and China–Burma–India (CBI) Theaters combined. Of the eleven US Army field armies that were deployed in the war, only the 6th, 8th, and 10th Armies went to the Pacific, where they nonetheless made a vital contribution to the eventual victory, particularly in the Philippines and at the battle of Okinawa.

There were also key differences within the US Army regarding Pacific tactics and unit composition. In the Pacific, US divisions and regiments were often "lighter" in composition, particularly in terms of armored support and mechanization, when compared to ETO and MTO formations, a situation dictated by the unique geography of the Pacific combat zones, and the need to deploy almost everything through amphibious landings. Indeed, in 1942–43 the US Army even formed three specialist light divisions purposely for the conditions of jungle warfare, although ultimately these were replaced in theater by regular Army divisions.

In contrast to the US Army, the other major ground forces component of the US armed services—the USMC—was almost exclusively deployed to the Pacific, where its amphibious warfare rationale and training meant that it naturally formed the vanguard of the "island-hopping" campaign through the Central Pacific. In June 1939, the USMC consisted of 19,432 officers and enlisted men. Around 25 percent of that figure belonged to the Fleet Marine Force (FMF), an amphibious landing component separated into the 1st and 2nd Brigades. Each brigade had the backing of a Marine Aviation Group (AVG); like the Army and the Navy, the Marines could call on their own aviation support. In February 1941, the FMF brigades were renamed as divisions as the USMC grew; by November 1941, the Corps' strength was at 65,881. By the end of the war, that strength had spiraled upwards to nearly half a million men, which included 128 squadrons of air support. The Marines were also active in the development of special forces units suited to guerrilla-style actions in the Pacific, such as the four Raider battalions, the first (1st and 2nd) formed in February 1942 but all four combined to create the 4th Marine Regiment in January 1944.

Like the Army and Marine Corps, the US Navy was also transformed both materially and tactically by World War II, not least by the huge naval combat and logistical demands placed upon it by the war in the Pacific. Manpower climbed from just under 161,000 in July 1940 to

Top: *US Marine Corps Raiders, an elite amphibious warfare unit, conduct a training exercise in the United States.*

Above: *Boeing workers gather to hear an address by Captain Hewitt T. Wheless, a bomber pilot who served with distinction in the Pacific Theater.*

Far right: *An American mother reads a letter from one of her four sons, all of whom enlisted to serve in the armed forces.*

3.4 million by August 1945. In June 1940 the Navy had 1,099 ships (all types) at its disposal, but 67,952 by June 1945, representing one of the greatest achievements of US industry. Furthermore, the US Navy's air arm—both carrier based and land based—swelled to become a major component of American airpower, with nearly half a million air personnel by the end of war, and operating some 75,000 aircraft during the war years.

At its highest level, the US Navy was split into two main commands, the Atlantic Command and the Pacific Command. The beating heart of the Pacific Command at the start of the war was the base at Pearl Harbor, Hawaii, home to the Pacific Fleet. Just prior to the Japanese attack on Pearl Harbor, the Pacific Fleet consisted of nine battleships, three aircraft carriers, thirteen heavy cruisers, eleven light cruisers, sixty-seven destroyers, and twenty-seven submarines. Backing up the Pacific Fleet was also the oft-forgotten Asiatic Fleet, based principally around the Philippine Islands and Borneo. In December 1941 it was organized around three cruisers, thirteen destroyers, twenty-nine submarines, six

gunboats, and two seaplane tenders. What is apparent in the fleet compositions in the Pacific is that US naval development prior to the onset of war was heavily focused on battleships, cruisers, and destroyers, rather than the true future of naval warfare—submarines and aircraft carriers. For comparison, in December 1941 the IJN had sixty-eight fleet submarines, fifty midget submarines, and fourteen aircraft carriers, with seven more aircraft carriers under construction.

Of course, US industry more than made up for the deficit in hardware as the war went on, far outstripping Japan (and indeed everyone else) in one of the greatest feats of shipbuilding the world has ever witnessed. The ships that went to the Pacific Theater, prior to February 1943, were divided between the South-West Pacific Area, South Pacific Command, and Central Command, which in 1943–44 became the 7th, 3rd, and 5th Fleets respectively. To confuse matters somewhat, in June 1944 the 3rd and 5th Fleets were combined into one mighty fleet, but alternated between the 3rd and 5th Fleet titles depending on who was commanding it.

The Pacific fleets, subdivided into mighty task groups and task forces, eventually came to rule the Pacific, albeit at a high cost in lives and ships. Their eventual dominance of the submarine and carrier war in particular, plus the mastery of amphibious warfare and associated logistics, meant that the United States was able from late 1943 to achieve air superiority, strangle Japan of supplies, and maintain a thumping tempo in the advance across the Pacific toward Japan itself.

The USAAF boasts wartime growth figures every bit as impressive as those of the other services, rising from just 2,470 aircraft and some 25,000 personnel in 1939 to nearly 80,000 aircraft and 1.9 million personnel in 1945. In the Pacific, however, it took time and the progressive capture of advanced island bases to enable the air force to build up its capacity against the Japanese. Thus in January 1942, the USAAF was able to deploy just 1,622 aircraft to the Pacific, but by July 1945 there were 7,260 in-theater. Note that these figures were small against the 14,648 US Navy and USMC aircraft deployed by the July 1945 date. Much of the USAAF effort in the Pacific was concentrated in its specialties of strategic bombing and tactical support. The main air forces sent to the Pacific War were the 5th, 7th, 10th, 13th, 14th, and 20th.

Above: Japanese troops in the China Theater find a novel way of moving around the countryside. China became a huge drain on Japanese manpower resources as the attrition of the Pacific War bit hard.

There are many factors behind the eventual US victory in the Pacific War, apart from just the industrial muscle the country brought to the conflict. The US armed services became relentless innovators, at both technical and tactical levels, so that deficiencies at the beginning of

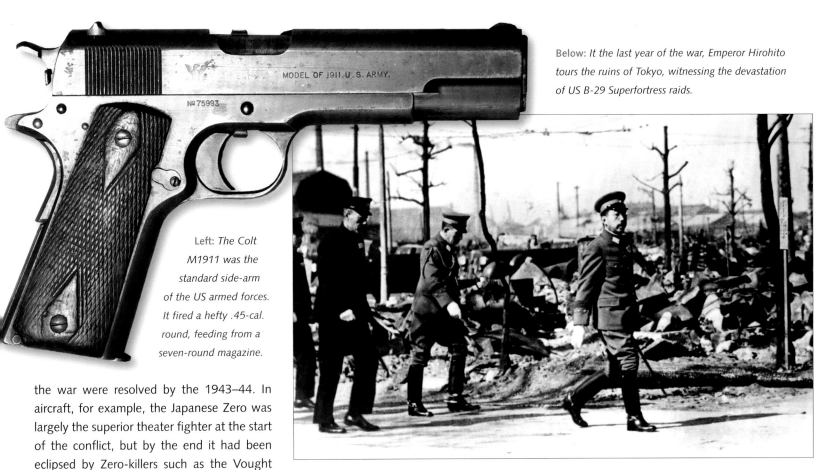

Left: *The Colt M1911 was the standard side-arm of the US armed forces. It fired a hefty .45-cal. round, feeding from a seven-round magazine.*

the war were resolved by the 1943–44. In aircraft, for example, the Japanese Zero was largely the superior theater fighter at the start of the conflict, but by the end it had been eclipsed by Zero-killers such as the Vought F4U Corsair and the Grumman F6F Hellcat. US Army and Marine Corps firepower came to be utterly superior to that of the Japanese soldiers opposing them, right down to the level of an individual rifle (in the M1 Garand). US amphibious tactics became more fluid and faster than anything the Japanese could match. Training was also superior, especially as the war progressed and the Japanese were forced to cut once-rigorous

training schedules down to ineffective minimums. Wayburn Hal, who joined the Marine Corps in 1943, remembers the essential toughness of training at Boot Camp: "At Boot Camp, everybody got the same training. You were considered a non-person until the day you graduated in Boot Camp. . . Any Marine who goes through Boot Camp takes the same kind of training. It is based on infantry, military training. We learned close-order drill and marching. We had to go through the gas tents, learning to use the gas mask. You had to jump off a thirty-foot tower with your gear on. That is just part of daily training. . . . We did some practice [amphibious] landings, because we were right on the bay, from Higgins Boats in December [1943]. You got soaking wet and you froze to death. It got a little tough at times. If we made one mistake . . . they would take us out on the hard surface, which they called the 'Boondocks.' That's the sand that comes up off the beaches out there. They would get us in a circle and make us run around holding our rifles at high port. You almost dropped. . . . You marched about two weeks without a rifle and learned how to close-order drill. Then they issue you with the M1 rifle. It comes packed up in a box, maybe six rifles to a box packed in cosmoline, which

Left: *A Japanese 70mm howitzer team in action. Although the Japanese invested in heavy militarization during the 1920s and 1930s, meaningful weapons development was poor during the war years.*

is some kind of special grease for guns and rifles. You get the rifle issued to you, the serial number is recorded, and you immediately learn that serial number and it stays with you . . . My first rifle that I ever had. I never wrote it down or anything."

The United States had many allies in the war in the Far East, not least the United Kingdom and its imperial forces. During the 19th century, Great Britain had forged the greatest empire in history, its colonies including Canada, Egypt, South Africa, India, Burma, Malaya, and Australia. By the time the Pacific War broke out in December 1941, cracks were starting to appear in Britain's imperial marble. Two years of war against the Germans, first in Northern Europe, then extending down into the Balkans and North Africa, had left the nation overstretched in terms of prosecuting another war across its Asian possessions, territories which were often showing signs of internal dissent over imperial rule anyway, especially in India. The fight for survival of the British mainland in Europe, plus the effort of defeating Rommel in North Africa (to protect Britain's oil reserves in the Middle East), would always take priority, hence deployments to the Far East were relatively limited in terms of the British

Above: At the height of the "Battle of Britain," RAF pilots race toward their Hurricane fighters to meet incoming German aircraft. By 1942, Britain had limited air resources to deploy to the East Asian Theater.

Left: British troops who escaped the German occupation of France unwind on a street in London in 1940, thankful to be at liberty.

Army. Thus during the war 2.64 million British soldiers served overseas in the Army, yet of those only 390,000 were deployed to the Far East. After the initial, disastrous, loss of Malaya, Hong Kong, and Singapore, most of these troops were deployed to India and Burma. We should not forget that 399,000 colonial Indian troops also served during World War II, enabling Britain to bolster its field manpower under the pressure from the Japanese. Tens of thousands of Australians and New Zealanders also fought for the Allied cause in the Pacific, largely alongside American rather than British forces.

In December 1941, the British Army presence in the region was embodied in two major commands: Far East Command, responsible for

land forces defense of Malaya and Hong Kong, and India Command, which looked after India and Burma. Burma had previously been within the purview of the Far East Command, but was transferred to India Command in December 1941. The grevious losses and gathering threats both commands suffered in the opening Japanese campaigns forced command restructuring. At the beginning of 1942, the Allied forces in the region collectively formed the American-British-Dutch-Australian (ABDA) Command, or ABDACOM, a unified cross-service command under the British Army general Archibald Wavell that was meant to protect territories from Malaya down to the northern Australian coastline. Yet the command's apparent inability to stop the Japanese juggernaut meant that it essentially ceased to exist by March 1942. In its place eventually came the more extensive South-East Asia Command (SEAC), which held sway from 1943 until 1946.

The inclusion of British forces within wider multinational commands became the norm for the ships and crews of the Royal Navy in the Pacific. Although the Royal Navy remained one of the world's most powerful maritime forces at the beginning of World War II in 1939, its ability to project that power into the Pacific and Asian waters in

late 1941 was severely limited by commitments in the Mediterranean and the Atlantic. The major British naval command in December 1941 was the Eastern Fleet, formed on December 2, 1941, from the previous China Station Command plus the two battleships *Prince of Wales* and *Repulse*, which together with a force of destroyers constituted "Force Z," meant to act as a naval shield protecting Malaya and Singapore. The destruction of both of the capital ships by Japanese carrier strikes, plus subsequent British defeats in the Indian Ocean eventually drove the Eastern Fleet back to bases in British East Africa, where it remained, relatively impotent to affect events further east.

This was not the end of the Royal Navy's efforts in the Pacific. In March 1944, the Eastern Fleet formed the heart of a new naval force called the British Pacific Fleet (BPF), founded at the urging of Prime Minister Winston Churchill, who was eager to reinstate some naval prestige in the theater. Together the BPF plus the associated Fleet Train formed Task Force 57, a sizeable naval force that accompanied the US Navy through the later phases of its Pacific campaign, between March and August 1945. This was no mere token force—it ultimately offered two battleships, four aircraft carriers, five cruisers, and fourteen destroyers, and was at the forefront of some of the bitterest offshore fighting, including enduring the kamikaze attacks off Okinawa in April–June 1945. This contribution rightly bolstered the pride of the Royal Navy in the

Below: On paper, Britain's Royal Navy was mighty, but many of its warship types were becoming obsolete. HMS Hood, *seen here, was pride of the navy until it was destroyed by a shell from the German battleship* Bismarck *on May 24, 1941.*

Opposite, left to right: Three Allied sleeve patches. From left to right: the US Navy 102 Patrol Bombing Squadron; the British Combined Operations insignia; and the "Bulldog" patch of the US Marine Corps.

Pacific, although when compared to the sheer might of the US Navy, it was clear that the days of the Royal Navy as the world's greatest maritime power were emphatically over.

For the Royal Air Force (RAF) in the east, the war in Asia was also something of a dispiriting experience, especially when compared to the public accolades garnered during the Battle of Britain in 1940, or to the earth-shaking power of the strategic bombing campaign against Germany between 1942 and 1945. There is no denying that the British in East Asia were woefully under-served for airpower at the beginning of the conflict, and the almost instant loss of air superiority to the Japanese was a significant factor in the rolling victories of the Japanese offensives. The situation was compounded by almost willful underestimations of requirements by the British Chiefs of Staff (CoS). In 1940, British estimates for air defense in the RAF Far East Command, covering all of Burma, Malaya, Singapore, Hong Kong, and Borneo, were put at 528 aircraft, but the CoS downgraded the requirement to 336 aircraft. In fact, when the Japanese offensive was unleashed against the British forces in Asia, the RAF had at its disposal just 265 aircraft, of which only 181 were actually of a serviceable condition. Many of these aircraft were also of obsolete types, easy prey to the maneuverable and fast-flying Zeros.

As with the experience of the Royal Navy, the RAF in the Far East recovered sufficiently to make a practical contribution to the eventual Allied victory. Under the umbrella of the SEAC command, the 3rd Tactical

Air Force was formed in December 1943, and went on to provide invaluable close air support to the soldiers of the 14th Army fighting in Burma.

So what of the Allies' opponents, the Japanese? It is obvious by the speed and breadth of their early war victories that the Japanese experienced the benefits of a heavy investment in military technology, tactics, and training in the prewar years. Yet there were certain faultlines running through the Japanese military organization that would eventually affect its ability to deliver an effective defensive campaign.

The Japanese armed forces consisted of the Imperial Japanese Army (IJA) and the Imperial Japanese Navy (IJN), each with their own air units. Both technically came under the overarching authority of the Imperial General Headquarters (IGA), although throughout the war the two branches largely acted without coordinated consultation with one another, even to the level of failing to share important intelligence. In general, the Japanese had appallingly ineffective processes of intelligence gathering, a situation that made a not-insignificant contribution to the eventual Japanese defeat.

While the IGA lay at the theoretical top of the command tree, all authority ultimately emanated from the Emperor himself. Emperor worship was fused with various *Bushido* traditions, plus aggressive notions of nationalism, to produce a harsh military philosophy of obedience, sacrifice, and brutality. Excerpts from a military code issued to soldiers in 1941 clarify this point: "The essence of discipline in the Imperial Army lies in the lofty spirit of complete obedience to His Majesty, the Grand Marshal (the Emperor). High and low must have deeply engraved in their minds the solemnity of the right of command. Those above should exercise the right in all seriousness, while those below should obey the commands in the utmost sincerity. Essential to victory and requisite for maintaining peace is the condition

LET'S GO GET 'EM !

U.S. MARINES

Left: This US Marine Corps recruitment poster emphasizes the American appetite for vengeance after the Japanese attack on Pearl Harbor.

wherein the entire Army, united in the bonds of absolute loyalty, moves as one in response to a command. Especially on the battlefield is the utmost observance of the spirit of obedience necessary. The spirit of the soldier is best exemplified by those who silently do their duty, joyfully braving death in obedience to a command given at a time when they are undergoing great

Left: The classic Australian bush hat, a practical item of headgear for the tropics.

hardships." Such codes were not mere chest-beating, but were actively expressed in the war through horrors like suicidal *banzai* charges or the turning death ride of a kamikaze aircraft.

At the outbreak of the war in 1941, the Japanese armed forces had reached a position of undoubted regional strength. The Army had 1.5 million men under arms, a figure that rose to 7.2 million by the end of the war. Of the 2.1 million men who served overseas, 1.1 million went to China, 700,000 went across the Pacific, while 300,000 fought the war in Southeast Asia. Two of the great strengths of the IJA were its flexibility in designing formations and units specifically for a tactical purpose, and its excellent and intensive training in the skills of night-fighting and amphibious warfare. Such training bred the confidence that led to the impressive victories of late 1941 and the first half of 1942.

The IJN was also a first-rate force, although its traditions were far more Western-looking than those of the Army, with the IJN having a

Above: A wartime can of that most famous drink, Budweiser beer. The PTO was in many ways "drier" than the ETO in terms of alcohol consumption.

H.M.S. MANUKA

training hours under his belt by the time he went into combat; a comparable Allied pilot might have had just 150 hours.

Given the evident strengths of the IJA and the IJN at the beginning of the war, it begs the question why their military capability became degraded so significantly as the war went on. There are several factors at play here. The first is that Japan's primary opponent, the United States, simply became supremely powerful on the back of a virtual military and industrial revolution. As the American strength swelled, the attrition equation became unsustainable for the Japanese, as soldiers, sailors, and pilots were lost in unimaginable numbers. With attrition came a collapse in, or at least the compression of, the training standards and durations

Above: A Douglas A-20 Havoc makes a flight over Oahu in 1941. The Havoc was a light bomber and ground-attack aircraft.
Left: The minesweeper HMNZS Manuka is launched in New Zealand on April 4, 1942. Australia and New Zealand made an important contribution to the Pacific War, including in supporting roles to American operations..

particularly close historical relationship with the Royal Navy. It had made a heavy investment in shipbuilding during the prewar years, not least in new carriers, developing the carrier warfare tactics that would shake the world with the attack on Pearl Harbor in December 1941. Training in other areas was also superb, especially in night-time gunnery, as the US Navy would experience to its cost during later battles around the Solomons and the Philippines.

Although both the IJA and the IJN had air units, it was the IJA Air Fleets that were the most important Japanese aviation force during the Pacific War. At the beginning of the war, the Japanese pilots enjoyed the benefits of superb aircraft and of extensive training, making them tough opponents for Allied air crews, who often had less experience and training. A Japanese aviator in 1941 would typically have 300–800

that had served the Japanese so well in the 1930s and the early 1940s. Moreover, Japanese investment in military technology became appallingly retrograde, the military leadership falling back on starved notions of willpower and spirit, which had no currency when faced with the massive coordinated firepower the United States brought to bear. Furthermore, we return to the point made earlier about intelligence. While the Allies took immense strategic and tactical advantage from its signals intelligence (SIGINT) intercepts, the Japanese either appear to have failed to make significant inroads into cracking Allied codes, or did not adequately distribute or analyze the information it did extract. Japan began the Pacific War as a potent and confident aggressor. Its aggression largely did not fade, but in the final analysis it did not have the strategy, men, or material to hold on to its victories.

PART 2
The Missions

Pearl Harbor and the Japanese Offensive

"I laid down on a shell deck bench and was reading a book when the attack came. It didn't take but a minute to know what it was."

—Charles Sehe, gunner's mate aboard the USS *Nevada* during the Pearl Harbor attack

The Japanese offensive in Southeast Asia and the Pacific was a stunning demonstration of offensive speed and strategic ambition. Its opening stroke was delivered on December 7, 1941, with the attack of Vice-Admiral Chuichi Nagumo's carrier force against the US Pacific Fleet at Pearl Harbor. The Japanese intention was to take the strategic advantage from the outset—cripple the Pacific Fleet, and thereby give Japanese forces freedom of maneuver for subsequent Pacific/East Asian thrusts.

The first bombs and torpedoes began dropping over Pearl Harbor at around 0755hrs, and the attack finally ceased at 0945hrs. During this brief period, the Japanese emphatically demonstrated that the era of the aircraft carrier had arrived. Final American losses were six battleships sunk and twelve other warships either sunk or damaged. Around 300 American aircraft had been either destroyed or needed repair, strafed up on their airfields. A total of 2,403 servicemen and civilians had been killed, and another 1,178 wounded.

As egregious as these losses were, however, they were not conclusive. The targets that the Japanese desired the most, the three US aircraft carriers, were at sea during the attack, and so were spared to fight another day. Moreover,

Left: This truck, riddled by machine-gun fire from Japanese aircraft at Hickam Field, Hawaii, illustrates the intensity of the attack on Pearl Harbor on December 7, 1941.

many of the sunken and damaged ships were subsequently refloated or repaired, and put back into service. On the psychological level, furthermore, the entire American nation was galvanized for revenge, not submission. The US industrial base swung into action to produce what would become the most powerful military force in all history.

Yet for a time, during late 1941 and the first six months of 1942, the situation in the Far East seemed irredeemably bleak for the Allied forces. The Japanese onslaught appeared unstoppable. Britain's empire contracted with the rapid loss of Malaya, Hong Kong, Singapore (where more than 70,000 Allied troops surrendered), British Borneo, and Burma. For the Americans, Guam, Wake Island and, especially, the Philippines were the most devastating Japanese conquests. The Netherlands lost that most prized jewel in its imperial crown—the Dutch East Indies—a territory that offered the Japanese the rich prospect of extensive oil reserves. New Guinea and the Solomon Islands were also absorbed, and Australia was directly threatened by the Japanese frontline.

By mid 1942, the Japanese defensive perimeter covered a truly vast section of the earth's surface. It reached from the Aleutian Islands in the icy North Pacific almost down to the northern coastline of Australia, and from the Burmese-Indian border in the west to the Marshall Islands in the Central Pacific. Now the Japanese just had to hold onto their gains.

Target Pearl Harbor

The attack on Pearl Harbor in December 1941 has generated huge analysis and controversy ever since. The core of the debate has been about whether the US government and the forces at Pearl Harbor could have responded more effectively to the intelligence inflow, and prepared for or even forestalled the attack. What is clear is that those who subsequently bore the brunt of the onslaught were caught by surprise on that fateful day.

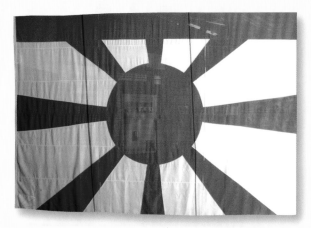

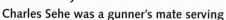

Left: The "rising sun" was adopted as the war flag of both the Japanese Army and the Japanese Navy during the 19th century, and was a potent rallying symbol for Japanese forces in World War II.

Charles Sehe was a gunner's mate serving aboard the battleship USS *Nevada*, and he remembers both the pre-attack innocence and the shock when the bombs and torpedoes finally started falling: "After a few months of at-sea exercises, we'd come into port, then we'd go back out. Since I was only a seaman second [class], my job was to clean pots and pans in the scullery. One of the reasons I was in the scullery was that I was put on report. I'd washed a few pieces of clothing, but you were not supposed to leave them hung out on exposed decks, but I had put them by an air vent. The Master at Arms came by and he gave me five days working in the scullery. The Friday before December 7th, December 5th, I went aboard the *Arizona* to see my home town friend, Charles Leroy Thompson. He suggested, why don't we go out Saturday night and live it up. It only cost us a dollar. I told him I can't, I got to be in the scullery Sunday morning. He said, 'No, we can do it. You

can sleep over.' I said, 'I can't, then I'd really be on report.' So I declined. And he said, 'Loan me a dollar. I'll pay you back Monday.' I said, 'Sure.' But, Monday never came for him. December 7th."

Sehe remembers that at the time of the attack, on the Sunday morning, he had just finished his breakfast at about 0730hrs: "I was a member of the 5th Division. The 5th Division was the deck division that manned the 5"51 [caliber] surface guns, the so-called casemented guns. The main batteries were 14in turreted mounts. The 6th Division, which was our neighboring division, was the antiaircraft division. They manned the 5"51 guns: five on each side, port and starboard sides. At the time of the attack, we'd just finished breakfast about 7:30, so I went to the enlisted men's after head, there were about six of us there, and I picked up the Sunday paper, the *Honolulu Star Bulletin*, and I was looking at 'Orphan Annie.' I heard the whistling, a loud noise, and 'All hands, man your battle stations. General Quarters. We're under attack.' I got up, and I had to remember what they told me when I first got on the ship. Movement throughout the ship requires two things in your mind. Up starboard and forward, down port

Above left: The Japanese attack plan relied upon each pilot efficiently identifying and attacking a specific target. This scale model was built to aid the pilots' orientation in the attack.

Above right: Just prior to the assault on Pearl Harbor, Japanese pilots aboard the aircraft carrier Kaga receive a briefing from a senior officer, who illustrates the lines of attack on a table map.

Above: A Japanese military map of Pearl Harbor, showing the positions of American shipping. Japanese spies had been observing the US base for weeks by the time of the attack in December 1941.

and aft. So that everyone can move in sequence, and some people forgot that. My battle station was the searchlights on the mainmast, and obviously the searchlights weren't being used, it was daylight. So I had a choice to make: either climb the ladder and help out somewhere. So I chose the ladder, which others did. Already the bombing had started. We heard this noise, a terrific noise, and that was the one torpedo that the *Nevada* got. My friend was in casement port four. His name was R.H. Kirby, seaman first class. Years later he said, 'Charles, I saw that torpedo coming right at me.' The ship shuddered. Then we got more bomb hits."

Robert Clark, a sailor aboard the USS *Tennessee*, also remembers the shock of the attack, and how the crew had to respond to the threat presented by the blazing ships nearby: "My breakfast was over and it

was Sunday and I didn't have to do anything in particular so I went into the turret and laid down on a shell deck bench and was reading a book when the attack came. It didn't take but a minute to know what it was. And pretty quick the announcement was 'Man your battle stations, this is not a drill.' So the turret crew all got together in the turret, of course, and the officers would tell us when they needed somebody out on the deck and we would go out to do whatever they wanted done. One time it was to throw the cables off that connected the USS *West Virginia* to us, to the *Tennessee*. The *Tennessee* was up against the docking keys on Ford Island so it was not hit by torpedoes, but the *West Virginia* was on the water side of the *Tennessee* and was hit by torpedoes and began to sink and it began to pull us over. So we threw off the cables from the bits and in the process we were out there on the topside and here came a flight of Japanese and none of us knew that. Somebody said over the loudspeaker, 'Clear the weather deck, clear the weather deck. Attack is coming in.' So we all hauled our backsides over underneath the turrets. Another time I was sent out to remove the burning tarpaulins that had been spread for shade . . . the 5in guns when they fired had ejected their casings, and the casings set those things on fire. I was sent out, tied up with a marine to get fire hoses to come up and blow the oil—the burning oil that was between us and the *West Virginia*—hose it off so that it would not burn the ship. . . . Well, there we were, the *Arizona* was sunk behind us, blown up, the *West Virginia* was sunk alongside us, and the *Oklahoma* was turned over in front of us and the *Maryland* was tied up by the *Oklahoma* and she got under way. She was alright."

As this account suggests, much of the damage done by the Japanese attack was inflicted in the first minutes. In fact, in these minutes alone five battleships— neatly presented to the Japanese torpedo bombers in "Battleship Row"—were hit, plus the target ship *Utah*. Within thirty minutes, most of the American aircraft had been wiped out. The base was struggling to survive.

Right: Isoroku Yamamoto stated, before the war, "I wonder if our politicians (who speak so lightly of a Japanese–American war) have confidence as to the final outcome and are prepared to make the necessary sacrifices."

Going for the Kill

forward to set watertight integrity. Watertight integrity is when you close the ports; you close and put the dogs down on all the hatches and that compartmentalized your ship so that if you did get hit in one part that part might flood but your ship wouldn't sink. You had plenty of air space to keep you going. That was my first job. The second job was to set up the after-battle dressing station, in the after part of the ship."

Left: *The battleship USS* Nevada *was hit by at least one torpedo and six bombs, and took 169 casualties during the attack, including sixty dead.*
Below: *A damaged door from the* Arizona, *which was destroyed during the Pearl Harbor attack. The hole in the door was cut by divers in an attempt to see if there were any survivors inside the compartment.*

The Pearl Harbor attack consisted of two principal waves of carrier aircraft, launched from positions to the north of Oahu island. The first wave included a major contingent of torpedo bombers, which had as their primary targets the vessels of "Battleship Row." The second wave, which made its approach at 0850hrs, consisted of dive-bombers, high-level bombers, and fighters, but met with a more ferocious defense from the American antiaircraft gunners, and therefore took some more noticeable losses. In total, the attack was to last for just under two hours.

George Allen Barrett was a medically trained serviceman aboard the destroyer USS *McDonough*. His account illustrates how training enabled the crews to respond with efficiency to a truly unexpected and violent event:

"I was aboard ship on December 7, 1941, and in fact, I was just finishing shaving, getting ready to take a shower and I heard the general alarm sounding and I thought well it's probably fire and rescue and I don't have the duty, so I don't have to worry with it. About that time the Chief Gunner's Mate came by and yelled in 'Hey Doc, the G.D. Japs are after us.' 'Oh come on Gunner, go get another drink.' 'No,' he says, 'honest, look.' And, by golly I looked out the port, and sure enough there's Japanese aircraft and one of the ships was turning over. I went immediately down below to get some clothes on and then I went

The *McDonough* was fortunate in that it took only two casualties during the attack, one of which was treated by Barrett: "I had a sailor with a bad burn . . . . [antiaircraft] shells were being fired and the gunners were in their positions and they were turning their handles sideways and up and down. As the gun fired, the brass would come flying out. It was practically red hot and you had a catcher there and he had a glove on and a catcher thing in the other hand. When a bomb exploded aft of us this kid was

Above: *The most immediate form of air defense at Pearl Harbor came in the shape of these Browning .30-cal. machine guns, hastily mounted as antiaircraft weapons.*

Right: *A US Navy officer's sword and scabbard, which was recovered from the locker of one Ensign Jones, who served aboard the USS* Arizona. *A total of 1,177 men lost their lives aboard the ship during the attack.*

knocked down and as the shell casing came out this kid grabbed it with his bare hands. It was hot, so he had some bad burns."

Gunner's mate Anthony Ganarelli, aboard the USS *Tennessee*, remembers some of the challenges in providing a defensive response to the Japanese attack: "They came in over Honolulu and then when they hit Hickham Field [one of the major air bases around Pearl Harbor], they came in from two different sides. With us, if we had to shoot our 5in guns, we would have been shooting right into the city of Honolulu. That was the main problem that we had. The .50-caliber machine guns, when we got them up there, we used those. We had one man who fired the gun so long without cotton in his ears, he couldn't hear anything for about three or four days. . . .

"That morning, on December 7, I went to the sick bay because I had a cast on my left leg. I had been injured the week before and the doctor was supposed to remove the cast. While I'm there is when all the things started happening. My battle station was

all the way aft in turret number 4. I snaked my way back to my battle station. I didn't know what was going on up above. We could hear the noise and all that, but my battle station was down in the shell room in gun turret number 4. When things settled down we found out we had to flood our magazine because it was all afire around us from the *Arizona* and the *West Virginia*. We flooded all our magazines. When things settled down, we figured there would be no more planes so we started pumping out all these magazines and inspecting all the 14in powder. We worked on that until wee hours of the morning. By that time, this cast that was supposed to come off just fell down around my ankles, so I cut it off myself.

"We left there about a week or so later and went to Bremerton Shipyard and we removed all our 14in guns and replaced all of them with new guns, repaired the ship from the damage. We had gun turret number 3 and number 1 had damage. We had a few strafings. One of my friends was killed in gun turret number 3. He was burned to a crisp. That was a sad day, I remember that. A lot of people have asked me, 'Were you scared?' Well, I can't say that I was scared, but I was just mad that we had to be in such a situation when we had everything we needed to protect ourselves."

One of the critical failings of the Japanese strike against Pearl Harbor was Nagumo's decision against launching a third wave, to target shipyard repair facilities and oil storage depots. By leaving these features largely untouched, Nagumo allowed the Americans to bring its Pacific Fleet back to life with speed after the attack. Nevertheless, a huge amount of damage had been done to the American fleet, and it would take months for the Pacific navy to get back to strength.

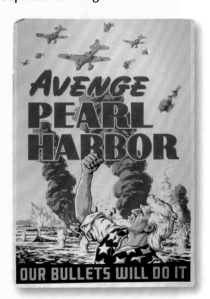

Above right: *The spirit of retribution was very pronounced across American society just after the Pearl Harbor attack, and provided a clear motivation for the US switch to a war economy.*

Pearl Harbor - The Reaction

Once the attack on Pearl Harbor ended, it was time to do the final accounting. The following ships had either been sunk or damaged: the battleships *Arizona*, *Oklahoma*, *West Virginia*, *California*, *Nevada*, *Pennsylvania*, *Maryland*, and *Tennessee*; the cruisers *Helena*, *Honolulu*, and *Raleigh*; the destroyers *Cassin*, *Downes*, *Helm*, and *Shaw*; the minelayer *Oglala*, the auxiliary ships *Curtiss*, *Sotoyomo*, *Utah*, *Vestal*, and *YFD-2*. A total of 169 aircraft had been destroyed and 159 damaged. Japanese losses were nine fighters, fifteen dive-bombers, and five torpedo bombers.

Whatever strategic isolationism existed in the United States, dissolved almost instantly. The very next day, President Roosevelt addressed the nation from Congress, delivering a short speech with an emphatic message: "Yesterday, December 7, 1941—a date which will live in

Above: *In the foreground lie the destroyers USS* Cassin *(left) and* Downes. *Both ships were wrecked in the attack, but subsequent salvage helped create new boats.*

Above: *The battleships* West Virginia *(foreground) and* Tennessee *burn vigorously after hits from Japanese bombs and torpedoes. Both ships, however, were restored and lived to fight another day.*

infamy—the United States of America was suddenly and deliberately attacked by naval and air forces of the Empire of Japan. . . . As Commander in Chief of the Army and Navy, I have directed that all measures be taken for our defense. But always will our whole nation remember the character of the onslaught against us. No matter how long it may take us to overcome this premeditated invasion, the American people in their righteous might will win through to absolute victory. I believe that I interpret the will of the Congress and of the people when I assert that we will not only defend ourselves to the uttermost, but will make it very certain that this form of treachery shall never again endanger us. Hostilities exist. There is no blinking at the fact that our people, our territory, and our interests are in grave danger. With confidence in our armed forces, with the unbounding determination of our people, we will gain the inevitable triumph—so help us God. I ask that the Congress declare that since the unprovoked and dastardly attack by Japan on Sunday, December 7, 1941, a state of war has existed between the United States and the Japanese empire."

To gauge public opinion, the US government also commissioned Alan Lomax, Assistant in Charge of the Archive of American Folk Song, to collect interviews with the regular "man on the street" across the Untied States. The responses were fascinating, showing a mix of anxiety about the future but also a fervent desire for payback. The prominent Reverend W. J. Faulkner, of Nashville, Tennessee, was clear about what he saw as previous US complacency and the need for robust action:

"This sudden and unfortunate attack of the Japanese on our country has revealed in stark outline a tragic attitude of unpreparedness and selfish indifference on our part to the real dangers confronting our nation and our democratic way of life. Too long have we been divided at home. For we have been dissipating our vast strength and straining our national unity through labor conflicts and class bickerings. And in practices of stupid and costly racial discriminations, our enemies have conspired to destroy us. I earnestly hope that at last we have become struck wide

Top right: A Douglas B-18A Bolo bomber on Hawaii. Most of the thirty-three such aircraft around Pearl Harbor were destroyed in the attack.

Lower right: The USS West Virginia was nursed back to health after Pearl Harbor, and is here seen undergoing an upgrade in April 1943.

Below: A shot-down Japanese Aichi D3A "Val" is recovered from the waters in Pearl Harbor. Note the telescopic gunsight on the top of the engine cowling.

awake to the real threats to our national safety at home and abroad. And that we will be galvanized into effective action by uniting all of our people and resources on a basis of equality into one invincible army of patriots who will work for the triumph of Christian democracy and brotherhood throughout the world."

Matt Allen, of Denver, Colorado, expressed his sense of the future in less poetic, but equally dramatic, terms: "Well, I've been looking, I've been talking about it across the bar for quite some time now with different army men, different navy men. I formed this opinion that this thing was coming and while it was a complete surprise when it came so soon at the same time, I think it's been coming on us for quite some time, although we didn't expect to be stabbed in the back. I would, myself, like to see the United States start right out and give Japan everything she's got right off the start."

Revenge was indeed a common sentiment across the United States as the dawn broke on December 8, 1941. Now the US war machine had to galvanize itself for action.

Guam and Wake Island

Two early objectives for the Japanese offensive in December 1941 were the American Pacific outposts of Wake Island and Guam. The latter, located in the south of the Marianas chain, fell in just two days, the 549-strong Marine and US Navy garrison overwhelmed quickly by nearly 6,000 invaders. The battle for Wake Island, however, ran on for nearly two weeks, the US troops putting up a trenchant resistance.

Frank R. Mace was actually a naval base construction worker and group chaplain on Wake Island when the Japanese invaded on Deember 11, after preparatory air strikes. Mace reveals both the ingenuity and the determination of the American defenders:

"[Regarding our] 3in [antiaircraft] guns, when they [the Japanese] would go over and bomb us one day, we would move those 3in guns away from where they were and set up a dummy in its place with 4in

Above: *The wreckage of F4F-3 Wildcats lies on Wake Island following Japanese aerial attacks, December 23, 1941. The US airfield was attacked by thirty-six G3M3 medium bombers.*

soil pipe. Then we would move that 3in gun, maybe 700 or 800yds [641 or 731m] away. The next day when they would come over and bomb, they would bomb that dummy. They had taken pictures when they went over, of course. They didn't hurt us any that way. We were moving the 3in guns one night at midnight and Gunner Hammus was in charge of the moving. We were pushing these 3in guns over on to Peale. We went across the bridge. Just as we were going across the bridge, I said, 'Gunner Hammus, there are three blobs out there in that lagoon that don't belong out there.' He said, 'Well Mace. you go take care of it.' I took six hand grenades and eight guys with .30-caliber machine guns

and we went down to the only place where they could bring these barges in. You could see they were barges by that time. We got down close to the shore. When they got in and were about 150ft [46m] from shore, I threw a hand grenade on each one of them. They were loaded with dynamite and black powder and had all their .30-caliber machine guns aboard. They were coming in to blow up all of the buildings on the island and figured they could kill what Americans they ran into with their .30-caliber machine guns. The next morning we found a hundred pairs of those little flip-flops that the Japanese use for footwear floating in the lagoon. So I figured I killed one hundred men. There were none alive at all. The guys with the .30-calibers said, 'You never gave us a chance.' So I told Gunner Hammus that we took care of that. He reported that to Major Devereaux and Commander Cunningham. They both said, 'We're putting you in for the Medal of Honor.' He said. 'We'll see that you get the Medal.' Of course four years later we were war prisoners for forty-four months and I never did get it. I said, Well, It's a little late in life now but it would still be pretty nice to have it."

As Mace's narrative indicates, the American defense of Wake Island would eventually run into the ground, particularly once a US relief attempt was forced to turn back because of reports of IJN carrier forces in the area:

Above: *An aerial view of Wake Island prior to Japanese occaption. Anchored off the coastline are seven US Navy PBY patrol planes.*

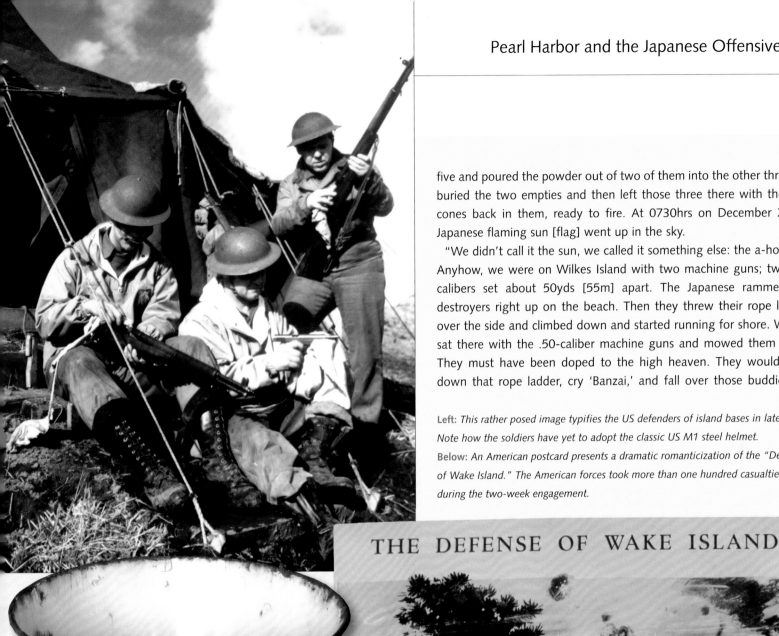

five and poured the powder out of two of them into the other three and buried the two empties and then left those three there with the nose cones back in them, ready to fire. At 0730hrs on December 23 the Japanese flaming sun [flag] went up in the sky.

"We didn't call it the sun, we called it something else: the a-hole sun. Anyhow, we were on Wilkes Island with two machine guns; two .50-calibers set about 50yds [55m] apart. The Japanese rammed two destroyers right up on the beach. Then they threw their rope ladders over the side and climbed down and started running for shore. We just sat there with the .50-caliber machine guns and mowed them down. They must have been doped to the high heaven. They would come down that rope ladder, cry 'Banzai,' and fall over those buddies and

Left: This rather posed image typifies the US defenders of island bases in late 1941. Note how the soldiers have yet to adopt the classic US M1 steel helmet.

Below: An American postcard presents a dramatic romanticization of the "Defense of Wake Island." The American forces took more than one hundred casualties during the two-week engagement.

THE DEFENSE OF WAKE ISLAND

Above: A simple Japanese feeding bowel, used by the occupation troops on Wake Island. The Japanese garrison were subsequently starved by a US submarine blockade.

"On the 23rd, all the guns had run out of ammunition except the one 3in gun that they had hit in the breech and split it, about 3 or 4ft [0.9 or 1.2m] up from where you put the shell in. The boys took that over to the machine shop and they grooved that out and welded it all back in and blued it all back in. You couldn't tell that it had ever been hit. We had five shells left for that 3in gun. We took the nose cones out of all

come right at you. We just kept shooting them. We only had four planes in the sky because there were eight of them sitting on the runway the first day and they had hit them all with incendiary bullets and burned them."

With such meager defensive resources left, the result was inevitable—Wake Island surrendered on December 23.

British defeats — End of Empire

Ill-prepared for the professionalism and tactical tempo of the Japanese assault, the British Empire suffered a succession of rapid hammer blows from the Japanese offensive in the Far East. In Malaya, the Japanese 25th Army under Lieutenant-General Tomoyuki Yamashita invaded on December 8, its two-pronged assault running southwards down both sides of the country. By January 31, 1942, the surviving British forces had been squeezed out of the peninsula onto the fortress island of Singapore. Yet despite having a force of about 80,000 troops (including Australians, New Zealanders, and Indians) available, the British commander on Singapore, Lieutenant-General Arthur Percival, was forced to capitulate on February 15 to a numerically inferior Japanese army.

Len (Snowie) Baynes was a British Army NCO on Singapore at this time. He vividly remembers the impact of the news about the British surrender:

"At a quarter to three, I received what I hope will remain as the greatest shock of my life, as a messenger came with the order to lay our weapons down in front of us and surrender. I find it quite impossible to describe my feelings. Until now we had felt that we were holding our own, and anticipated pushing the Japanese back off the island before many more days had passed (we were still optimistically awaiting the arrival of Allied aircraft).

"Our wildest guesses did not take into account the possibility of abandoning the territory to the enemy—we had been told that the island must be retained at all costs, since it was an essential link in our communications with Australasia. In any case we did not think of throwing in the sponge [surrender] while any of us remained alive—that was not the British way. I crept round the position passing on the order, adding the instruction to remove the rifle bolts and bury or otherwise hide them.

"Private Tanner stood 6ft 2in [1.87m], and had proved himself in the fighting to be a very brave soldier—when he heard the order, he stood there unashamedly with tears streaming down his cheeks. His were not the only tears that sad day. I felt as

Left: The Japanese Army worked hard to perfect its amphibious warfare, which gave it tremendous tactical maneuverability. Here infantry and armor make a river crossing.

though my bowels had been painlessly removed, my mind refused to work properly, and I was unable to grapple with the situation.

"Hardly a word was exchanged between us, as we awaited further orders. Talking about this afterwards, we agreed that we were still undergoing a feeling of bitter shame, with our arms lying useless on the ground and our country's enemy only a hundred yards away.

Although the surrender was imminent, these were still extremely dangerous moments for the British troops, as Baynes discovered when he tried to move positions:

Above: The fall of Singapore was not just a disaster for the British and Empire armed forces. In addition, thousands of civilians were captured by the Japanese, and were sent to internment camps across the Japanese territories.

"We seemed to wait in our trenches after the arrival of the cease-fire order for a very long time, without anything happening. An hour and a half after we received it, men dug in 50yds [46m] away, in the centre of a lawn, decided to climb out of their trenches—a machine gun opened fire on them, and they all lay still around their position. I ran back to our RAP [Regimental Aid Post] to try to borrow a Red Cross flag to take out over the lawn, and fetch in any wounded.

"Dodging a hail of bullets from that same machine gun, I found our Medical Officer and explained my mission, but was told that since some of our men had fired on Japanese stretcher bearers, they had ceased to respect the Red Cross, and were firing indiscriminately at

Above: *Japanese soldiers advance through Hong Kong. The attack on Hong Kong began on the morning of December 8, 1941 (local time) and the final British surrender came on the following Christmas Day.*

Above: *The Japanese victory in Malaya was a stunning slap in the face for the British. Although not necessarily jungle warfare experts, the Japanese soldiers exhibited a mastery of maintaining momentum in the offensive.*

both stretcher bearers and ambulances. I was told to stay quietly with my men until further instructions were received. . . .

"Stepping out through the front door of the house where the RAP was situated, and seeing an ambulance standing there, I looked in over the tailboard. Within seconds I came under machine-gun fire from an unexpected direction, and tracer bullets whizzed past me like fireworks and into the ambulance. Although it seemed that I could have touched these bullets, again they all missed me. I jumped to cover into an alcove built in the wall of the house, and as I did so the ambulance burst into flames—a tracer bullet had penetrated the petrol tank. The fire spread and the ambulance became an inferno. The firing did not ease up, and

I began to feel the intense heat. Soon I had to choose between roasting and stepping out again into the line of fire.

"The house was built on a slope, and like most of the dwellings in that area it was built on piers, high off the ground. I leapt out of the alcove and fell flat on the ground in a spot where I could roll back under the house, and managed to accomplish this in one movement. I lay there for a few seconds, getting my breath back, and watching the tracers fly past, almost within reach of my hand. Then the heat increased, and I realized that the fire had spread to the house, so crawled to the rear of the under-floor space." **Len survived this encounter, and like some 30,000 of his comrades, went into Japanese captivity.**

The Sinking of *Prince of Wales* and *Repulse*

It was not just the British land forces that were suffering egregious defeats during those first terrible months of the Japanese offensive. The Royal Navy also gained cruel first-hand experience of the professionalism of the Japanese forces, particularly in terms of their mastery of carrier warfare.

The battleship *Prince of Wales* and the battlecruiser *Repulse*, two jewels in the crown of the British fleet, had been sent to Singapore in October 1941, designated Force Z. As the Japanese invasion of Malaya began to play out, Force Z was sent to interdict a possible landing at Kuantuan; actually the intelligence was incorrect, and there was no landing taking place there. Yet they were spotted by the Japanese and on December 10, at 1015hrs, Japanese carrier forces launched a merciless attack on the two vessels. Commander R.V. Ward, of the Prince of Wales, remembers that day:

"We sailed north-east around the Anamba Islands, as the water around the actual coast of Malaya had been heavily mined. On the morning of the 9th, we were spotted by a high-flying enemy aircraft off Khota Bahru. By mid-morning waves of Jap planes were coming over, some bombers, some torpedo carriers. The enemy had a very early success, when a bomb hit our port side propellers, distorted them and so, as the shafts continued to spin, the distortion caused them to open up gaps in the hull so there was considerable flooding especially in the engine rooms. These were evacuated. Now both ships were taking water and

Above: HMS Prince of Wales *leaves Singapore harbor in 1941. The ship was a King George V-class battleship launched in May 1939. It saw limited action in 1940, and subsequently became one the first ships to be sunk by airpower in open water.*

the tragedy was that because of the grounding of the carrier *Indomitable* off the US earlier on, we had no defense against air attack.

"P.O.W. was listing 40 degrees to port. The cypher office was flooded, and so with others I moved into the nearby lower steering position where Commander Lawson was in charge. Main power had been lost, ventilation failed and only emergency lighting was available, six decks down from the bridge, in that lower conning tower. I was standing near the 'plot', where the actual course of the ship was being recorded and I saw that the course was one of ever decreasing circles, obviously because we had power on the starboard side only and the rudder had been damaged so that we had actually lost control of the ship.

"Now the ship was sinking lower and the list increasing, so the Commander ordered us to get out on deck—he stayed behind and was lost. We left through the escape 'tube', inside which were small footholds, but the tube was too narrow for us to enter it without first removing our life jackets— obviously an unwise, though inevitable, thing to do, considering our prospects for the next few minutes. A young sub-lieutenant was ahead of me and part way up the tube he declared he could go no further, at which I gave his bottom a huge shove so that he struggled to the hatch at the top

Left: The Prince of Wales *(left, front) and* Repulse *(left, behind) twist and turn in an attempt to evade the Japanese bombs raining down. The destroyer in the foreground is actually an artist's insertion.*

Above: An aerial view of the two British warships under attack. The total Japanese attacking force numbered more than 130 aircraft.

Naval antiaircraft fire

During World War II, naval warships evolved increasingly toward becoming antiaircraft (AA) gun platforms, as the threat from land-based and carrier-based aircraft grew. For example, the American battleship USS *Texas*, on its commission in 1914, essentially had just eight antiaircraft guns. Following its major 1942 refit, however, it boasted 6 x 5in guns (which could be used for AA purposes), 10 x 3in AA guns; 40 x 40mm Bofors AA guns, and 44 x 20mm Oerlikon AA cannons. This extraordinary increase in AA firepower meant that ships such as the *Texas* could almost blanket the sky around them with protective fire. The efficency of AA fire improved alongside its volume. The use of director firing, allied to proximity-fused shells, meant that AA fire became 50 percent more effective by 1944. The US Navy in the Pacific therefore became ever more proficient at destroying the Japanese air forces. In 1942, US Navy AA gunners shot down an estimated 243 aircraft, but in 1943 that figure climbed to 372. (These figures include kills against German aircraft, but about 85 percent of the kills were in the Pacific Theater.) During the first half of 1945 alone, however, 945 were downed, as the gunnery tactics reached their perfection.

Above: British Mk VIII "pom-pom" guns, officially known as the QF 2-pounder. Each gun was fed from a fourteen-round steel-link belt and could fire at a rate of 115rpm and to an altitude of 13,300ft (3,960m).

(fortunately it was not clipped shut) and we were out on deck seeing the damage for the first time. HMS *Express* was alongside; men boarding her along ropes, jumping from P.O.W. Some missing the deck and being caught between the two ships. Some wounded were successfully transferred to safety. Because the rising keel of the P.O.W. was threatening the stability of *Express*, she withdrew to a safer position. The last person I spoke to was Captain Leach—I gave him a message from Commander Lawson—but the captain was lost, together with Admiral Tom Phillips and 327 men from P.O.W. and 513 from *Repulse*. I slid down the starboard side of the ship as far as the armored layer and then jumped clear into the oily sea and put a fair distance—say 5yds [4.5m] between me and the fated ship. . . . We swam for a total of one and a half hours and then *Express* returned, P.O.W. having gone under—gracefully but tragically—so we swam towards her and safety."

The survivors of this tragic event were the lucky ones, as within the three-hour attack a total of 840 British lives were lost. The destruction of the two ships also exposed the fact that the sun had set over the era of the battleship.

The Fall of Burma

The Japanese offensive overwhelmed the British forces on many fronts, not least in Burma. This British colony was defended by the British Burma Corps plus three Chinese armies, but none were able to halt the Japanese push up from the south made by the Japanese 15th Army, which launched its main invasion on January 20 near Moulmein. Rangoon fell on March 8 (despite some dogged delaying actions on the Salween and Bilin Rivers), Mandalay on May 1, and the northerly point of Myitkyina on May 8.

General William Slim was the commander of the "BurCorps." In his memoirs, he gives despairing account of the Japanese air superiority over Burma during the campaign: "Now great wedges of silver bombers droned across the sky and one after another

Above: The Japanese Type 14 Nambu pistol was an 8mm recoil-operated handgun with an eight-round magazine.

a few sticks at a time, and keeping one in suspense. With the Japanese it was all over quickly; you had either had it, or were alive till next time. Whatever the method, it was effective enough with the civil population. The police, hospital staffs, air-raid precaution units, public services, railways, collapsed. Labor vanished into the jungles; towns were evacuated. Only a few devoted British, Anglo-Burmans, and Burmese carried on."

On the frontline of the British retreat was James Palmer of the Royal Tank Regiment. In February 1942 his formation was caught up in the defense of Rangoon, a defense that Palmer understood could not be sustained against the Japanese momentum:

"The situation was desperate and we knew that Rangoon could not be held, but would have to be evacuated and the remains of the army of

the cities of Burma spurted with flame and vanished in roaring holocausts. Prome, Meiktila, Mandalay, Thazi, Pyinmana, Maymyo, Lashio, Taung-gyi, largely wooden towns, all crumbled and burned. The Japanese used pattern bombing, coming over in faultless formation, giving themselves a leisurely dummy run or two, and then letting all their bombs go in one shattering crump. They were very accurate. We always said they had in each formation only one leader capable of aiming and all took the time from him. It was certainly effective, but I personally preferred it to the methods of the Italians and the French when they also had no air opposition. They had cruised round, dropping

Above left and above right: The Japanese offensive moved quickly through Burma, despite British attempts to slow it down, such as blowing up bridges (above right). Logistics and movement were always tough in the jungle terrain (above left).

Burma retreat northwards towards Burma and Assam. It was not going to be a 'tactical withdrawal,' it was a full-scale retreat and we would have to live off the land.

"There was no way that we could be supplied to establish a defense line and we had to move fast. The docks and warehouses at Rangoon and all the port facilities had to be blown sky high. Nothing would have to be left

Above: *Japanese troops are welcomed by the citizens of the Rangoon, after the Burmese capital fell in January 1942.*

so we took what supplies we could from the storage sheds. Then we began the demolition.

"Everything that stood up had to be blown down. The whole of Rangoon was blazing as we moved out towards the Prome Road leading northwards towards Mandalay, passing the Swegon Pagoda, glistening in the sun.

"Meanwhile the Japs had moved from the east, north to Rangoon towards Pegu, and our tanks had to move towards them to hold them away from the Prome Road, which was the only exit from Rangoon. Here we hit trouble. Around Pegu we were confronted by pockets of Japs who had infiltrated through and we came under devastating mortar and heavy machine-gun fire, but we couldn't see the little yellow men in the dense jungle growth. This was no place for tank warfare. . . . The Japs seemed to be everywhere and were playing cat and mouse. It was nerve-

Below: *A Japanese war bugle, used for ceremonial puporses and for galvanizing troops in the attack.*

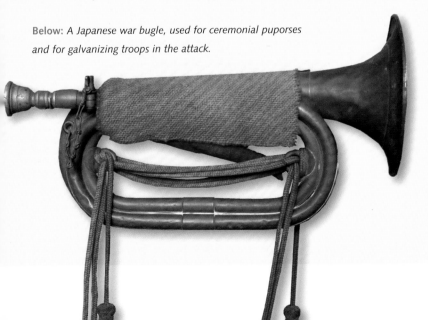

wracking and demoralizing. Planes sometimes strafed the road and dropped leaflets after the raids. The leaflets showed crude drawings of British women being raped by American soldiers and said,'Go home and protect your loved ones.'

"It was about this time that I had an accident with my foot, to add to my misery. A five-gallon drum of petrol toppled off a lorry when we were refilling a tank and crushed my foot. My infantry role did not help much and for the rest of the journey northwards I limped along. The big toe festered and my leg became swollen, but there was nothing I could do but get along as best I could. It wasn't bad when I went out in the scout car as a gunner, but during the most essential patrols I was a dead loss.

"Most of us were now covered with jungle sores caused by thorn scratches festering and bleeding. Dysentery and diarrhea were rife and jungle fever hit everyone.

"Excessive sweating and perpetual nausea drained us physically and we were becoming a sorry sight indeed. We were limping along and every

Above: *The Yenangyuang oilfields lie wrecked, having been destroyed by the British during the retreat from Burma.*

mile seemed longer than the last. The damp heat of the jungle drained us even in the shade, and we all felt so tired and weary we just wanted to curl up and be let alone. Sod the yellow bastards—they wouldn't leave us alone, but followed us like a swarm of bees, stinging and taunting us."

Such a grim picture of demoralized retreat must have played itself out across the lives of tens of thousands of men, not only in Burma but across the entire sphere of the Japanese offensive.

Life in Japanese Captivity

More than 140,000 Allied soldiers fell prisoner of the Japanese during World War II, the majority of them captured during the first six months of the Japanese offensive. They, along with hundreds of thousands of Asian civilians, provided the Japanese with a ready source of forced labor, manpower that could be utilized with an utter lack of concern for humanitarian considerations.

POWs were sent across the territories conquered by the Japanese, with major concentrations in Burma (building the infamous Burma–Thailand railroad), Taiwan, Singapore, the Dutch East Indies, but also in the Japanese homeland itself, which had seven major camp areas distributed across the home islands. The work performed by the POWS was varied but always punishing, including mining, handling logistics, building railways and bridges, earth-

Left: A group of POWs present themselves for a group photograph. The men captured in 1941 and 1942 would endure three years of hardship before their release, if they survived at all.

moving, stone-breaking, and other highly physical tasks. The fact that such duties, which were typically performed across a twelve-hour day, had to be sustained on a camp diet of around 600 calories a day goes part way to explaining why only one

Below: A canteen and mess kit used by an American POW in the Fukuoka 17 prison camp. The soldier had been captured in Bataan.

Right: A prisoner artwork shows a moving scene in the Cabanatuan prison camp in the Philippines.

in three prisoners managed to survive the camps. Standard fare in the camps was a thin stew, seaweed, soy beans, and barley, with a rare piece of meat or fish thrown in every few weeks or so. Torture and random executions, plus untreated disease, explain the other causes behind the attrition.

Brutality was endemic in the camps, not only from the Japanese guards but also from Japanese-allied camp personnel, such as the Koreans. One man who fell foul of this treatment was US Navy serviceman John Reas, who after capture eventually found

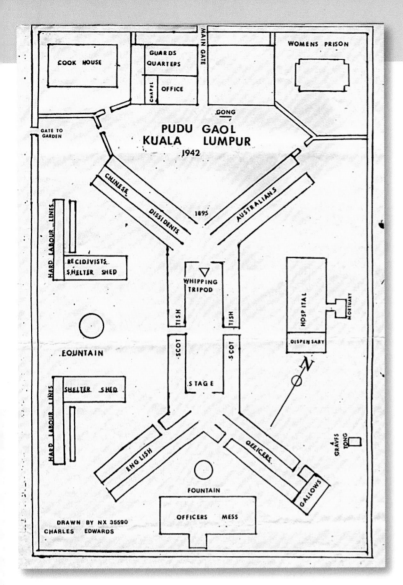

Above: Rough mapwork showing the layout of the Pudu gaol in Kuala Lumpur. Note the segregation of the POWs by nationality, plus the presence of gallows and a "whipping tripod."

himself working on the Burma–Thailand railroad, where he remembers the following incident: "This evening around dusk there were three or four of us up there sitting on a log by a little fire heating the water and treating the ulcers on our legs or whatever with the salt water. And here come a Korean guard [who said] 'ook ook ook.' I turned around and looked . . . he didn't say get up, but said wait a minute. . . . He lined us up because we didn't bow to him, salute him, . . . enough to satisfy him. He lined us up in a row. He went down the front of the line hitting you in the chest with the butt of his rifle, and he came around the back and hit you in the back. He got me in the back of the head instead, and I saw fire, almost passed out and staggered forward, and I didn't know much for a while and a couple of days even. When I got back to Dallas after the war, what shows up on the X-ray—residue of a fractured skull." **Given such treatment, it is little wonder that around 50 percent of surviving POWs showed evidence of psychiatric disorders after the war.**

Letters Home

While British and American POWs were reasonably entitled to write letters home in the European Theater of Operations, the same was not true in the Pacific Theater. The Red Cross did act as a humanitarian postal service in the Far East, but on average the prisoners were only allowed to write one letter a year, averaging twenty-five words only, although some longer versions were occasionally permitted.

Letters received by the prisoners from home were like gold. J.S. Gray, a prisoner from the Army Air Corps, was being held in Manila when he received a piece of exciting news. "When we got there an interpreter told us what a good deal we were getting. He said we were getting POW boxes from our folks back home. I got one and it had a razor in it and about three blades. It had been torn open and I got about one hundred and fifty letters from my mother. Everybody in the world had written to me, but you could only have those letters for fifteen minutes. A lot of people didn't get any so you would pass them out. Of course, you could hardly read them because they had been cut up and censored. I didn't get too much out of my box." The frustration experienced by Gray must have been near overwhelming.

Below: A letter from a US POW, who was captured on Wake Island in December 1941, is written with an evident awareness of the Japanese censor looking over his shoulder.

Zentsuji War Prison Camp, Japan
23 August, 1942.

Mrs. C.T. Sloman
Rt. 1, Box 136,
Texas City, Texas, USA

Dear Mother. This is the first chance I've had to write in nine months and I still don't have much to write, but I will try and use up the 350 words we are allowed to write. Wake was captured on December 23rd, 1941. We were captured and sent here to Japan. I have received very good treatment since I was captured. Once a week we go on a hike through the city and up in the hills, which is very interesting. Commander Newman, got letters from his sister and one from his father and he let me read them so I got most of the news about the home town. I would like for Mildred to know where I am and that I would like to hear from her, but I can only write one letter so I want you to be sure and let her know. Tell all the family hello and that I am thinking of them and expect to be with them soon, but for them to write just in case I don't make it. We are going to get 500 books in our library in a few days and they should keep us busy until we get out of here. Well Mom, I'll knock off for this time and wait to hear from you. Love to all   Wiley

Wiley W. Sloman PFC USMC
Zentsuji War Prison Camp, Japan

Spreading web — the Dutch East Indies

The Dutch East Indies were of special importance in Japan's overall war plan. With Japan unable to supply more than 10 percent of its own oil requirements, the oil fields of the Dutch East Indies promised a solution to Japanese oil starvation under war conditions. Attacks on the Dutch East Indies began shortly after the Pearl Harbor assault, and despite the formation of the American-British-Dutch-Australian (ABDA) Command on January 15, 1942, the combined Allied forces could not prevent the takeover of the island chain, which fell by March.

Left: A Dutch Air Force F2A-3 Brewster Buffalo. The Dutch forces in the Dutch East Indies simply didn't have the military resources to defend such an extensive island chain.

The American war reporter Cecil Brown remembers the raised eyebrows as youthful and inexperienced pilots flew reinforcements into Java during the early stages of the campaign:

"A few minutes later twelve P-40Es, the Kittyhawks, came in. This is a huge field at Daly Water—in many respects a perfect field. There are no barriers and visibility is excellent on all sides. We stood beside our bombers watching the Kittyhawks circle to follow their leader down. The leader made a perfect landing, the next one bounced but got down. The next one seemed to be coming down too low, short of the aerodrome, and heading for a field. He came down in the field and hit a ditch. The next one did the same—down on the field and half turned over. The following Kittyhawk did the same. Lieutenant Rose was shouting and screaming, 'What the hell's the matter with them? They've got all the field in the world here to land in and they are coming down in the grass and weeds.'

"The others came down all right, until the final one of the twelve. He made five attempts to get down but when four or five feet off the ground he decided he couldn't make it, put on the gas, and zoomed up and away again for another circle. Five times he did that. . . . 'These boys are going to be slaughtered out here,' one pilot said."

The focal point for resistance to the Japanese invasion was Borneo, although the Japanese managed to capture most of the key installations of that territory by the end of December 1941. With military resistance limited, the civilians of the islands had little between them and captivity, as the young Frans W. Doelman, living in Java at the time, remembers:

"When we got to the Dutch East Indies—my father took us into a mountainous area to a town called Batoe, which was just a few miles from Malang. We had a flat-roofed house there and some servants. The peace continued until December 7, 1941, the fateful day of Pearl Harbor. It didn't take the Japanese very long to take over the Dutch East Indies, about three or four days. There was very little resistance. The people who did try to fight didn't have enough armament. The next phase of the Japanese was to ship all of the

Left: Japanese infantry in the Dutch East Indies use long sections of jungle grasses and foliage to camouflage their trucks and armored vehicles from aerial attack or observation.

Above: The Palembang oil refineries on Sumatra were a major center of oil production in the Dutch East Indies. The refineries were owned by Royal Dutch Shell, but they were extensively destroyed by the Dutch forces just prior to the Japanese takeover of the area in February 1942.

able-bodied men away. My father was already sixty-seven at that time and had high blood pressure so he stayed with us. Then the Japanese started to round up all the Caucasian families, the British, Dutch, and so forth. They put us in a restricted area in Malang. One of the things that the Japanese did was to make my mother report to the Japanese almost daily. She was allowed to go back home later. The decision was then made to go ahead and send us to an internment camp because my mom couldn't be away that long from my father. We were all ordered to go to these internment camps or whatever you want to call them. They made us make mattresses by taking a sheet and stitching it about every 10cm [3.9in] apart and fill it with cotton. It was probably a little over 2ft [0.6m] wide and probably 6ft [1.8m] long. You had to make those to have a place to sleep. We were also only allowed to take a minium of baggage. We took what we could.

"From Malang they decided to ship us to a different, more restrictive camp. In Samarang, in the middle of the island is also a fort, and the Japanese decided to put all the internees around that area. That's how they controlled the Caucasian people. They took us to Samarang. It was pretty drastic, kind of like Dr. Zhivago's movie that you've probably seen. It was unbearably hot. People couldn't sleep very well. We didn't

know what our fate was going to be ultimately. We finally arrived at a huge camp, Karang Panus, which used to be a church and grounds. The Japanese lined us all up and took everything that they wanted. They left us very little. . . . In this initial camp, our little family of four was assigned a large room, probably about 25 x 20[ft] and that was to be my home for the next year and a half. There was another family assigned to the rooms. They had a boy about the same age as I, in fact he was even born on the same day, but he suffered from epilepsy. Sometimes he would fall down and twist and turn in his game with death. We got separated later and I don't know whatever happened to him. My father became ill and went to what was sort of a hospital. But because of the lack of food and his age, he only lasted a few months and then he died in August of 1944. I have no idea what he died of exactly." **The Dutch East Indies remained under Japanese occupation for the entirety of the war, Douglas MacArthur's proposal to liberate the islands in 1944–45 being rejected by the Joint Chiefs of Staff.**

Above: Indonesian civilians wave to Japanese troops as the invaders move through their town. Such scenes were at first common across the Japanese sphere of occupation, but within weeks the locals usually understood that the Japanese were there as conquerors, not liberators.

The Battle of Java Sea

Although later naval battles such as those at Midway and around the Philippines have tended to capture much of the historical press, the first major fleet action of the war was actually the the battle of Java Sea, fought on February 27, 1942. The clash was the result of a mixed ABDA force of five cruisers and nine destroyers, under the command of Dutchman Vice-Admiral Karel Doorman, attempting to resist a Japanese covering force of four cruisers and nine destroyers, which were protecting a landing on Java. Without air cover, and outclassed by Japanese firepower, torpedo technology, communications, and night-fighting ability, the ABDA force was in for a rough ride.

Frank Gallagher was aboard the cruiser USS *Houston*, as part of a US Marine contingent:

"…there was the battle of Java Sea in which we were in the company of several friendly ships. One was the HMS *Exeter* which had been involved in the action that resulted in the sinking of the German battleship *Bismark*. There were some other British ships and I've forgotten their names. [Apart from *Exeter*, the other British ships were the destroyers *Electra*, *Encounter*, and *Jupiter*.] That battle was a running battle along parallel lateral lines with considerable distance between us. We didn't close action with any of the Japanese ships. We did close fire on a couple of them and set one of them on fire. Nightfall came and that terminated that naval action. We proceeded at that time into Jakarta and from Jakarta we were on our way to Sunda Strait…"

Once in the Sunda Strait, *Houston* and the Australian cruiser HMAS *Perth* managed to surprise and engage a Japanese landing fleet at anchor, sinking two ships and damaging three others. At this point, however, the covering force returned and began to exchange fire:

"We were being hit but to my knowledge not with any heavy shells on the topside. We did take three torpedo hits, one of which disabled one of the fire rooms and reduced our speed to about 5 knots. There was another solid shot that went through the forecastle and out the other side of the ship. I don't recall anything else that struck us at that time. I was well up in the forward part of the ship and aft of me there were several hits. . . . The ship was being maneuvered by the captain and it was going through all kinds of configurations. We were keeling over from one side to the other and going in circles. I was sitting on the Director [gunfire aiming station] hanging on. I remember that turret two was trained aft, at [a] right angle to the ship and it was not more than 20ft [6m] from me. These three 8in guns went off and I just shuddered

Above: *The light cruiser HNLMS* De Ruyter *lets loose with its main 5.9in (150mm) guns at Java Sea.*
Left: *The light cruiser* Java *of the Dutch Navy struggles to escape from Japanese bombs. The ship was sunk on February 27, 1942.*

because I thought we were being hit. It was a few minutes before I realized that it was our own guns and we were not hit. It was quite an exciting moment for me.

The excitement would soon wear off. Having suffered multiple "Long Lance" torpedo strikes, and with the captain (Albert H. Rooks) eventually killed by a shell strike at 0003hrs, the *Houston* capsized and sank, with hundreds of men going into the water:

"As I stepped off of the quarterdeck and into the water there was a life raft that came along with a lot of our mess attendants clinging to it. We

his heart started again and it did on a couple of occasions. He said, 'I don't think this is going to work.' The poor guy died right there. I decided I'd better leave that life raft because it wasn't making any headway. I left the life raft and I don't know what happened to it. Then I was alone in the Sunda Straits. The interesting part of that experience was that I swam a long time and eventually reached Java. I knew it was Java because in the Sunda Straits that night there was a full moon and there must have been a million stars in the sky. It was perfectly clear and I could identify a mountain on the southern tip of Sumatra as the volcanic peak of Krakatau. The current through the Sunda Straits, a key avenue of sea traffic between the Indian Ocean and the South China Sea, was swift north and south at about four and a half knots. I wasn't

Above: The British cruiser HMS Exeter *lists heavily as its sinks. Subsequent to this picture, the ship was hit by two torpedoes on the starboard side.*
Far right: An Allied warship under air attack during the battle of Java Sea. The multiple bomb impacts indicate an attack by a level bomber, rather than a dive-bomber.

had a lot of Chinese mess attendants hanging to the side of the life raft and they were terrified because not many of them knew how to swim. For a moment I grasped a hold of the life lines that are tied to this rectangular life raft and I found myself next to the ship's chaplain, whose name was Rentz. . . . This chaplain was an elderly person and he kept saying, 'My heart keeps stopping.' I kept urging him to raise and lower his legs in a kicking action like on a bicycle to get

making much headway. I had a life jacket on and it kept me vertical. I didn't start making headway into Java until I got into the lee of the island. It was an extraordinary experience. For most of the time I was alone and an extraordinary thought crossed my mind, no one knew where I was, no one."

The final toll of the battle of Java Sea reflected a terrible defeat for the ABDA force. In total, the Allies lost two cruisers and three destroyers, with many other Allied ships seriously damaged. About 2,300 sailors had also died. The Japanese covering force lost none of their ships, suffering just one damaged cruiser.

Right: A pack of Code Flag Cards issued by the US Naval Aviation Training Division; Morse code details of the flag were given on the back.

Invasion of the Philippines

The great General Douglas MacArthur had been appointed the commander of US Forces in the Far East (USFFE) in July 1941, and hence when war broke out he presided over a mixed American and Filipino army in the Philippines. In total, this army numbered nearly 180,000 men, but only 19,000 were well-trained American troops and they had limited air cover. Many of the local troops were poorly trained reserve or police units, and they were facing the Japanese 14th Army supported by excellent air cover from more than 500 combat aircraft.

Andanto D'Amore was a US flight surgeon with the 19th Bomb Group, and was present for the opening phases of the Japanese onslaught: "And so we arrived at Clark Air Force Base in the fall of '41 around about October. Clark Field, of course, was the landing strip base at Fort Stockton in the Philippine Islands on the main island of Luzon . . . . And as you know, on the great day of December the 8th, we were all alerted that something was going on in Hawaii. And we were in the Philippines and of course we were closer to Japan and we expected to get hit also. Everything was quiet for the morning, and at about 11 o'clock . . . the Japanese decided to attack Clark Field and our airplanes. At noon on the same day that they were doing Hawaii. So we were then, as you say, under an air bombardment and I got my first experience at running between different abutments taking care of the soldiers that were injured, and [performing] triage. There was so much to do, but . . . we didn't have too many facilities and the hospital at Fort Stotsenberg was a small, active facility for the active soldiers because all the real surgeries and sick ones were sent to Manila, to the main general hospital. That was my first experience of the bombing and strafing by the Japanese. . . .

"Since there wasn't much we could do, because most of the damage was done by the original strafing and very few airplanes were able to get into the air, after about two or three weeks it looked like there wasn't much to do and the Japanese would probably invade. General MacArthur went into his wartime role of going into Bataan, which was the peninsula across from Manila Bay in central Luzon. . . . By January, of course, the Japanese were in control of the area and the military formed their lines of defense on Bataan. But the 19th Bomb Group was . . . selected, not to stay there, but to move to the island of Mindanao, which was a southern island in the Philippines where they had a potential airstrip being made at Malaybalay, on the plains, in a great big pineapple plantation, where, of course, they leveled off a runway there. . . . Of course, the fighting in Bataan got very serious and the Americans really had plenty of ammunition but no food; the food rations got to be very slim up there, although ours wasn't a problem. By April they surrendered Bataan and technically the surrender included us and all the islands of the American troops. So we were picked up by the Japanese at Malaybalay and moved to the prison there in Davao, the largest city in Mindanao on the gulf."

Below: Japanese troops head towards a landing beach in the Philippines. The principal landing craft for Japanese amphibious troops was the Daihatsu-class boat, which could carry up to twelve troops.

Left: In this small-unit action in the Philippines, a Japanese machine-gunner, armed with a Type 11 machine gun, prepares to deliver supporting fire.

By the end of December, 1941, General MacArthur could see the writing on the wall for the Philippines, especially following the main Japanese landings at Lingayen Bay on December 22. On December 23 he announced his decision to withdraw his troops into the Bataan Peninsula, leaving Manila to its fate—it fell to the Japanese on January 2, while in Bataan the defenders prepared to meet the enemy.

US Army artilleryman Dwight Pendleberry was one of those American troops who were pushed back into the Bataan Peninsula, caught between a north–south pincer movement from the Japanese forces. He also remembers the evident Japanese air superiority:

"Here came the Jap planes. I was right between two hills so I stopped and everybody else stopped around me. This plane came up and the engine didn't sound too good but it flew along alright. And he dropped a bomb right where we were just after we left. I never went back to see what happened. But I saw that. Then they moved us back to Bataan and we were on a pretty high hill. . . . And in the valley ahead of us, between that and north of us, was where our artillery was. And we were parked on that hill and the Jap bombers would come along and bomb the artillery. They were actually flying below us or right out from us and I was still under orders not to fire until fired upon. And so you have to do that, you know. Didn't agree with it, but that's what you have to do. And we did give them a burst one day, but they were a little bit too far out of range. But they bombed every day, several times a day. And they pretty well ruined a lot of the artillery.

"Then we moved again, clear back on to Bataan. We were pretty well back on the tip and we were there for awhile. Then we ran out of gasoline and I had to help build a sort of a stove so they could cook their rice on it. Beside that when we moved back to Bataan . . . they cut us to one-tenth rations. We got rice and gravy twice a day and coffee, that's all we got. We were on that for over two months. So when Bataan fell, we were pretty darn hungry by then."

Right: In an attempt to protect their city from destruction, citizens of Manila display an "Open City" sign as the Japanese enter.
Below: A Japanese artillery battery lays down fire in support of operations in the Philippines. Japanese artillery production lagged behind the frontline requirements for most of the war.

Bataan and Corregidor

Joseph Lazjer was a US Army tank man. He was one of the 80,000 troops who retreated back into the Bataan Peninsula, an arduous movement dogged by extreme hunger and the destruction of anything that could be of value to the Japanese:

"I was on the retreat for four days. I was with the 1st sergeant, and we rode a six-by [truck]; we had ammunition and gasoline on it. So they told me I couldn't go to tanks because I knew too much about guns. So anyway I was with the 1st sergeant and helping him drive the six-by. We didn't have nothing to eat for about thirty-six hours after the retreat was still moving, and we finally caught up to them down the road somewhere and we had two hot cakes. . . .

Left: *Japanese troops ride into the assault on Corregidor island; the presentation of the rifles feels like a rather theatrical device for the camera.*

Above and lower right: *Prisoners of the Japanese, captured in their thousands in the Philippines, faced a brutal future. The men pictured to the lower right show the traumatic expressions of those on the "Bataan Death March."*

So we went all the way down then we stopped somewhere along the way. There were some spotlights and a lot of gasoline tanks over there, drums filled with gasoline, so we stopped, the sergeant and I, and we destroyed the lights. They had searchlights—we destroyed them by breaking the glass. We emptied the gasoline out as it was getting close to dark. Before we left we put a match to that gasoline we dumped. I can remember some screaming going back in the back yard because the Japs were really coming up on us. I guess we burned up a few of them. . . . First thing you know we found out that General [Edward] King [Commanding General of the Philippine-American Army in Bataan] surrendered us to the Japanese because he figured it was useless. We had no ammo, no food, no medicine and it would just waste the lives, he said, so he surrendered us."

Every type of American soldier was pressed into the defense of Bataan, including Army Air Corps medic Robert Brown, who here describes one of his unexpected adventures: "When we got back to Bataan, we were put on half rations food wise and there was no quinine available at all. And Bataan was infested with malaria mosquitoes. So no quinine, half rations, issued with Enfields and Springfields [rifles] from World War I, and put in the infantry. That was something I told my mother would never happen, that I would be in the infantry. I'd be in the Air Corps and behind the front lines. Wrong. Dead wrong. Anyway, we started down through the jungle in the 17th Pursuit Squadron like a bunch of Boy Scouts. They put us in three flanks. Left flank, right flank, and middle flank. And I was in the middle flank with the squadron commander . . . and here come three Filipinos running up this little trail, like on top of the ridge. So Captain Stone says 'Joes, where you going?' [They replied]'Oh my companions are wounded and shot . . .' and blah, blah, blah. Captain Stone says 'Well, if you got companions down there, you go down there and get them. And medic you go with them.' I had to put a gun on them to make them go. I put a .45 on them. I said get going ahead of me, down this trail. We got down there about 50yds [46m] maybe and heard

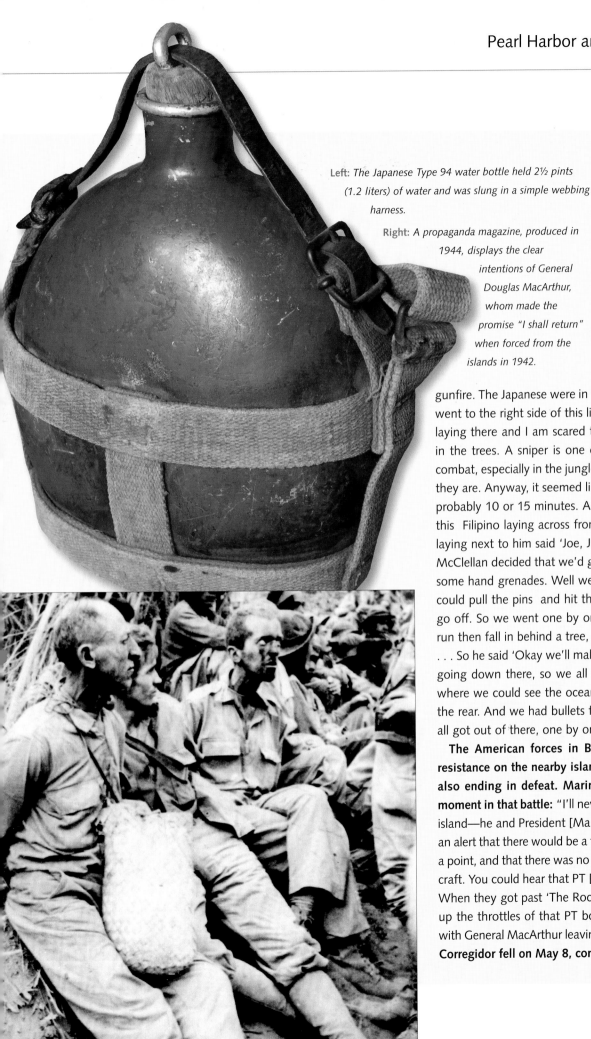

Left: The Japanese Type 94 water bottle held 2½ pints (1.2 liters) of water and was slung in a simple webbing harness.

Right: A propaganda magazine, produced in 1944, displays the clear intentions of General Douglas MacArthur, whom made the promise "I shall return" when forced from the islands in 1942.

FREE PHILIPPINES

GENERAL MACARTHUR LANDS WITH HIS TROOPS AT HOLLANDIA

"I shall return"
MacArthur

gunfire. The Japanese were in the trees, snipers. And these three Filipinos went to the right side of this little trail. I went to the left side and we are laying there and I am scared to death as you couldn't see these people in the trees. A sniper is one of the worst things you can ever have in combat, especially in the jungle because you don't know where the hell they are. Anyway, it seemed like we had been there for hours, but it was probably 10 or 15 minutes. And another shot went off. Pow, pow! And this Filipino laying across from me, his back bowed up and the Filipino laying next to him said 'Joe, Joe, my companion has been hit. . .' So Lt. McClellan decided that we'd go off on the left flank and he would throw some hand grenades. Well we had World War I hand grenades and you could pull the pins and hit them with a baseball bat and they wouldn't go off. So we went one by one down the left flank as fast as we could run then fall in behind a tree, and all of us made it down to the bottom. . . . So he said 'Okay we'll make it to the beach.' There was kind of a trail going down there, so we all made it to the beach. We go all the way where we could see the ocean and the Japanese opened up on us from the rear. And we had bullets flying all over. . . . But believe it or not, we all got out of there, one by one."

The American forces in Bataan were surrendered on April 9, but resistance on the nearby island of Corregidor went on into May before also ending in defeat. Marine Glenn McDole remembers a poignant moment in that battle: "I'll never forget the night that MacArthur left that island—he and President [Manuel] Quezon of the Philippines. There was an alert that there would be a friendly craft leaving at a [certain] time from a point, and that there was no need to challenge it as it would be a friendly craft. You could hear that PT [patrol torpedo] boat coming through there When they got past 'The Rock' [Corregidor], you could hear them open up the throttles of that PT boat wide-open as they went to Mindanao, with General MacArthur leaving General [Jonathan] Wainright in charge." **Corregidor fell on May 8, completing the Japanese conquest.**

The Japanese Home Front

Japan's society was fully mobilized for war between 1941 and 1945. Partly this was out of patriotic fervor—the Japanese government was never slow to emphasize that everyone was implicated in the struggle for empire and survival. Yet it was also out of necessity, as the labor force and the economic structure of Japan required radical reconfiguration to meet the demands of feeding an insatiable war machine.

Even in the early years of the war, Japanese civilians would have noticed a distinct tightening of food supplies and consumer goods. Severe rationing bit hard in 1942, and shops began to close as they ran out of basic goods. Austerity took hold, despite the fact that Japan had added vast swathes of supposedly productive territory to its empire; imports were almost all diverted towards war production. Thus even the most basic foodstuffs such as rice, salt, sugar, and soy could only be obtained via ration coupons. Furthermore, rationalization of the war economy from late 1942 meant that many small and mid-sized businesses were forced to close in favour of larger government production enterprises, changes that further hit standards of living among the Japanese people. The country's struggle to find fuel supplies also meant that private vehicular travel became virtually impossible.

For the Japanese industrial authorities, a key priority was to ensure that there was an adequate workforce to maintain output, especially as a major percentage of the country's working-age men were now in uniform overseas. The main labor reservoirs were therefore women and older

Right: *Infantry and cavalry present themselves on parade during Army Commemoration Day in Japan, 1944.*

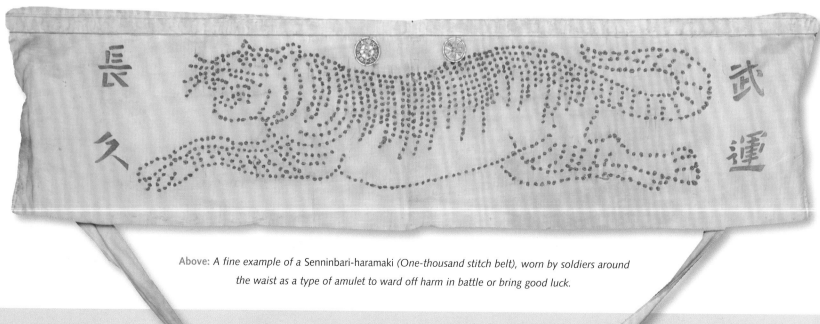

Above: *A fine example of a* Senninbari-haramaki *(One-thousand stitch belt), worn by soldiers around the waist as a type of amulet to ward off harm in battle or bring good luck.*

Right: Although gender notions restricted the employment of women in the labor force, thousands of Japanese women did find themselves in war industries.

students. The exploitation of female labor was aided by the centralization of all women's patriotic groups in 1942, forming the Great Japan Women's Association, which had a total of 20 million members. Japanese cultural sensitivities about women at first limited their vocational use, unlike the mass conscription of women in, say, the UK. In particular, the government was keen to preserve the breeding capability of the Japanese mother, and thus excused most married women from arduous employment. The increasing threat of defeat in 1943, however, meant that in September of that year all unmarried women under the age of twenty-five were compelled to sign themselves into a labour volunteer corps.

Some 3.4 million students were also drafted into industry, working 10–15-hour days that did little to enhance performance in their studies. Yet even they were treated better than the tens of thousands of Koreans and Chinese who were shipped in as forced labour workers in the Japanese homeland, dying by the dozen in factories, mines, and other industrial facilities.

At the same time as working its citizens hard, the Japanese government also looked to infuse it with patriotic spirit. The streets of every village, town, and city were strewn with exhortatory posters and messages, such as "Deny one's self and serve the nation" and, more ominously, "Serve the nation with one death." Focus on the indoctrination of youth was regarded as especially important, for it was they who would provide the military manpower of the future. School life was radically re-engineered in 1941, the curriculum being contorted to emphasize militaristic physical training and imperialistic thinking, rather than subtle intellectual reasoning. By 1943, the war conditions also merited a reduction in middle-school education from five years to four years. In universities and colleges, the Japanese Army emplaced military personnel to ensure that the right mindset was being inculcated in its future leaders.

From 1941 to 1944, Japanese society became painfully familiar with the loss of its soldiers on far-off fronts. In 1944–45, however, death came to visit the Japanese homeland itself in the form of a crushing strategic bombing campaign. Evidence seems to suggest that the innate orderliness of Japanese society did not break down entirely even under this violent pressure. Yet there were definite problems. Industrial enterprises suffered from high rates of staff absenteeism, either through the death of their workers or through workers being driven far afield to look for food. The transportation system also almost entirely collapsed. More than 600,000 Japanese civilians would eventually die in the war, paying the ultimate price for imperialism.

Above left: Fire held a deeply embedded fear in Japanese culture. Here we see a firefighting crew conducting an air raid drill.

Above right: Type 3 Chi-Nu medium tanks under production. Japanese industrial output was a tiny fraction of American productivity, even under war conditions.

The Threat to Australia

Prior to the attack on Pearl Harbor, Australian public opinion about the country's active participation in the European and Mediterranean war was variable, the conflict being such a long way from the homeland. The opening shots of the Pacific War changed all that rapidly. The Japanese offensive surge created a southern perimeter that directly threatened northern Australia with invasion, and events such as the fall of Singapore demonstrated that massive defeat at the hands of the Japanese was a perfectly viable prospect.

As in the more distant theaters, however, the Australian forces proved themselves a resilient and aggressive opponent to the Japanese. Ian Morrison, a correspondent for the London *Times* who covered the Malayan campaign, remembers Australian troops initiating a highly effective and sizable ambush on the advancing Japanese:

"The scheme was to let the Japanese through, and then fall upon them from each side of the road. The men took up their positions and were given four days' rations. Only two days' rations would have sufficed, for the Japanese appeared very much earlier than we thought.

"They cannot have expected anything at all. They came marching along the road in the afternoon of January 15 in small groups, many of them wheeling bicycles. Several companies came over the bridge and walked down the road blissfully unaware that keen eyes were watching them from out of the jungle on each side. The officer in charge of blowing the bridge [a road bridge to the north of Gemas] decided at last that he had let enough Japanese over. He waited until there were as many actually on the bridge as he thought were likely to be at any one moment and then released the fuse. There was a tremendous explosion. The Japanese on the bridge were blown sky-high. Bridge, bodies, and bicycles went soaring up. The explosion was the signal for the battalion to fall upon the Japanese, which they did with loud yells. Rifles barked, tommy-guns sputtered, many of the Australians dashed in with their bayonets. Nearly all the Japanese who were on the hither side of the bridge were killed. Later it was estimated that between eight hundred and a thousand of the enemy were killed, while the Australians suffered less than a hundred killed and wounded. The Australians then fell back south of Segamat. It was a triumphant beginning. It set all the Australians cock-a-hoop [jubilant]. It had a tonic effect on all the British forces. But more was still to come."

More was indeed still to come, and despite this early and stirring victory, the Australians, like the rest of the Allied forces in Malaya, were eventually driven out the peninsula, and thousands were captured in Singapore. In early 1942 the war also came directly to the Australian mainland, in the form of bombing raids on bases and installations along the northern coastline. The biggest of these raids was the first, launched on February 19 against the naval anchorage and

Above left: *The cargo vessel MV* Neptuna *is blown to pieces after being hit by Japanese bombs in Darwin on February 19, 1942. The bomb strikes detonated a cargo of one hundred depth charges.*

Above right: *Oil tanks burn ferociously in Darwin after the February 19, 1942, Japanese air strike. The attacks on northern Australia represented the southernmost extent of the Japanese aggression.*

Above: The war drew in people from all sectors of society. Here Maori volunteers in the New Zealand Army stand for inspection on April 4, 1942.

facilities at Darwin. Bob McMahon was a USAAF fighter pilot with the 21st Pursuit Squadron, based at Darwin. He was present on the day of the Japanese raid, but just prior to this event he had been in dogfight with Japanese Zeros, shooting down three before being wounded and having to ditch his damaged plane in a mangrove swamp. Others in his flight were also shot down and injured, but many, including McMahon, were rescued by PBY and taken to Darwin:

"... we watched the RAAF [Royal Australian Air Force] and Darwin airports go up in reddish brown smoke. It looked like later pictures of an atom bomb when they dropped everything. That was the first time that day I had seen any flak from the Australian side but they were well below and behind the formations as they came in. The Aussies were shootin' old 75mm antiaircraft guns that had a range probably up to about 18,000ft [5,486m]. Only two or three bursts got up in the vicinity of the bombers but never connected with anything. But we were cheering for 'em. Then the PBY crew brought me back across the harbor. Fortunately an Aussie soldier was coming along in a jeep and took me out to a hospital called 'Burma' and by the time I got in there, four of the other guys preceded me. Walker greeted me, then I found out what happened to him. There was Glover under a bed, and the other pilot, Rice, had his head all bandaged up so he couldn't see. Glover couldn't

see either but he recognized my voice. He was bandaged head to toe. We had been together through all the training from primary flight on. We were operated on (by the time they got to me, they were out of anesthetic. So the 'Doc' gave me a shot of whisky—after I had him take a shot first!) put in bed and I sorta dozed off. Early the next morning . . . [the] whole base was deserted except for gunners, (Aussie machine gunners) and the tactical recce unit which was the reconnaissance Hudson unit. They were picking over their planes or what was left of 'em. The rest of the base was deserted. The Aussies got an order to evacuate and they streamed out of Darwin with all the civilians."

During the raid a total of 236 people were killed, thirty aircraft were destroyed, eight ships sunk, and twenty-five ships damaged. Air attacks on Australia continued throughout 1942 and 1943, albeit of lesser intensity.

Left: Japanese naval aircraft are here seen en route to targets in Australia. In total, more than one hundred Japanese raids were launched against northern Australia.

Above: Soldiers begin the clear-up operation in Darwin following an air raid. The city of Darwin had to adjust to a major disruption in its utilities, especially in relation to its water supplies and electricity.

The Indian Ocean Raid

What we now know as the Indian Ocean Raid was another demoralizing blow for the Royal Navy at the hands of a confident Imperial Japanese Navy (IJN). It began when Nagumo's Carrier Striking Force sailed into the Indian Ocean in March 1942 to raid Ceylon and destroy British shipping there. Admiral James Somerville, commander of the British Eastern Fleet, was aware the attack was coming, and had at his disposal three carriers, five battleships, and five cruisers. On paper, the British had a potent force at their disposal, but in reality it was completely outclassed by the Japanese in terms of carrier aircraft capability.

Left: Leonard Joseph Birchall was an officer in the RCAF, known for warning the Allied forces about the Japanese attack on Ceylon.

Fighting began in earnest on March 31, and was sustained over the next ten days. Stan Curtis was aboard the carrier HMS *Hermes*, and he recounts what happened on April 9:

"The dawn came up that morning as it only can over the Indian Ocean, the sky filled with red and gold streaks. During the morning watch our captain spoke to us over the Tannoy system; he read out a signal he had received from the C in C, to the effect that the Japanese had sighted us and we could be expected to be attacked at any time, but the fighter aircraft were being sent out for our protection. . . .

"We waited and waited but no aircraft put in an appearance, only Japanese. At 1030hrs we had the report, 'enemy aircraft in sight.' Immediately our AA opened up. *Hermes* was a sitting duck, our antiaircraft defence was inadequate against the number of dive-bombers that attacked us; there were eighty-five of them. Zero dive-bombers each carrying a 250lb [114kg] bomb that was delay fused; they went through our flight deck (we had no armor plating), exploding below decks.

"The planes dived out of the sun and apart from a few near misses every bomb was on target, they went through our flight deck like sticking your finger through tissue paper, causing absolute destruction below decks. One of the first casualties was our forward lift, it received a direct hit, was blown 10ft [3m] in the air to land upside down on the flight deck eventually sliding into the sea; all personnel

in that area were instantly killed. Wave after wave of these Zeros came at us. Our captain was doing his best to dodge the bombs by using the speed of the ship. We were moving flat out at about 20–25 knots, shuddering from stem to stern, not only from the speed, but from the continual pounding we were getting from those little 'Sons of Nippon' up in the air. Where oh where was our fighter cover? We never did get any. Up until then we had a commentary on what was happening up top.

"The AA guns crews did a magnificent job. To assist them, because the planes at the end of their dive flew along the flight deck to drop their bombs and because the guns could not be fired at that low angle, all the 5.5s [5.5in guns], mine included, had orders to elevate to the maximum so that as the ship slewed from side to side [they could] fire at will, hoping that the shrapnel from the shells would cause some damage to the never-ending stream of bombers that were hurtling down out of the sun to tear the guts out of my ship, which had been my home for the past three years.

"Suddenly there was an almighty explosion that seemed to lift us out of the water—the after magazine had gone up—then another, this time above us on the starboard side, from that moment onwards we had no further communication with the bridge, which had received a direct hit,

Right: HMS Hermes *blazes in the Indian Ocean after being bombed to destruction by Japanese aircraft on April 9, 1942. A total of 307 men died aboard the ship.*

Above left: *The IJN fleet sails into the Indian Ocean in March 1942. From left to right are:* Akagi, Soryu, Hiryu, Hiei, Kirishima, Haruna, *and* Kongo. *The photo was taken from the carrier* Zuikaku.

Right: *The British heavy cruisers HMS* Dorsetshire *and* Cornwall *under Japanese air attack on April 5, 1942. Both ships were eventually sunk, with* Dorsetshire *hit by ten bombs and* Cornwall *by eight bombs.*

Above: *Command of the Indian Ocean had implications for adjacent theaters. A Vought SB2U Vindicator from the USS* Ranger *flies over a convoy en route to Cape Town, the transport ships carrying soldiers from the US 18th Infantry Division.*

as a result of that our captain and all bridge personnel were killed. Only about fifteen minutes had passed since the start of the action and the ship was already listing to port, fires were raging in the hangar, she was on fire from stem to stern. Just aft of my gun position was the galley, that received a direct hit also, minutes later we had a near miss alongside our gun. Talk about a tidal wave coming aboard—our crew were flung yards, tossed like corks on a pond. Picking myself up and finding no bones broken, I called out to each number of our crew and got an answer from all of them (no-one washed overboard). We were lucky; our gun was the only one that did not get hit.

"At this stage *Hermes* had a very heavy list to port and it was obvious that she was about to sink. As the sea was now only feet below our gun deck I gave the order 'Over the side lads, every man for himself, good luck to you all.' Abandon ship had previously been given by word of mouth, the lads went over the side and I followed, hitting the water at 1100hrs; this is the time my wristwatch stopped (I didn't have a waterproof one). As she was sinking the Japs were still dropping bombs on her and machine-gunning the lads in the water. In the water I swam away from the ship as fast as I could, the ship still had way on

and I wanted to get clear of the screws and also because bombs were still exploding close to the ship. The force of the explosions would rupture your stomach, quite a few of the lads were lost in this way after surviving Dante's Inferno aboard, so it was head down and away."

By the end of the Indian Ocean Raid, the British had lost one carrier, one cruiser, two destroyers, three other naval vessels, and twenty-three merchant ships. Japanese losses were minimal; around twenty carrier aircraft had been destroyed in the action.

The Doolittle Raid

enemy or anything. They just looked down there and they stood up and some waved. But there was no feeling that they knew who we were. We turned and then as we came out, back towards the bay, we did drop a couple of those 500lb [227kg] bombs in the army area. Then, as we came out, we dropped incediary bombs, with scatter bombs raining down on

Left: Lieutenant-Colonel Doolittle (center right) stands with other crew members of the Doolittle raid, plus officials from the Chinese government.
Below: A bombed-up B-25 bomber struggles to gain lift from the flight deck of the USS Hornet as it sets out on its sortie to Japan.

The Doolittle Raid was a legendary retaliatory strike against Japan, one that had almost neglible military effect but gave a critical boost to morale back in the United States. On April 18, 1942, sixteen B-25 bombers lumbered off the deck of the USS *Hornet*, laden with bombs they intended to deliver over the Japanese mainland itself. As that mainland was 750 miles (1,207km) away, a range prohibiting a return journey to the carriers, the intention was to fly on to mainland China after the raid. The attack was led by Lieutenant-Colonel James H. Doolittle, and James H. "Herb" Macia was the navigator/ bombardier of the fourteenth aircraft in the flight: His aircraft had the city of Nagoya in its sights:

"We knew that there were some army installations in Nagoya, in the northern part of Nagoya. There were things like a barracks for an army unit or something like that. We came up in from the sea here and that is when we started climbing. Up to this time, we had been still staying pretty close to the deck. A little higher, a little higher than we had been out further. As we went up there, the object was to go up and look Nagoya over as we came in and then we could fly by the city rather than over the city. Now we flew clear up to the end and we make a turn. The aircraft plant was right down on the water. It was way down. We looked over the city as we went in and Jack [Hilger, the pilot] would point out something. . . . [The Japanese] didn't recognize us as an

them. That really worked. We just continued right straight over this great big building. All I had to do was just drop the bombs."

With their bombs released, each B-25 crew then had to make the perilous journey to China, and ensure that they landed on an area not occupied by the Japanese. Hilger's official after-action report states what happened next: "About 300 miles [483km] off the China Coast we encountered rain squalls and lowering ceilings and about 100 miles [160km] off the coast at 20:15 the weather got so bad that we pulled up to 1,000ft [305m] and went on instruments. At 21:05 we estimated

Above: Another B-25 prepares for lift-off from Hornet. *Each aircraft carried four 500lb (225kg) bombs, one being an incendiary cluster munition.*

we should be over the coastline and started climbing to 7,000ft [2,133m]. We saw a few breaks but very few lights on the ground. At 22:20 we estimated we were over Chuchow and still on instruments. We had about 40 gallons [151 liters] of gas left and I changed altitude to 8,500ft [2,591m] and ordered the crew to jump. The crew abandoned the ship quickly and with no confusion. After the co-pilot jumped I trimmed the ship for flight at 170mph [274km/h] . . . and abandoned ship. I heard the plane crash shortly after my chute opened and the site was later visited by the co-pilot. The ship was badly smashed and had been stripped by vandals.No injuries to crew members other than bruises and sprains. The entire route was flown at 100ft [32m] except when making the bombing runs and when on instruments near the China coast. . . . When I landed from my jump I was shaken up but not seriously injured. I was on a very steep mountain so I made a tent of part of chute and rolled up in the rest of it and spent the night there. The next morning I discovered a small village at the foot of the mountain and one of the villagers took me to a road where I met a military party out searching for us. I was taken to Kwang Feng, about 15 miles [24km] from where I landed and then sent to Chuchow the next night."

Targets struck by the Doolittle Raid were Kobe, Nagoya, Yoksuka naval yard, Yokohama, and Tokyo. About fifty Japanese citizens were killed, and nine of the US aircrew also died on the mission, some executed by the Japanese when captured in occupied China.

James H. Doolittle

For a brief period in April 1942, James H. Doolittle became the most famous man in America. The US public, dispirited by a string of grim news from the Pacific Theater, were euphoric at the Doolittle-led raid against the Japanese homeland, seeing it as part payback for Pearl Harbor and a defiant threat for the future. Born on December 14, 1896, in Alameda, California, James Harold Doolittle began his love affair with military aviation in 1917, when he became a flying cadet in the US Army Signal Corps. With an academic performance as strong as his flying skills, Doolittle rose smoothly through the ranks, working primarily as a test pilot until called upon to command the raid on Japan in April 1942. In fact, the raid actually missed many of its intended targets, and Doolittle returned from the action fearing disciplinary action. By contrast, he was awarded the Medal of Honor and promoted to the rank of brigadier-general. Doolittle went on to hold very senior command positions, including being the commanding general of the 8th, 12th, and 15th Air Forces. He was also a tactical pioneer, refining the relationship between bombers and their fighter escorts.

Above left: *The execution of some of the captured crewmembers from the Doolittle raid provoked a trenchant desire for vengeance in the American public.*
Above right: *James H. Doolittle became a heroic figure following the raid against Japan, and his subsequent career was little short of stellar.*

Carrier Battles—Coral Sea and Midway

"I looked over there and all I could see was the cloud of smoke and nothing under it. Of course the torpedoes hit it, the other bombers hit it . . . there were a lot of hits."

—SBD pilot Stanley Vejtasa, the battle of Midway, June 4, 1942

The Pacific War was, from a naval perspective, fundamentally dictated by two types of vessel— submarines and aircraft carriers. When thinking about carriers, we must not take this point too far. Carriers were not unilateral warfighting machines; their very importance meant that they required heavy escort protection (including from submarines), plus continual logistic support. In essence, carriers were ships around which the fleet structure had to be built.

The most important virtue of aircraft carriers was, however, the range of power projection. While a capital warship could strike an enemy only within the limits of its big guns—about 20 miles (32km) at maximum range— carrier aircraft could have a combat radius of 300 miles (482km). Such range was a burden as much as an opportunity. Carrier forces had to chose the right moment, based on sound intelligence and a defined objective, to launch its squadrons. Get that timing wrong, and the result could be a carrier group stripped of its aviation defense at a critical point in the battle. Get it right, and a distant enemy could be overwhelmed by a surprise strike.

American, Japanese, and British carriers did not come in uniform sizes. They ranged from diminutive escort carriers,

Left: The American aircraft carrier USS Yorktown *was severely damaged during the battle of Coral Sea, with a Japanese bomb penetrating below decks and causing sixty-six casualties.*

carrying fewer than twenty aircraft, to major fleet carriers with more than 130 aircraft. For example, the US escort carrier USS *Casablanca* (CVE-55) had a standard displacement of 7,800 tons and carried twenty-eight aircraft, with a complement of 916 men. The USS *Midway* fleet carrier, by contrast, was commissioned just as World War II ended, but had a 45,000-ton displacement, carried 137 aircraft, and had a crew of 4,104 sailors and aviators.

The two battles that dominate this chapter were both demonstrations of America's emergent ascendancy in carrier warfare, plus turning points in the strategic picture of the Pacific War. In these two battles the Japanese lost five carriers, stripping the IJN of much of its capability to provide air cover to invasion forces or to strike at American shipping. Morever, these losses most be considered in an industrial context. Between 1937 and the end of the war, the Japanese commissioned twenty-two new carriers, five of which were small escort carriers. In the same period, the United States produced and commissioned more than one hundred, including eighty-six escort carriers (some carrying up to thirty-six aircraft) and seventeen fleet carriers of the *Essex* class.

In 1942, the year of Coral Sea and Midway, however, this astonishing disparity in strength had yet to come to fruition. A huge amount still depended on the tactical perception and courage of the fleet commanders, as these great ships engaged in a lethal game of cat and mouse.

New Guinea and the Prelude to Coral Sea

The context for the battle of Coral Sea was the Japanese intention to seize Port Morseby, which was the capital of Papua and a vital staging post for Allied aircraft and shipping transiting to and from the northern coast of Australia. The Japanese had already invaded New Guinea to the north on March 8, 1942, putting forces ashore at Lae and Salamaua, and developing their control during the following April.

Norman Sterrie was a pilot with VT-2 flying from the USS *Lexington*, and in March 1942 he made some of the early US air attacks on the Japanese bridgehead. Terrain was as much of a threat as the enemy:

"Well, our first mission was a surprise attack on ships that were gathering in Salamaua, New Guinea. That's a small community on the north shore of New Guinea. We were on the south side, about a hundred miles south of the shoreline. To get there we had to cross the mountains over a pass that I think was 9,000ft [2,743m]. The question was, 'Can a torpedo plane carry a torpedo at 9,000ft?' Nobody had ever been that high with one, so we just had to see. The group commander went into Port Moresby to get information about the route and he returned with a map that was probably drawn from a National Geographic magazine. So we were all equipped with mimeographed copies of this penciled out thing and that was our intelligence. Well, then came time for the takeoff. . . . We took off and the torpedo planes approached this mountain. I was turkey under-the-line, it looked like the lead plane was taking us right into the side of the mountain and we got almost to the mountain and I was ready to make a turn ahead of time. But the squadron commander made a flip over on the side, made a turn, and we went back and started over. It was about, I suppose, a 5-mile [8km] ascent which was all that we could get out of it. The next time we cleared the pass at 50 to 100ft [15–30m] I'm sure, and then descended on the other side and found very few ships there, and made an attack. I think we lost one bomber in that episode. The group commander was stationed over the pass because he had to report if the pass was closing, which it did everyday around noon, I guess. We returned airight. The pass had not closed over yet on the return and got to the ship on the other side."

During April 1942, the IJN formulated a plan to take Port Moresby by amphibious invasion,

Above: The Grumman TBF Avenger aircraft was a torpedo bomber that first entered service in 1942, although just slightly too late to take part in Coral Sea.

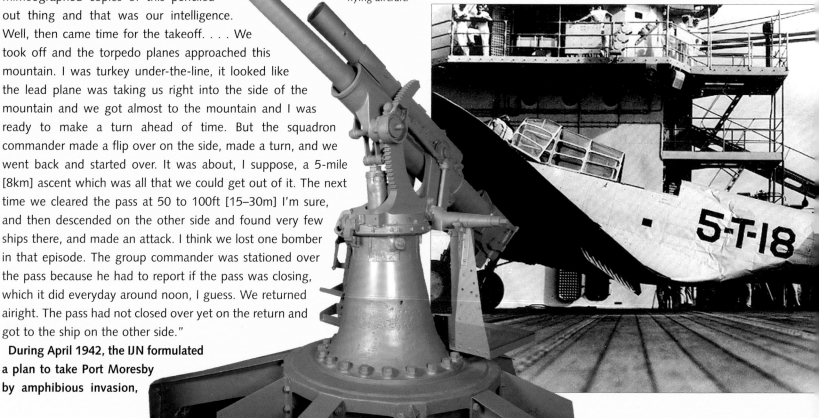

Below left: A Type 3 80mm Japanese Navy antiaircraft gun. Because the gun could be lowered three degrees below the horizontal, it could engage low-flying aircraft.

along with an assault on Tulagi in the southern Solomons. To protect the invasion forces from US surface and carrier threats, the IJN also deployed two covering forces, which together included the carriers *Shoho*, *Shokaku*, and *Zuikaku*. It was these forces that were intercepted by, ultimately, three US task forces in the Coral Sea (TF 11, 17, and 44), with TF 17 operating the carrier *Yorktown* and TF 11 the carrier *Lexington*. Battle began on May 4, and Stanley Vejtasa, an SBD pilot on *Yorktown*, remembers the call to action: "They [the Japanese] were going to take Port Moresby. Initially an Army Air Corps medium bomber sighted this Japanese fleet. There was one carrier with accompanying vessels and a number of troop ships and supply ships with escorts. They were north of New Guinea in the Bismarck Sea. Immediately the word had come 'Attack!' so we loaded up and the order was given to attack."

Below left: Aboard the USS Yorktown, *a damaged TBD from VT-5 sits on the flight deck, awaiting removal and repairs.*

Below right: New Guinea, 1942. Here we see Australian troops ready for action aboard the Universal Carrier, a diminutive tracked vehicle intended for light reconnaissance duties. The central armament of these vehicles is the Vickers machine gun, but the Bren Gun was more common.

Chester Nimitz

Fleet Admiral Chester W. Nimitz (1885–1966) was, alongside General Douglas MacArthur, one of the formative figures in US Pacific War strategy. Born in 1885 in Texas, Nimitz originally attempted to enter the US Army through West Point, but in the absence of available appointments he instead entered the US Naval Academy in 1901. As history would show, it was a fortuitous move, and Nimitz rose fluidly through the ranks, serving aboard submarines (his main specialty), cruisers, battleships, and refueling vessels. In 1939, he was appointed Chief of the Bureau of Navigation. Now in the upper circles of military governance, he impressed President Roosevelt sufficiently that in December 1941 he was appointed to commander-in-chief, United States Pacific Fleet (CINCPACFLT), ranked as an admiral, just days after the Pearl Harbor attack. In the Pacific Theater,

Nimitz proved himself as an aggressive combat commander, seeking out the enemy actively and appointing like-minded individuals to senior commands. He once said: "It is the function of the Navy to carry the war to the enemy so that it is not fought on US soil." From April 1942 his authority extended well beyond just the US naval forces, when he was appointed the C-in-C Pacific Ocean Areas (CINCPOA), with control of all land and air forces within his strategic area. In this role, he worked to refine and perfect the tactics and logistics of amphibious warfare. His leadership was a driving force behind the victories at Coral Sea and Midway, and he came to dominate the Japanese through his strategic decisions.

Top right: The great naval commander of the Pacific War, Admiral Chester Nimitz. He served in the US Navy for more than fifty years, and was known for his strategic acuity and solid leadership.

Coral Sea — First Kills

On May 3, 1942, aircraft from the *Yorktown* conducted raids against the successful Japanese landings at Tulagi. For the next few days, however, the US and the Japanese fleets attempted to locate one another, with the IJN Carrier Striking Force, commanded by Vice-Admiral Takeo Takagi, entering the Coral Sea area on May 5, where Vice-Admiral Frank Fletcher had gathered the three task forces. On May 7, the two forces began to come to blows, with Japanese aircraft first locating and sinking the destroyer *Sims* and damaging the fleet oiler *Neosho*. The clash culminated in *Yorktown* and *Lexington* launching their aircraft against the carrier *Shoho*, part of the Japanese Covering Group under Rear-Admiral Aritomo Goto.

Norman Sterrie was torpedo-bomber pilot in VT-2 aboard the USS *Lexington*, and was soon in action: "I recall a lot of things about the battle. The first day, it would have been May 7 I think, the *Yorktown* had spotted this carrier at Tulagi and I think it was a support ship for the fleet that they anticipated coming through later on. But on May 7 I think the *Yorktown* got to it first. It was a bright sun-shiny day and from a distance we could see the smoke from the carrier. I think we probably made a pretty routine approach to the thing, but as I looked over my shoulder I spotted a plane diving on me and sure enough my gunner opened fire and nearly shot my tail off. I didn't know about that until I had returned to the ship. The ship [*Shoho*] had slowed down by the time we had got to it and it presented a perfect target from the broadside and the twelve

Above: *The USS* Neosho, *a Cimarron-class fleet oiler, burns in the Coral Sea after being hit by more than seven Japanese bombs. The ship sank on May 11, 1942.*

of us dropped our torpedoes at it from an ideal location. I think there were five hits recorded on that, but who did what was anybody's guess. We returned to base and everybody was feeling good."

Another American pilot participating in the strike upon the *Shoho* was SBD pilot Stanley Vejtasa, flying off the *Yorktown*: "We found the carrier. It just happened that I had the staff gunnery officer in my rear seat. He wanted to make a combat flight. He was one brave man because I don't think he had ever done any dive-bombing or had even ridden in a dive-bomber before. This is a pretty rigorous trip, you know, not only going high, but it was cold as hell up there, because there was no heat or anything in our SBDs and we had to have oxygen, that had to work, and of course there was the business of doing the dives and releasing the bomb. So for the rear-seat man, it's rigorous. Anyway this was the best coordinated attack I ever participated in, mostly due to our skipper because he had everything timed. We had broken radio silence and he was talking to the other air group so they could coordinate and time everything and he was also talking to the torpedo planes. He knew just how far to go so the torpedo planes could break formation and be in

Above: *The INJS* Zuikaku *launches numerous Mitsubishi A6M Zero aircraft from her flight deck. The carrier had a total of seventy-two aircraft on board, including eighteen Zeros and twenty-seven B5N2 "Kates."*

Right: *A pair of goggles worn by a US dive-bomber pilot, to protect against dust and airflow.*

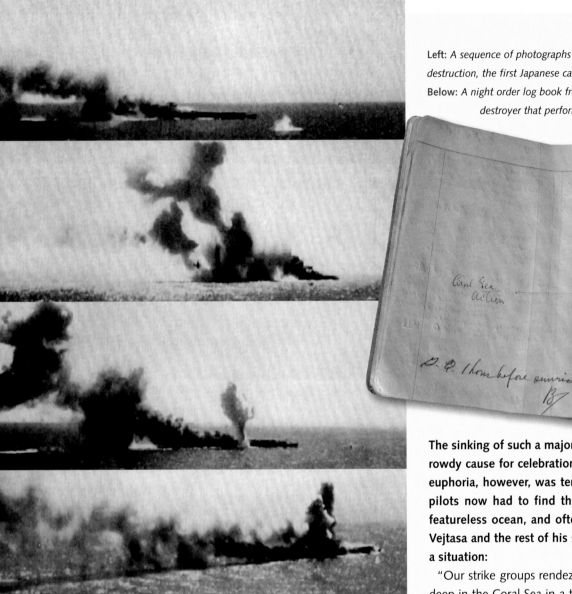

Left: *A sequence of photographs shows the INJS* Shoho *being bombed to destruction, the first Japanese carrier sunk in World War II.*

Below: *A night order log book from the USS* Phelps, *a US Navy Porter-class destroyer that performed escort duty for the carriers at Midway.*

position for their attack right after our bombing runs and we did that. . . . He was flying an SBD. He was the leader. I was right behind him in the dive. I saw his 500lb [227kg] bomb leave the airplane, wiggle a little bit, then steady down to hit right into the middle of the flight deck about a third of the way back from the bow.

"I looked over there and all I could see was the cloud of smoke and nothing under it. Of course the torpedoes hit it, the other bombers hit it, and we hit it so there were a lot of hits. You'd never count the hits. It went down, right down, a complete loss of life. We rendezvoused down there and back through, this is an interesting thing. This was actually the first phase of the Battle of the Coral Sea—the sinking of the *Shoho*."

The sinking of such a major target as an aircraft carrier was obviously a rowdy cause for celebration amongst the US carrier combat pilots. The euphoria, however, was tempered by the dawning realization that the pilots now had to find their way back to a distant carrier, across a featureless ocean, and often in conditions of complete radio silence. Vejtasa and the rest of his squadron now had to wrestle with just such a situation:

"Our strike groups rendezvoused to return to our carriers, which were deep in the Coral Sea in a tropical front. Raining! Foggy! High winds! It was a mess. We're on radio silence again now. The ship is not putting out any signals. You've got to find that thing by dead reckoning. I tell you we were all tucked in close to the skipper. He was a good one and all the rest of us were good on instruments as we had been doing searches for over a year, I guess. Well actually we had been doing searches longer than that because we started doing them even in the Atlantic. Out and in, that sort of thing. I was timing the whole thing and almost at the exact moment, I looked down and there was the *Yorktown*. I could see it through the fog right below us."

The sinking of the *Shoho* had been a stunning early victory for the US carriers. It sank at 1135hrs with the loss of more than 600 lives, having been struck by at least seven torpedoes and thirteen bombs. The Japanese were keen to enact revenge.

Flying from a Flat Top

Carrier operations required a special breed of pilot, not easily given to anxiety. Carrier operations pose readily understandable challenges. Compared to a conventional land airfield, a carrier deck is an extremely small and crowded area on which to perform take-off and landing. The deck of the USS *Lexington*, for example, was 866ft 2in (264m) long and 105ft 11in (32.3m) at its maximum width. Adding to the pilot's problems was the fact that this surface was in sympathetic movement with the sea.

The chief challenge of a carrier take-off was gaining sufficient airspeed to avoid dropping into the sea off the end of the deck. The carrier would turn into the headwind, thereby adding the natural windspeed to that of the aircraft, and the aircraft would run its engine at full revs before being hurled down the deck by a hydraulic catapult system. As long as the pilot could keep the airspeed above a stall, he would be OK.

Landings were the real challenge. John Nash undertook pilot training for the US Navy in 1942–43, and remembers the basic training methods: "We went out to one of the auxiliary fields. . . . They took one runway and painted a carrier deck on it in white paint and even had the landing wires. They didn't have the wires but they had stripes across it to tell you where they would be. Then we learned to make carrier approaches and landings without an LSO—landing signal officer. Then for graduation from that little portion; it only took us about a month or maybe less than that to do that; then they brought us brought for a final [test with] an

actual LSO, who would bring us in for a landing. You had to come in and set down and get one of those six wires. Our aircraft had no hooks on them. When you graduated from that then they took twenty-five of us to Glenview Naval Air Station in Illinois for carrier certification, I guess you would call it that. I think that's about all I can tell you, although it was all in my logbook.

"When we got up to Glenview they had procured an old ore boat called the *Wolverine* on Lake Michigan and they had built a flight deck on it and put in the six landing wires and a crash net. Then we went up, five of us at a time. One guy would come around and make his five landings and takeoffs in a row. You didn't alternate with the second guy coming in; no, you did your five landings in a row, but with no catapult. Just flyaway. You would come in and hit the wire. . . . If you missed all the wires they had a crash net to stop you. They back you up and drop the crash net and then you rev up and take off. That is your first takeoff and then you come in and make the second landing and the third landing and fourth landing and the fifth landing. Then you circle while the other three guys do it."

Below: The Vought F4U Corsair was one of the finest carrier-based fighters of World War II. It was maneuverable, fast, and capable of withstanding all manner of punishment. Not only was it used in the fighter role, but it also excelled in the ground-attack role, delivering close air support.

Above: Douglas SBD-5 Dauntless dive-bomber was the key aircraft at the battle of Midway, largely responsible for the destruction of four Japanese carriers. Note the dive brakes on the aircraft's trailing edges.

Left: A Helldiver prepares to touch down on a carrier deck, with its wheels, air brakes and arrestor hook all in the lowered positions. Landing was one of the the most dangerous phases of a carrier aircraft flight.

Right: An oil-spattered naval work uniform, such as might be worn by an LSO on the carrier deck. Any flight deck carrier work was uncomfortable, dangerous, and dirty.

The LSO was a critical part of the success of a carrier landing. Through signal paddles he would provide visual guidance to the pilot about how to adjust the landing attitude and speed to ensure that the plane's arrester hook connected with one of the arrester wires. At night, however, the LSO would often just have to determine the plane's approach pattern by aircraft lights (which changed color with altitude) and by the engine sound. The LSO played an absolutely critical role, and his influence over carrier safety was fundamental. Nevertheless, carriers landings always remained dangerous; more than seventy aircraft were lost during night landings in the battle of Philippine Sea.

Victory at Coral Sea

At around 0815hrs on May 8, the Japanese and US fleets located each other once again, and Takagi launched a major strike, as did the _Yorktown_ and _Lexington_ once again. The US carrier aircraft located and attacked the _Shokaku_. Norman Sterrie was again part of these attacks:

"The anticipation of what was going to happen was anybody's guess. The 8th was the early launch of airplanes and I imagine that the Japanese did the same thing because whoever got there first had the best target. When we got the report from the scouts of where the location was of the enemy, we took off and the bombers took off ahead of us instead of waiting for us and away they went. We generally had counted on doing a coordinated attack, but I don't know what happened there, but anyway, they got to where they thought the target was and it wasn't there. And likewise for us, so we undertook what they call an expanding rectangular search, but in the middle of our search, or towards the beginning at least, we had a call from the group commander saying that he had spotted the enemy and that they were some 40 miles [64km] to the south of us, so we headed back there. In the meantime, the bombers had run out of gas and were dumping their bombs in the ocean and returned to base. We located the Japanese and made a descent into the level through rainy weather, which really saved us because we did not encounter any opposition coming in. The squadron commander led us in the attack and I think he himself overshot a bit and wanted a better target so he went around. I was his wingman, but I had already made my drop into the carrier, which was making a turn at the time. I did not realize that he had failed to drop until I got closer to him and could see the torpedo underneath. I followed him around and he went in on the fleet and I went in with him about a quarter to a half mile away. I had nothing to offer except diversion for their antiaircraft fire. As we got closer in we got bounced around encountering very rough air, which I deduced was the slipstream from the 5in shells. I thought to myself I cannot go any farther with this because we were getting a little too close. By that time the skipper, Nagan, made his drop and we got out of the way and we gathered the rest of the squadron."

Left: Naval binoculars used by an officer aboard the USS Yorktown. Constant surveillance was critical in the Pacific Theater, both of the seemingly endless ocean and of the huge Pacific skies.

Above left: *A huge explosion curls up from the deck of the USS* Lexington *during the battle of Coral Sea. The badly damaged carrier was eventually scuttled by US forces on May 8, 1942.*

Above right: *The Japanese carrier* Shokaku *is pounded by US bombs. US dive-bombers managed to secure three hits upon the carrier at Coral Sea, forcing the vessel back to Japan for repairs.*

The *Shokaku* had been hit and disabled by the US attack, but meanwhile worse punishment was being meted out to TF 17 and TF 11, which came under Japanese air attacks at around 1115hrs. *Lexington* was struck by numerous bombs and torpedoes, and Norman Sterrie was present as the ship descended into conflagration: "Anyway, I landed aboard and I was spotted on the front elevator and as I proceeded to jump off the plane, there was a tremendous explosion underneath the plane and me and everybody else in it went up about three or four feet. There were explosions all around. The fuel lines had been ruptured on the *Lexington* below decks and they could not get the fuel so we and the planes and everything else were destined to remain aboard.

"After I got out of the plane, I tried to go below deck, but everything was sealed off. I had a good clarinet down there and a bottle of scotch that was full, and they had to go down with the ship. In the meantime, about half the crew was on the bow and the other half was on the stern. I was toward the stern and for about two hours of so we stood back there wondering why we were still aboard waiting for the 'abandon ship' [order] because there were explosions after explosions all through the afternoon and we thought that when it gets to the magazines, maybe that'll spur a little action.

"Finally the call came after they'd taken all the wounded off, I remember trying to get below deck to my cabin and having to cross a gun emplacement on which somebody had neatly piled up about half a dozen bodies. That was my introduction to real war. When the 'abandon ship' came, people went into the water anyway they could get there and I went to my plane and took out a raft. I blew it up and lowered it and looked down and it was all full as soon as it hit the water: any port in a storm. I went to another plane, got a rail and told a friend that I was going to lower this down and I want you to go with it and hold a place for me, please, which he did, but the place was about one hand width around a line surrounding the raft. We were in the water for probably fifteen minutes to a half an hour [when] a lifeboat from one of the surrounding ships came and picked us up and it happened to be the *New Orleans*, I think. We ascended up on a rope ladder to the safety of the *New Orleans*. That was the battle of the Coral Sea."

With the sinking of *Lexingon*, the battle of Coral Sea ended in an apparent draw, with both sides losing a carrier. Yet there were three factors that tipped the balance of the final reckoning somewhat in the Americans' favor. First, the Japanese had lost more aircraft—ninety-two as opposed to sixty-nine. Second, the amphibious invasion of Port Moresby was called off. Finally, and looking ahead, Coral Sea set the scene for a truly decisive American victory at Midway just a month later.

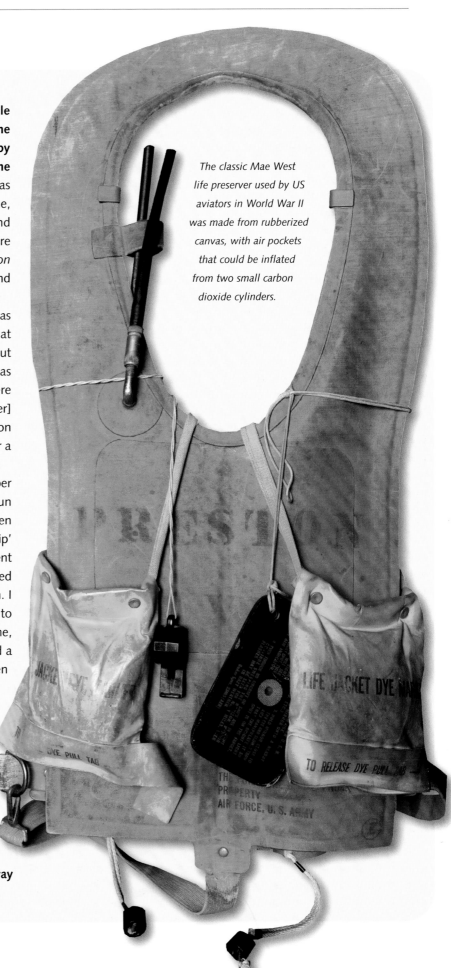

The classic Mae West life preserver used by US aviators in World War II was made from rubberized canvas, with air pockets that could be inflated from two small carbon dioxide cylinders.

Aleutians and the Build-up to Midway

The battle of Midway was the outcome of a complex gathering of events. Following the battle at Coral Sea, Admiral Isoroku Yamamoto, the commander-in-chief of the IJN, opted to extend the Japanese defensive perimeter of the new Japanese Empire by capturing the island of Midway in the Central Pacific, scheduled for early June. The three main components of the Midway operation were the First Carrier Striking Force, with the carriers *Kaga*, *Akagi*, *Soryu*, and *Hiryu*, plus two other sizable naval formations containing the invasion troops, two light carriers, and multiple other warships.

As a sleight of hand to lure US naval forces away from Midway, the Japanese also invaded and occupied Kiska and Attu in the Aleutians in the North Pacific, an action that prompted a bloody and largely forgotten campaign in the frozen north. Richard Salter was a B-26 pilot in the Aleutians in 1942, and was tasked with making strikes against the Japanese shipping: "So now we were at Adak, and in the first mission

Left: A Zero fighter is caught on camera going down in flames over Akutan Island in the Aleutians. The aircraft was recovered by the US forces, and it was subsequently labeled the "Akutan Zero."

out of there—with a torpedo underneath the belly of my airplane—I was leading an element of three B-26s, and we made a torpedo run against a Japanese ship anchored in what we called Gertrude Cove at Kiska. We were told the altitude and air speed to fly at. I'm not sure, but I think they said to fly at an altitude of 200ft [61m] and an air speed of 180mph [290km/h]. So I started in on my run, and I had never been in combat before. As I was proceeding, I looked ahead and saw all these big black puffs of smoke up ahead. I was momentarily confused as to what it was, but I very quickly realized that they were shooting at us. Fortunately, we got out of there without any loss, but the mission had a negative result. Very shortly after that . . . a very young crew was on a mission to the same target, and they were shot down."

The Japanese Aleutians ruse was not taken by the US Navy; Nimitz knew of Yamamoto's real plans by virtue of intelligence intercepts. Thus he sent TF 16 and TF 17, which included the carriers *Yorktown*, *Enterprise*, and *Hornet*, to intercept the Japanese forces at Midway. The commanding officer of the *Enterprise*, Captain George Murray, later reported the build-up to contact from June 3:

"1. On the afternoon and evening of June 3, 1942, the general situation prior to the battle was as follows (times throughout are Zone plus 10): Task Force Seventeen and Task Force Sixteen had previously rendezvoused in the general vicinity of 'Point Luck,' approximately 350 miles [563km] northeast of Midway Island and were operating in that area closing Midway during darkness and opening during the day, remaining east of the longitude of Midway. Both Task Forces has completed fueling to capacity and the oilers dispatched to their rendezvous. The Senior Officer Present Afloat and Officer in Tactical Command

Left: African-American soldiers serving in a labor battalion in the Aleutians tuck into some basic food after a field kitchen was set up on a beach.

Above: *A Consolidated PBY-5A Catalina amphibious patrol bomber conducts a patrol over the Aleutians in late 1942. The landscape of the Aleutian islands was radically different to that of the rest of the Pacific Theater, being characterized by deep snowfall and sub-zero temperatures.*

Right: *An aerial view of Midway Atoll, showing the eastern island with its airfield.*

Far right: *An aerial photograph of Attu village. At the time of the Japanese invasion the population of the village was just forty-five people.*

was in YORKTOWN. The two task forces were separated but were within visual contact. They were operating independently but generally conforming in their movements. At 2150 course was changed to 210° T. toward a 0630, June 4, rendezvous (31° 30' N; 176° 30' W) designated by Commander Task Force 17. At 1812 a radio message from Flight 312 to Radio Midway was intercepted '2 enemy destroyers 2 cargo vessels course 020 speed 13.'

2. At 2000, June 3, 1942, ENTERPRISE, Flagship of Commander Task Force 16 was in position 33° 16' N, 175° 46' W, in the center as guide of Cruising Disposition 11-V, axis 270° T, course 100°T, speed 15 knots and zigzagging according to Plan Number 7. Wind south 9, clouds cumulus 7, visibility 30, sea smooth.

3. The following significant messages were received during the night of June 3–4:

At 0447 – from Flight 44 to Radio Midway 'large enemy forces bearing 261° T, distance 500 course 080 speed 13 x ten ships.'

At 0734 – from Flight 58 to Radio Midway 'enemy carriers'.

At 0753 – from Flight 58 to Radio Midway 'many planes heading Midway bearing 320 distance 150.'

At 0803 – from Flight 92 to Radio Midway '2 carriers and battleships bearing 320° distance 180 course 135 speed 25.'

At 0807 – from Commander Task Force 17 to Commander Task Force 16 'proceed southwesterly and attack enemy carriers when definitely located.'"

By this time, the Japanese fleet had already begun its offensive action, launching a wave of carrier aircraft strikes against Midway island at 0430hrs, and beating off an attempted counter-response from land-based aircraft on Midway. Yet the commander of the First Carrier Strike Force, Vice-Admiral Nagumo, was about to be confronted with some critical decisions. He decided to rearm his second-wave aircraft, which had been equipped with antiship weaponry, with land-attack munitions for another strike against Midway. Around 0830hrs, his first-wave aircraft returned to the carriers. The upshot was that his carrier decks were crowded with refueling and rearming aircraft.

Midway — June 4

The US carriers began launching their first strikes around 0752hrs. An unescorted force of US torpedo bombers was virtually massacred by enemy fighters when it attempted to make its assault at 0930hrs, a fact that gave Nagumo some complacency. Then, in a game-changing action, a cloud of US dive-bombers found the three carriers at around 1025hrs, the ships' decks cluttered thickly with aircraft undergoing refueling and rearming. Captain Jack Kleiss was a dive-bomber pilot during this action:

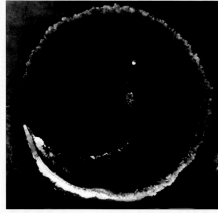

Left: In this striking image, the Japanese carrier Soryu circles widely in a desperate attempt to avoid bombs dropped by a B-17 Flying Fortress bomber above. The ship was damaged by dive-bombers and was scuttled.

"Sure enough, we looked there and here were three aircraft carriers close and 20 miles [32km] away was another one. McClusky says 'Dick you take the one on the left, Earl and I will take the one on the right.' Within two minutes, as we started our dive the one that was the closest was the *Kaga* and Dick Best took the *Akagi*. They were just like a haystack on fire. . .

"When we hit there I saw two bombs miss. Earl Gallaher was determined that he was going to get involved. He came in and hit a plane that was near the stern of the deck as it was just starting to move forward. His bombs landed right smack on top of it: a 500lb [227kg] bomb and two 200lb [91kg] incendiaries, just left and right. Immediately, this thing was a mass of flame 50ft [15m] tall. . . . There were two planes ahead of me and I was so busy with my run that I didn't see where they hit. But I did notice the fire had gone up towards mid-ship. Now whether it was another bomb or bombs or whatever, anyway the fire had moved forward against all the wind for some reason. Then the red circle right at fore of the ship was uncluttered and I put one right on top of it and my two incendiaries on top. I turned around and took a look and immediately it was just a great big bunch of fire. [It was reported] that this hit a large gasoline tank and forced this gasoline tank up underneath the bridge, which set up a great big fire. At that point, I was a little bit busy, and here was a fighter coming at me.

John Snowden got him or made him go away. Then another one came in and we got him. Then came the antiaircraft [fire]. I couldn't really see what was going on until I got far away. But even when I got 10 or 20 miles [16 or 32km] away, I could see pieces of items of the ship going up the air a thousand feet high. A lot higher than I was, throwing these pieces up. Then I could see there were these two flames and here was the third flame over here. Now within two minutes two [Japanese carriers] were in massive flame and within less than two minutes more the third one was on fire.

Kleiss was witnessing a truly remarkable event in the history of the Pacific War. In a matter of five minutes, the Japanese fleet had lost three carriers—*Kaga*, *Akagi*, and *Soryu*—ripping the heart out of the

Right: The USS Yorktown *heels to port after a torpedo strike on June 4, 1942, at Midway. The damaged ship was torpedoed by a submarine two days later, and sank.*

Left: *A lifesaver such as this one was essential kit for US air crews operating in the Pacific, as ditching was common during carrier battles.*

I was twelfth position in the formation so there were eleven ahead of me in the dive. You see four or five ahead of you in the dive and you see the bombs dropping and they pull out. I went down at a dive angle of about sixty to seventy degrees. The plane has split flaps and . . . 240 knots is about the maximum speed with the split flaps. In those days you had what you call a gun sight, which is a tube with cross hairs in it. You look through that and in the meantime you are flying the plane and you have to keep it balanced. I put the cross hairs on the leading edge of the carrier. The radioman called out the altitude, five thousand, four thousand, three thousand, twenty-five hundred because when you are

Above left: *An SBD-3 Dauntless is forced to ditch during the battle of Midway, landing by the side of the USS* Astoria.

Above right: *Survivors from the embattled USS* Yorktown *are transferred from the USS* Portland *(right) to the USS* Fulton.

IJN's carrier force. Lewis R. Hopkins was an SBD pilot flying off the *Enterprise*, and also remembers this startling attack:

"I did not see any torpedo planes and the amazing thing was there were no fighters. There were no fighters until we got down. We didn't have any resistance. They didn't even have any [anti]aircraft fire. They didn't see us. The Japanese side of this tells about people on the deck and they don't see the SBDs until some of them are actually in their dive. They see at that point in time that it is too late to do anything about it.

looking in the cross hairs you can't see the altimeter. He calls twenty-five hundred and a Zero [is] coming from the right. I went ahead and released the bomb and immediately turned in to the Zero in a defensive maneuver. I think post analysis showed that I didn't get a hit. Usually you can drop your bomb and make a left turn and look back over your shoulder and see your bomb hit. I didn't have that opportunity since I was busy with the attacking Zero. I got down on the water as close as I could and Anderson the gunner says, 'Let's get the hell out of here.' I said, 'What do you think I'm trying to do?' Basically we are in the middle of the Japanese fleet when we pull out."

Despite the sudden victory, the US fleet was still in danger, as the *Hiryu* carrier remained active. It launched its aircraft just before midday on June 4.

US propaganda

Every country during World War II engaged in propaganda to a greater or lesser extent, and the United States was no exception. It must be remembered that for many years prior to the Japanese attack on Pearl Harbor, the American public at large had been equivocal about US involvement in distant overseas conflicts. The Japanese assault of December 7, 1941, changed that perspective through direct threat, but the US government was ever mindful of the need to marshal the population behind broader war aims, and to focus their efforts into meaningful action.

A key practical step in the creation and distribution of propaganda was the establishment of the Office of War Information (OWI) in June 1942. The ostensible purpose of the OWI was to educate the public about the war and its aims, but it also had deep links with the creative industries, including the Hollywood film-makers. Thus it was that the OWI began a prolific propaganda campaign, the output of which covered all manner of creative media, from posters and press adverts through to motion pictures and comic books.

Looking back at the materials from modern times, it is easy to be struck by the gratuitously racist portrayal of the Japanese people, especially in poster art. The exaggeration of Japanese facial features was grotesque,

Above and right: While the poster above encourages civilians to engage in war production with maximum effort, the poster to the right promotes enlistment to one of the less-understood sections of the US armed services.

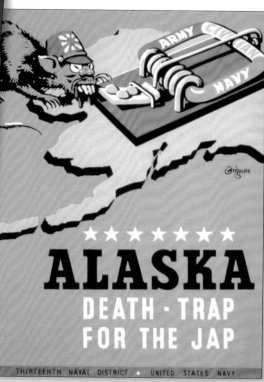

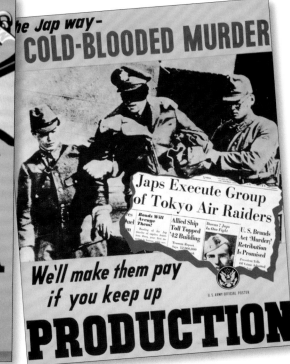

This page: The racial stereotyping of the Japanese people in US propaganda is egregious to modern eyes, but at the time tapped into a very focused desire both for American vengeance and a conclusion to a prolonged war.

with the Japanese often characterized as vermin such as rats, or as predatory underworld creatures like sprawling octopuses, the tentacles wrapping around the globe. Such degradation was generally contrasted with the image of the US soldier, airmen, or sailor, who was strong, clean-cut, patriotic, and noble. The depiction of the Japanese, which ran through all media, can be revealingly contrasted with that of the German forces. While the OWI could sometimes make an almost forgiving distinction between the politically rabid Nazis and the rest of the population, which itself needed to be free from Hitler's domination, the Japanese were universally and unswervingly regarded as grotesque creatures, deserving of little but their own destruction.

In fact, posters were among the most influential types of OWI propaganda produced during the war, and more than 20,000 designs were created, often to extremely high standards of artistry and color print. They were displayed widely in public places, such as train stations, post offices, schools, restaurants, and shops. The themes of the posters was varied. Sometimes they just aspired to give focus to the American desire for revenge, but they had a range of far sharper goals, especially to attract recruits to the major armed services, to encourage new heights of industrial production, to encourage acts of conservation, and to promote the purchase war bonds.

Beyond poster art, the OWI had many other tools at its disposal. Hollywood used its imaginative power and its celebrities to project an anti-Axis message through either ridicule or through sombre information. One particularly important series of films was entitled *Why We Fight*, and was produced by Italian-American file director Franz Capra, at the request of General George C. Marshall, Chief of Staff of the US Army. This seven-episode documentary series explained the essential reasons why the United States was involved in all the major theaters. The Pearl Harbor film was entitled *War Comes to America*, and explained why it was imperative that Japan be defeated. Although the series was originally made with the purpose of giving political and geographical orientation to new recruits, it was eventually released to the public at large.

The heyday of the Hollywood propaganda war film was between 1942 and 1944. At first many of them had a saccharine quality, with the experience of war given a heroic and glossary lamination. However, during the late war years, as interest in war films began to decline, the producers began to issue more nuanced depictions of conflict. *The Purple Heart* (1944) starred Dana Andrews and Richard Conte, and essentially dramatized the story of the US aircrew who fell into Japanese hands following the Doolittle Raid. The fact that it was the first film to deal with POWs shows the growing American confidence that victory was in its grasp.

Across the media, the American people heard one confident voice from its government, a voice that following Midway was grounded in reality.

Turning point at Midway

The aircraft from *Hiryu* found and attacked the US fleet for two-and-a-half hours during the first half of the afternoon of June 4. They preyed particularly upon the *Yorktown*, which was soon suffering grevious blows. Robert Daniels was a crewman aboard *Yorktown*, and was struggling for survival:

Left: An injured airman at Midway is lifted from his aircraft for medical treatment.

Below: Fire-control crews on the Yorktown struggle to quench the fires burning on the flight deck. US carrier flight decks were unarmored.

"...the Japanese were really clobbering us. We took torpedoes just ahead of us, bombs down the stack on the island, and the torpedoes rolled up the catwalk ahead of us like rolling up a curtain. There was a wall of water and debris all over us and scattered 20mm shells all over the place. Then the ship started listing to port and we thought sure she was going to roll over, but we stopped dead in the water.

"After a period of time, we were ordered to abandon ship over the starboard side but, being on the port side, that was easier said than done because we had quite a list to port. We managed to climb up the flight deck and down the starboard side to a boat pocket, where, for some reason, maybe expecting to come back, we took off our shoes and placed them along the side on the deck. We then went down a line to the water. I had on a kapok life jacket over a suit of anti-flash clothing and dungarees. I swam over to a raft which was already full and, about

that time, a very scared sailor, who couldn't swim, grabbed a hold of me to get on the raft. I broke loose from him and swam away, figuring it was easier to float by myself until I was picked up. I noticed I was floating quite a ways from the other ship. One time, a destroyer pulled along side and threw me a line. Just about that time, I reached out to grab it, the Japanese started strafing and the destroyer pulled away at full speed. I didn't feel too worried because I figured I would be picked up but, I noticed I was floating further away from the battle scene. At the same time, the kapok life jacket was soaking up the water and the water was lapping at my mouth. Now, I knew I was in trouble. I knew I had to get rid of some of the clothes under the jacket. Fortunately I had my hunting knife on me and I was able to cut the clothes off, all but the life jacket, belt, and hunting knife and a pair of shorts. That's all I had left on. Still that life jacket wasn't helping much to keep me afloat. All of a sudden, there it was. Floating towards me. A

Above: *A box of lead model ships made to help officers with their ship identification skills.*

Below right: *A US Navy flashlight, critical in the event of a power failure.*

Mae West life jacket, all inflated. I put it on, and I don't know how long a time it took, but finally, I was picked up by a destroyer, which came along. I was fortunate."

Yorktown's fate was sealed, and after suffering the further blows of being torpedoed by a Japanese submarine on June 7 (an attack that also sank the destroyer *Hammann*), the great carrier sank, with the loss of 141 lives. *Hiryu* now became the focal point of US efforts, as US Navy dive-bomber pilot Roy P. Gee remembers: "Upon entering the ready room, I was informed that we were launching on a mission to attack the Japanese carrier *Hiryu*. The attack group would consist of nine VS-8 SBDs carrying 1,000lb [454kg] bombs and seven VB-8 SBDs carrying the 500lb [227kg] bombs that we'd loaded on Midway. No VF escort would be available. The enemy ships were located approximately 162 miles [261km] out, bearing 290 degrees. I plotted my course for intercepting the enemy formation and returning to the *Hornet*. Lieutenant j.g. Bates, the VB-8 flight leader for this mission, briefed us on tactics for the strike. We were ready to go. . . .

"Just as we were approaching the dive point, we noticed several explosions on the ocean's surface, quite some distance from the target. Looking up, we saw a flight of B-17s high above us. They'd dropped their bomb loads right through our formation, missing us as well as the

Above: *The Japanese carrier Hiryu, a smouldering ruin at the battle of Midway, and later to be scuttled. Hiryu was commissioned in 1939 and had an aerial complement of sixty-four aircraft.*

enemy ships! We then tailed off into our dives. Lieutenant j.g. Bates had the lead plane (bomb fell 50ft [15m] off the starboard bow) followed by Ensign Nickerson (100ft [32m] astern). I was next (hit astern). The second section dove next with Ensign White first (miss), followed by Ensign Friez (miss wide), followed by Ensign Barrett (hit on starboard quarter), followed lastly by Ensign Fisher (no release). During the dive, what looked like orange balls were popping up at me and continued coming from all directions during my high-speed retirement at sea level. Following the strike, all sixteen of *Hornet*'s SBDs rendezvoused unscathed and returned to the ship, landing back aboard at dusk. VB-8 had at last lost its combat virginity."

By the end of June 4, the IJN had lost four of its major carriers, a blow from which it would never quite recover. Now not only had the balance of power changed in the Pacific, but the IJN had suffered a mortal dent in its confidence. The battle rumbled on, albeit with a lesser intensity, for three more days, during which time the US aircraft also sank one Japanese cruiser and damaged another. By the time the two forces separated, the Americans were celebrating an undeniable victory.

The Allies Fight Back

> "Don't let anybody tell you that when you've been in a
> firefight and your buddies are laying next to you all blown
> to bits that you're not scared from then on. I don't know
> of anybody that just didn't have knots
> in their stomach. . . ."
>
> —Martin L. Clayton, USMC, 5th Marine Regiment, 1st Marine Division

The battle of Midway was a pivotal moment in the history of the Pacific War. From this point onwards, Japan started its progressive fall into a defensive strategy, pressed by the swelling military might of the newly confident US armed services.

Following Midway, the US Joint Chiefs of Staff set about examining how to go on the offensive against Japan. The first targets in its sights were the Solomons Islands and New Guinea. If the Americans could begin to wrest control of these islands, then Japan's grip on its southern perimeter would be severely weakened, not least by the Americans isolating or taking the staging base at Rabaul. In early August 1942, US forces occupied Tulagi and embedded themselves at Guadalcanal, creating a vigorously contested anchor point in the southern Solomons. The US Marine Corps defense of the so-called Henderson Field became the stuff of legend, and the IJN's attempts to control the seas around the islands resulted in some of the greatest naval battles of the war. Nevertheless, the US effort paid off. The foothold on Guadalacanal survived the year. Meanwhile, Australian and US forces were struggling for survival in a grim battle in New Guinea. A major Japanese landing at Buna on July 21/22

saw the Allies pushed back under pressure over the mountainous Owen Stanley range, nearly to Port Moresby, before they returned on the offensive and undid all the Japanese gains, retaking Buna in January 1943.

At the beginning of 1943, a critical strategic decision was taken by the American high command. General Douglas MacArthur was given command of the South-West Pacific Area, with responsibility for operations in New Guinea, the Solomons, the Philippines, the Bismarck archipelago, and the Dutch East Indies (which included Borneo). Admiral Chester Nimitz took charge of the Pacific Ocean Areas, with responsibility for invading and reclaiming the myriad Japanese-occupied islands dotted across the Pacific Ocean. In essence, Japan was now caught in a vast pincer grip, with MacArthur's forces driving up from the south, and Nimitz from the east.

This vast, aggressive strategy paid off, although much blood would be spilled in the process. While Nimitz's forces ground across the Pacific in a series of amphibious assaults (covered in the next chapter), during 1943 MacArthur advanced steadily up the Solomons, passing through New Georgia and reaching Bougainville by November. From January 1943 until July 1944, New Guinea was also effectively reclaimed for the Allies, isolating Rabaul, which was reduced to a burning shell by air attacks. The Japanese were starting to see the beginning of their end.

Left: *Hellcats of VF-5 return to the carrier* Yorktown *after a strike against Wake Island on October 5, 1943. Fifteen Japanese aircraft were shot down during the attack.*

Henderson Field

On August 7, 1942, units from the 1st Marine Division were landed on Guadalcanal in the Solomons, against no opposition, while other elements occupied the islands of Tulagi and Gavutu. The Marines advanced quickly overland and took over what they called Henderson Field, where the Japanese had been constructing their own airstrip. Charles E. Loeschorn, a Marine with the 1st Marine Regiment, remembers the largely uneventful initial operations:

"Well, on August 7 I wasn't in the landing the first day. I was assigned aboard ship to unload ammo. I remember of course we went through some air raids. I remember one night somebody was working down in the cargo and we had an air raid and they forgot to shut the light off. We were arguing about who was going to go down to the bottom of the hold and shut the light off because it was a nice target for the planes. Anyway we had air raids for the next few days. I remember the ship we were aboard had steel plates, where apparently it had been a cruise ship or something and they took the glass out and put steel plates in there. When they [the Japanese] were strafing it sounded like marbles dropping on the steel deck. Quite exciting. We unloaded the ships and then we went ashore. As far as I know there wasn't much activity from the Japs at the time of the landing."

The peaceable situation was not to last. The isolated Marines soon found themselves under frequent air attack and naval bombarment, and from August 18 the Japanese began to land troops at Taivu, just 20 miles (32km) away, and then began a series of unrelenting attempts to dislodge the Americans from their positions. Robert Galer was a Grumman F4F Wilcat pilot, flying one of the American aircraft that were

Below: *Surrounded by the puffs of smoke generated by exploding antiaircraft shells, Japanese medium bombers fly in very low over the waters of the Solomons to attack the American landings at Guadalcanal.*

Above: *US Marines hunker down in their trench systems, carved into the ground in positions surrounding Henderson Field. Despite ferocious attacks in October 1942, the Japanese were unable to dislodge the Americans.*

based out of Henderson Field. As well as countering Japanese aircraft, he would also tackle offshore targets:

". . . if there were ships, we'd strafe them. We had Jap navy ships [approaching Guadalcanal] almost every night. It depended on how you worked it out. . . . if they were trying to land troops, we definitely would go strafe them, but we strafed or dive-bombed them or both. We had a lot of problems—poor food, dysentery, malaria. We took anybody [into the air] who was healthy and wanted to go. If he could get in an airplane, he got to come. . ."

In terms of creating the airbase, the US Navy engineers took the lion's share of the work, enduring the punishing Japanese shellings as they worked: "Well, the SeaBees [Navy CBs or Construction Battalions] did the work. They just worked day and night on it. You know, the worst night, I think, was on November 13 or something like that. Theoretically, when the Japanese battleships came down to shell us, they fired 972 big shells, 16in shells, that came in around Henderson Field. When they came in, I landed and taxied over, and thought that I had put my airplane where they couldn't see it. Well, then it rained like hell that night, and we were bombed that night. The next day we got an alert, and I got into my airplane and went back exactly the same way that I came in, except that there was a hole this deep full of water. I ended up like this..." Galer made a gesture indicating that the plane was standing on its front end with the propeller pointing toward the ground.

James R. "Rube" Garrett was a Marine corporal, an ammo chief for I Battery, 3rd Battalion, 11th Regiment. He kept a detailed diary of his experiences on Guadalcanal. He remembered an incident dated to September 15, 1942, which indicated that the Japanese were also suffering in the campaign:

"In our motor section—and anybody who's ever been around an artillery motor section knows they are more or less on their own– they lived off to one side and they were pretty careless about keeping night guards and so on. For some reason, I remember a Japanese slipped in on the motor section. Pfc. Tucker woke up, saw the Japanese, as I recall, lurking around there. He had been sleeping on top of the ground—he hadn't bothered to dig a hole—and the way I understand it, the Japanese threw a hand grenade at him but it didn't go off. I think Tucker shot the guy and finished him. After searching him, we found that he had taken some coffee, some sugar, and I think he had taken one of our American rifles and some ammunition. We buried him there in the motor section the next morning. He was probably starving . . . he was after anything which he could eat. We didn't have much food laying around so he didn't find much."

The Americans at Henderson Field had to hold out for as long as possible, with neither side quite capable of the offensive action required to force the battle to a conclusion.

Struggle for Survival

Life for the Marines at Henderson Field was punctuated by the daily threat of shelling, plus periodic land assaults. One individual who remembers some of the strange effects of the former was Marine ammo chief James R. "Rube" Garrett:

"One day, soon after the drive on the Matanikou, we go back to the battery—me and several troops from my section—went back to pick up whatever ammunition was left behind. I said 'Harry, lets make one last bucket of coffee.' So we lit a fire, and put the proper amount of water in there and the coffee was going good . . . it was like four o'clock in the afternoon, somewhere in that neighborhood . . . and we heard a creaking noise. It was a noise I didn't identify, and in combat one

Above: *December 1942, and Japanese dead litter a Guadalcanal beach following another failed resupply mission.*

Top right: *A US soldier sets up a loudspeaker in the jungle on Guadalcanal, to broadcast a message encouraging Japanese surrender.*

of the scariest things a man can do is holler 'uh oh.' Sombody says 'uh oh,' and you're saying 'What is it, what is it, what is it!' And I'm listening to that weird noise and somebody says 'uh oh' and takes off just running and those hard steel heels are just hitting that deck 'bloom, bloom, bloom' and we were on the edge of a clear field—we were back in the trees next to the airstrip—so we all just follow . . . we all run like crazy, run out into the opening and here comes a tree just tumbling

down—blom! Right on our tent! The tree had been cut through enough with naval shelling–shrapnel–that it was ready to fall, and when the wind hit it right, it just come right on over. When we heard one of our group running . . . they just stampeded, and I went with them. But some of us didn't know why we were running and I'm not sure the guy who was running did either. But that was frightening–that puts your heart up in your throat. You know, when somebody's out there shooting, that's a different kind of fear . . . this was sudden fright."

When the Japanese forces on Guadalcanal did make their attacks, they tended to be of ferocious intensity, committed with a near blindness to casualties and tactical sophistication. However, the Japanese confidence in night fighting meant that such attacks were often made in the confusion of the after-dark hours. USMC Sergeant Mitchell Paige remembers one such incident:

"All of us must have seen the Japs at the same time. Grenades exploded everywhere on the ridge-nose, followed by shrieks and yells. It would have been death to fire the guns because muzzle flashes would have given away our positions and we could have been smothered and blasted by a hail of grenades. Stansbury, who was lying in the foxhole next to mine, was pulling out grenade-pins with his teeth and rolling the grenades down the side of the nose. Leipart, the smallest guy in the platoon, and my particular boy, was in his foxhole delivering grenades like a star pitcher.

"Then I gave the word to fire. Machine-guns and rifles let go and the whole line seemed to light up. Pettyjohn yelled to me that his gun was out of action. In the light from the firing I could see several Japs a few feet away from Leipart. Apparently he had been hit because he was down on one knee. I knocked off two Japs with a rifle but a third drove his bayonet into Leipart. Leipart was dead; seconds later, so was the Jap. After a few minutes, I wouldn't swear to how long if was, the blitz became a hand-to-hand battle. Gaston was having trouble with a Jap officer, I remember that much. Although his leg was nearly hacked off and his rifle was all cut up, Gaston finally connected his butt with the Jap's chin. The result was one slopehead with a broken neck.

"Firing died down a little, so evidently the first wave was a flop. . . . Things got pretty bad on the second wave. The Japs penetrated our left flank, carrying away all opposition and were possibly in a position to attack our ridge-nose from the rear. On the left, however, Grant, Payne, and Hinson stood by. In the center, Lock, Swanek, and McNabb got it

Right: A Japanese Type 94 37mm antitank gun. The Japanese Army claimed the gun could penetrate 0.8in (20mm) of armor at 1,093yds (1,000m).

Antitank guns were often emplaced in well-concealed bunkers, for close-range attacks.

Above left: Marine troops rest during a march to the frontline on Guadalcanal in December 1942, by which time the campaign was effectively won.

Above right: A US soldiers displays a collection of war booty, including a battered-looking Arisaka rifle.

and were carried away to the rear by corpsmen. The Navy boys did a wonderful job and patched up all the casualties, but they were still bleeding like hell and you couldn't tell what was wrong with them, so I sent them back. That meant all my men were casualties and I was on my own. It was lonely up there with nothing but dead slopeheads for company, but I couldn't tell you what I was thinking about. I guess I was

really worrying about the guns, shooting as fast as I could, and getting a bead on the next and nearest Jap." **Paige managed to survive the subsequent close-quarters assaults. Indeed, the Marines' tenacity around Henderson Field steadily sapped the Japanese strength. The Marines were eventually replaced by XIV Army Corps in December 1942, and the Japanese evacuated Guadalcanal in early 1943.**

Life in the Tropics

It is difficult to overstate the physical shock many Allied troops felt upon their deployment to the Pacific Theater. For city boys from New York and Chicago, farm boys from the Mid West, fishermen from Alaska, or British men from the industrial north of England, the Pacific brought contact with a truly alien world of flora, fauna, and weather, an environment as dangerous as it could be captivating.

For those deployed into jungle combat zones, such as in the Solomons or New Guinea, the close confines of the vegetation could limit visibility to a matter of feet, producing a panicky claustrophobia, made worse by the potential threats the jungle hid, plus the fact that the overhead tree canopy could strain out the tropical sunlight, meaning that the men lived in a strange, sepulchral light. Then there was, of course, the heat and the

leather straps, shoes, fabric webbing, and other materials rotted quickly; fresh clothes were soaked in sweat within minutes of putting them on, causing rubbing and abrasions on the skin. Extra care had to be taken with weapons and ammunition, to prevent the build-up of rust or the degradation of shell fuses. Skin became prone to fungal infections, and even the slightest cut (commonly incurred from sharp foliage and thorns) could quickly become infected if not treated properly. One soldier, Private

Above: *A typical American tropical camp, here set up on the island of Saipan toward the end of the campaign there in July 1944.*

Right, above: *Troops of the 1st Marine Division cross the Matanikau River on Guadalcanal. River crossings were regular challenges in inland Pacific regions, and drownings were not uncommon.*

humidity. On maneuvers and in battle, heat stroke victims were commonplace, especially if supplies of water began to run low. On more exposed island bases, sunburn on pale city skin was a painful daily occurrence, although long-term exposure tended to toughen the skin up. Corpses rotted quickly in the heat, making some environments unbearable High tropical humidity also caused a whole host of problems. Clothing,

Above: *Indian troops advance warily through Burmese foliage. As is evident here, jungle vegetation could reduce tactical visibility to a matter of feet, resulting in sudden, explosive close-quarters encounters.*

Above: *Crewmen clean a 20mm antiaircraft gun emplaced at Eniwetok Atoll naval anchorage. Note the color of men's skin, turned a leather-like texture from incessant strong sunshine.*

First Class James Jones of the US Army 25th Division, eloquently described the experience of operating in New Britain: "The moist humidity was so overpowering, and hung in the air so heavily, that it seemed more like a material object than a weather condition. It brought the sweat starting from every pore at the slightest exertion. And unable to evaporate in it, the sweat ran down over their bodies, soaking everything to saturation. When it had saturated their clothes, it ran down into their shoes, filling them, so that they sloshed along in their own sweat as if they had just come wading out of a river."

In addition to the general humidity, the soldiers would also have to cope with the seasonal torrential rains, and occasionally typhoons. Such adverse weather turned landscapes into tortuous mud, which made overland navigation both physically exhausting and agonizingly slow. Storms or typhoons caused fatalities, such as when several Marines were killed around Cape Gloucester in January 1944, crushed by falling trees. There was also the matter of dangerous wildlife. One Marine battalion surgeon on Saipan briefed his men by saying: "In the surf . . . beware of sharks, barracuda, sea snakes, anemones, razor-sharp coral, polluted waters, poison fish, and giant clams that shut on a man like a bear trap."

The War against Malaria

There was a variety of diseases that plagued the Allied troops in the Pacific, including dysentery, dengue fever, and beriberi. Yet by far the most pervasive and debilitating, both at individual and unit levels, was malaria. The casualties from malaria could easily outstrip those from combat, especially in the early years of the Pacific War when anti-malarial drugs were in short supply. In 1942 in the Philippines, for example, some 24,000 of the Allied defenders—essentially around a division's worth of men—were suffering from malaria. Spread by the *Anopheles minimus flavirostris* variety of mosquito, malaria expressed itself in fever, headaches, chills, vomiting, and severe fatigue, but could lead to multiple organ failure and death. Basic prevention included mosquito nets and clothing discipline, but the medical treatments were Atabrine tablets and quinine. These medications produced a range of unpleasant side effects, such as yellowed skin, but they were vital to keeping the casualty count under control. Some Japanese units, given almost no anti-malarial treatments, were also 90 percent combat ineffective because of malaria casualties.

1000 Tablets

Quinine
Hydrochloride

Above and left: *This particular Marine, Jim Goodwin, contracted malaria thirty-six times during his Pacific deployments. Here we also see a bottle of quinine tablets, the primary prophylactic and treatment for malaria.*

Naval Battles - The Solomons

The landings by the US Marines on Guadalcanal triggered intense naval activity on both sides around the southern Solomons, as they attempted to keep their troops reinforced and supplied from the sea. The Japanese Navy's resupply runs would largely be delivered at night, and earned the nickname "Tokyo Express" from the American troops.

The presence of the US Navy and IJN inevitably resulted in some brutal engagements. The first major clash came around Savo Island on the night of August 8/9, 1942, in which a Japanese cruiser force effectively destroyed three Allied cruisers and damaged a fourth, demonstrating the Japanese superiority in night fighting. Just two weeks later, however, the US Task Force 61, commanded by Vice-Admiral Fletcher and including the carriers *Saratoga*, *Wasp*, and *Enterprise*, confronted a Japanese transport run supported by IJN combat forces that itself boasted three carriers: *Ryujo*, *Zuikaku*, and *Shokaku*. On August 24, *Enterprise* launched a carrier strike that sank the *Ryujo*, although in return Japanese carrier aircraft also severely damaged the *Enterprise*, and the two carrier groups broke apart. Yet the next day three Japanese ships, including a destroyer, were sunk by land-based aircraft.

Another major action, this time a night-time clash of naval gunnery, came on October 11/12, as an American force intercepted a Japanese supply convoy and covering cruiser squadron as they attempted to pass down between the Eastern and Western Solomons. A punishing

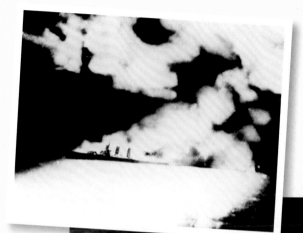

Left: *The USS* Quincy *illuminated by the searchlights of Japanese cruisers during the battle of Savo Island.*
Below: *An artwork depicting US cruisers on fire during the battle of Savo Island. The Japanese Navy had excellent night-fighting capabilities.*

Below: *The Japanese heavy cruiser* Aoba *under way. During the battle of Cape Esperance, this vessel was hit by around forty US naval shells.*

exchange of gunfire began at 2246hrs, and two IJN cruisers were hit and a destroyer sunk. Yet the cruiser USS *Duncan* was separated, and soon came under devastating fire, as a US after-action report explains:

"While making two torpedo hits on a Japanese cruiser from a position between our cruiser column and the enemy force, the *Duncan* was simultaneously hit by four or more shells, including several from our cruiser column. Her No. 1 fireroom had already been damaged by a shell hit, but the crew had remained at their stations in order to secure the forward boilers. This devotion to duty cost them their lives, for when the fire-room was hit again, all men in it were killed. Other shells burst and killed all personnel in the charthouse and the main radio room. Another hit near the charthouse killed four men on the wings of the bridge. One of these men was standing next to the commanding officer, Lt. Comdr. Ennis W. Taylor. Uncontrollable fires quickly broke out near the No. 1 fireroom and the main radio.

"No. 2 gun mount was a mass of flames, with fire and explosions from the handling room cutting off access to the forecastle. Everything from the bridge level up was isolated by fires roaring just below. The charthouse and after end of the navigating bridge were wrecked. The forward and after parts of the ship were two distinct units, separated by flames from the fire in No. 1 fireroom. All communications from the pilothouse to other parts of the ship were dead. The gyro-repeater was out. There was no answer from signals over the engine room annunciator. Bridge steering control was lost, and with her rudder jammed left the *Duncan* was carried clear of the line of fire and away from the battle area. She was still making 15 knots.

"The director crew and the uninjured personnel on the director platform lowered the wounded to the starboard wing of the bridge. But the bridge was isolated from all parts of the ship by increasingly serious fires raging beneath, forward and aft. Accordingly, Lt. Comdr. Taylor ordered the personnel gathered on the bridge to abandon ship. Efforts were made to reach the life net just beneath the port wing of the bridge, but the smoke was too thick and the flames too fierce. Escape from the bridge level was possible only by dropping into the water over the starboard wing. All bridge personnel left the ship in this manner.

"During their escape and for many minutes afterward, Lt. Comdr. Taylor strove unsuccessfully to signal the crew of gun No. 1 and the survivors from gun No. 2, who were gathered in the eyes of the ship [apex of the bow], isolated by fires which had spread to the magazines under gun No. 2. After a final effort to communicate with men in the after part of the ship, and when an inspection of the bridge level showed that the port

Above: *The USS* Chicago, *a Northampton-class cruiser, undergoes repairs in a dry dock in Sydney, Australia, following her torpedoing by a Japanese destroyer at the battle of Savo Island.*

Left: *The USS* Chicago *sailing off Guadalcanal. The ship was lost in January 1943 at the battle of Rennell Island, when it took multiple torpedo hits.*

wing was on fire and that all living personnel had got clear, Lt. Comdr. Taylor jumped from the starboard bridge shield at about 0100, a half hour after giving the order to abandon the bridge.

"The remaining personnel forward and aft made persistent efforts, despite continually exploding ammunition and intense fires, to bring the flames under control with fire and bilge pumps and the handy-billy. Both bilge pump and handy-billy failed. At about 0200, with the flames increasing in intensity and ammunition exploding ever more violently, Lieut. Herbert R. Kabat ordered all personnel to abandon ship."

Despite the loss of the *Duncan*, the "battle of Cape Esperance" was a US victory, and gave the American troops a new-found confidence in night-fighting, which would turn out to be misplaced.

Battle of Santa Cruz

The battle of Santa Cruz was one of the largest and most important naval battles that took place around the Solomons in the fall of 1942. A major Japanese land offensive on Guadalacanal was bolstered from the sea by a Japanese fleet consisting of forty warships, including three fleet carriers. Meeting this fleet were the US Task Forces 16 and 17, which locked horns with the Japanese around the Santa Cruz Islands on the morning of October 26. Both sides launched their carrier strikes at virtually the same time, the air units passing each other on the way.

Edward L. Feightner was a Wildcat pilot from *Enterprise*: "Jimmy Flatley was the VG skipper in charge of the strike. I remember going in there. We were at 20,000ft [6,096m] and we are just about to the point where we could see the ships. I looked up and saw a flight of thirty or more Zeros. I counted up to twenty-eight and they were still some distance away but they were coming right at us. They were over 30,000ft [9,144m] up and we were at 20,000ft [6,096m]. For some reason they never saw us. Jimmy Flatley said 'Don't anybody move, don't flash any canopies or any wings, I don't think they've seen us.' While this is going on and they are right overhead and he said 'OK, the fleet is down there.' He didn't want anyone duplicating diving on the same ship. Can you imagine anyone this cool? He said 'OK, Red

you take the one on the right, Bernie you take the left lead ship.' He assigned each bomber pilot a target. Unbelievable! We actually started the dives before the Zeros saw us. The minute we started the dive the people down on deck started shooting. The fighters went down and strafed. We had a rendezvous, which was about 3 miles [5km] east of the ships, which we had all decided where we would meet. The fighters went out there and covered the area and the bombers after the bomb runs came out and joined up. The next thing we knew we had Zeros all over us. We got through that and we lost only three or four people, total, out of that whole group. Then we all headed for Guadalcanal. Of course we just about out of fuel anyway. We got to Guadalcanal just before dark."

The strike from the *Enterprise* disabled the carrier *Zuiho*, a significant reduction of the Japanese fleet strength. However, the US carrier *Hornet*, aboard which was hospital corpsman Ronald Veltman, was also under heavy attack:

"I was up on the...my battle station was up in between the flight deck and the hangar deck. . . . [I] Got the word, 'Stand by for air attack.' I hit the deck opposite the Ready Room and there was a big explosion on the other side

Below left: A Japanese Nakajima B5N "Kate" torpedo bomber, attacking US shipping, prepares to drop its torpedo, visible beneath the centerline of the fuselage.

Left: Japanese dive-bombers attacking the USS Enterprise *are met with a cloud of AA fire on October 26, 1942.*

Below right: A US Navy Grumman TBF1 Avenger, flying as part of VT-10 from the USS Enterprise, *is prepared for takeoff.*

Above: *The USS* Hornet *comes under intensive bombing and strafing attack from Japanese dive-bombers at Santa Cruz.*

Right: *Evacuation of the stricken US carrier* Hornet *is underway, as fires take hold and all power is lost. Subsequent US attempts to scuttle the ship failed, and it was eventually finished off by torpedoes from Japanese destroyers.*

with my buddy, Bill Good, and word come over to abandon ship. Before that the *North Hampton* tried to get us in tow, but was no good . . . we were too close to any land-based bombers . . . they were still coming at us. So I told my buddy Bill, I says, 'Go down the line, get in the water . . . try and get one of the 5in shell casings as a buoyancy,' and I says, 'Don't be vertical in the water; be horizontal because the shock waves from any exploding bombs nearby . . . if you're vertical, you're finished.' So he went down the line and I said, 'Wait for me down there,' and I went down. I get down there . . . he went down too fast and he had rope burns . . . salt water took care of that. So I said, 'Okay, lay on your back,' I said, 'put my

of the bulkhead where I was lying . . . the door flew open and flames came shooting out. I got the wounded and everybody out, up onto the flight deck and went back to man the fire hose to try to control the fire in the Ready Room. But the [water] pressure was . . . minute. In the meantime, there was a 500lb [227kg] bomb on the other side of the compartment where we were fighting the fire. It was laying there and did not explode. The Japs came in with a kamikaze right into the Signal Bridge and we had twin quartermasters up there . . . brothers. And one of them was on fire and his brother saw him and he tried to get to him to save him and they both were consumed in the flames. I went up on the flight deck and got to the First Aid Station up on the port bow. We had a terrific starboard list . . . we thought we were going to capsize. So while up there I look up and I see a Zero coming down at us . . . right straight down at us. And I hit the deck. He sprayed the island and he got one Marine that was on the 20mm and his name was Victor Keebler . . . right through his mouth, cheeks, come out the other sidebusted up his teeth pretty bad, but he survived and we're still in contact. So then we got the USS *Mustin* (DD-413); [it] came along side . . . took off most of the personnel that were wounded and anybody that was not ship's company. Ship's company had to stay aboard. I was up in the port bow

toes under your armpits; I'll use my arms, you use your legs.' I see we're not moving. I look over . . . he's got his legs bent like he's riding a bike, so I straighten them out . . . I got that going. So we got over the USS *Anderson* destroyer and they hauled us aboard. I went down to the Sick Bay to see if I could help with anybody that may have been wounded and assist the medical personnel on the Anderson. . ."

With the *Hornet* crippled beyond repair, and left to burn, and the *Enterprise* seriously damaged, the Americans broke off the attack. The fact remained, however, that this Japanese "victory" had cost it a total of ninety-nine aircraft destroyed in aerial combat.

Naval Clashes around Guadalcanal

The naval battles around Guadalcanal rumbled on into the winter of 1942 undiminished, although both sides were now starting to feel the pain of their extensive losses. Another major engagement came on November 12, when the IJN attempted to land 13,000 men on Guadalcanal, protected by very strong covering forces, at the same time as US naval units attempted to deploy US reinforcements. The US Navy task force commander, Rear-Admiral Daniel Callaghan, attempted to launch a surprise attack, and the Japanese and US ships ultimately met each other in the early hours of the morning.

Robert D. Graff, US Navy, was serving aboard the light cruiser USS *Helena* during the action:

"November 12, 1942. We were a column of ships which consisted of four destroyers, four cruisers—the *San Francisco*, the *Atlanta*, the *Helena*, and I think *Juneau* was the last cruiser, followed by four destroyers. *Atlanta* had fire-control radar which could see far and accurately. The *San Francisco* did not. We made radar contact with enemy ships as did the ship behind us, the *Helena*. She had taller masts and could see farther, and she said they're out there at 12 miles [19km] or something like that. We were now in the heart of Iron Bottom Bay with Guadalcanal 3–5 miles [5–8km] on our portside, with Florida Island, Tulagi, 5–6 miles [8–10km] on our starboard side and 5 miles [8km] ahead, a little island called Savo. . . . We went forward. At 12 miles [19km] *Helena* got radar contact and very shortly thereafter, we made contact. Admiral Callaghan didn't do anything about it. We just kept seeing them come closer.

Above: Convoy resupply runs into the Solomons were perilous affairs for both sides. Here we see a US convoy under attack on November 12, 1944; the ship in the foreground is the USS President Jackson.

"The Japanese kept steaming towards us, we towards them. Finally we were at 6,000yds [5,486m] and our fire-control people up in the director were going crazy. When are we gonna shoot? Now we could see the ships, ghosts, but we could see them. And then the *San Francisco* decided to do what Scott had done effectively the last time in the Esperance fight. The Japanese came down in two columns and Scott took his single column of American ships right up the alley between them and turned around and then started to work, odd guns and even

Below: US cruisers and Japanese surface vessels slug it out with their guns in one of the numerous night battles around the Solomons.

guns, just shooting at everybody on the way down and doing terrible damage. Of course we might have been just obliterated but somehow we were not. We must have been too close to them, apparently, for their torpedoes to arm, which is fascinating, because they were lethal, terribly destructive, and in the course of the fighting around Guadalcanal Japanese torpedoes must have sunk ten cruisers of ours and maybe twenty destroyers. There weren't many battleships that bothered with them; it was left to the cruisers.

"So, Admiral Callaghan gave the orders for the task force to turn left . . . [and] decided this was now getting too dangerous and God knows why the people in the *San Francisco* didn't fire, but we were not allowed to fire until either the enemy fired at us or the task force commander gave the command. So, suddenly the destroyers start to turn left and Captain Jenkins said, 'I'm going to get our boys in here,' so he turned left for maybe ninety degrees or something like that, and then straightened out in our column.

Above: *A gunsight from the USS* Ward, *an American destroyer deployed to the Solomons area in 1943–44.*

"...The fire-fight broke into a million pieces which is so fantastic you couldn't imagine it. . . . There were just ships and people now shooting every side, lights, floodlights, illuminations, star-shells, illuminations, explosions, torpedoes coursing the waters, high-explosive shells, friendly fire by *San Francisco* raking the *Atlanta*'s superstructure. . . . In the process, either a Japanese destroyer or a cruiser, I don't know, exactly which, put two torpedoes in us . . . ."

During this epic clash, the Japanese lost two cruisers, with one battleship and numerous smaller vessels damaged, while the American forces lost two cruisers and four destroyers. The naval battles continued throughout the month, the Americans taking heavy losses in night engagements, but the Japanese also suffering through the American use of radar-controlled gunnery, which had become increasingly accurate. By the end of November, however, the Japanese had essentially given up on the prospect of reinforcing Guadalcanal significantly.

Above: *The USS* Boise *was a Brooklyn-class light cruiser, and was heavily involved in the battles around the Solomons. At the battle of Cape Esperance, the ship was hit by several Japanese shells, killing 107 of her crew.*

Above: *A US destroyer squadron (Squadron 23) on maneuvers around the Solomons in late 1943. Destroyers delivered a wide variety of combat duties, including antiaircraft and antisubmarine roles.*

On the Kokoda Trail

The battle across the Kokoda Trail in New Guinea has a legendary status in Australia, because of the privations that Australian and also US forces suffered there. Following the Japanese landings at Buna on July 21/22, 1942, the Allied forces were driven back across the Owen Stanley mountain range, under truly dreadful conditions. Australian private B. Findlay wrote an account of his physical experiences on the trail, where the environment was as much of an enemy as the Japanese forces against them:

"Some of the old units are so thin that you'd be shocked to see them. This trip is a physical nightmare. . . Yesterday we were twelve hours on the track and most of us were 'out on our feet,' but we had to keep going . . . You spend four hours rising 2,000ft [609m] step by step with your heart pounding in your throat, resting every 100ft [32m] of rise. And then when you reach the top it is only 15ft [5m] wide, and you immediately begin to descend 2,000ft [609m]. This is dangerous as well as painful, because you get 'laughing knees,' and only your prop stick in front of you

keeps you from falling headlong. The farther down you go the weaker your knees become, but you don't lie down and die, as you feel like doing; you keep resting and going on and on. . . .

"The first night out we tried to rest in a shelter of bushes many thousands of feet up, but none of us could manage sleep. Next day we were caught in a fierce storm, and staggered and slipped through it for two long hours. When we rested we lay out in puddles in the pouring

Right: *Buna, 1942. A US gun crew of the 32nd Infantry Division ready a 37m antitank gun against Japanese attack..*

Below: *A Pattern 1903 Sword Bayonet for a .303in Lee-Enfield rifle.*

Above: *Japanese bodies litter the ground thickly after a clash with Australian troops around Buna, c. January 1943. The Japanese tendency to resort to frontal charges resulted in unnecessarily heavy casualties.*

Above: *Terrain and weather were essentially the greatest challenges for both sides during the Kokoda Trail campaign. The mud and foliage sometimes reduced progress to just a few hundred yards in several exhausting hours.*

Above: *Australian troops search for Japanese troops in the jungle. Grasses such as these not only reduced visibility, but also imparted irritating cuts on bare skin, which could become infected if left untreated.*

Right: *After months of toil in New Guinea, Australian troops finally get the chance to relax and enjoy some entertainment.*

rain, panting and steaming and wet through in the fullest sense of the words. But you had to keep going. Everything was wet and heavier now. . . . At nightfall we staggered into a ramshackle native grass hut. It had no sides and the rain was driving in on us the whole time. . . . at an altitude of 4,000ft [1,219m] I lay on the bare ground in wet clothes. It was bitterly cold. As soon as we settled down the native rats started. One of them ran across my face and scratched my nostril with his sharp claws. They kept running over my body, and when I dozed off, they started nibbling at my hair."

At Ioribaiwa Ridge, just 25 miles [40km] from Port Moresby, the Australians made a defensive stand, which although was ultimately overcome by the Japanese actually marked the effective limit of the Japanese advance. Eric Williams, 2/16th Infantry Battalion, endured a Japanese bombardment on the Ridge:

"[There was] Bill Grayden and myself. I was the sergeant, he was the officer behind [his men]. Unfortunately these blokes had their heads against a tree and I suppose the Japs must have seen us from over there. The next thing we knew was this mountain gun was fired and exploded in this tree just above our head. And it killed the three blokes with their heads on the tree, because the percussion went straight down, split their skulls open. And knocked out Bill Grayden right alongside me, I was all right. . . . I could see they were dead, I thought Bill was dead.

"I made a bit of a boo-boo [an error], I should have made sure he was dead. So I grabbed all of the grenades and I thought, 'There is no good giving them to the Japs' and I chucked them down the side, and took the bolts out of their rifles, including Bill's, so the Japs couldn't use them, tossed those off and pissed off. And when I got back to battalion, which wasn't far, here to the gate and back, there was no sign of the Japs. Anyway I went back and reported that these three blokes were killed and Bill Grayden. And I suppose about a quarter of an hour later who should come lurching up the track was Bill Grayden. Silly as a weirdo, he had been knocked out. Of course I felt dreadful I had left him, I thought he was dead, same as the other blokes."

At their positions near Port Moresby, the Japanese offensive had finally run out of steam, and they were progressively pushed back down the trail until, by November, they were back in the Buna-Gona area. The brutality of the fighting during this phase of the campaign was remembered by Paul Cullen, who commanded the 2/1st Infantry Battalion during the Australian advance. He remembers taking part in awful hand-to-hand combat at Oivi-Gorari, where the Japanese made a futile attempt to prevent the Australians reaching the northern coast:

"And again, we encircled the Japanese position, and with another battalion from 7th Division, we killed over three hundred. And one of the [most] extraordinary sights I've ever seen, when we encircled these Japs so we could capture the position and kill them all, and vast stores of rice and things, a Japanese officer raced out with his sword, drawn sword, samurai sword, and Lieutenant St George Rider, great name, one of our lieutenants, grappled with him, and his, his weapon had jammed. Just luck of the game, you know, it happens in every battle I suppose. And they grappled together and any rate, someone else came up, one of our chaps, and shot this Japanese who had so gallantly and bravely raced towards us waving his sword. You know, extraordinary sight, you wouldn't think you would see it in this 1942 war would you?"

In the battle the Australians lost 121 dead and 225 wounded; the Japanese had 430 killed and about the same number wounded.

Hell in New Guinea

In 1943 and 1944, the United States poured substantial forces into New Guinea, a process that eventually isolated and trapped an entire Japanese army in the Huon Peninsula. However, US troops had also participated in the drive to push the Japanese troops back across the Kokoda Trail in 1943. George S. Mixell served with the 158th Infantry Regiment (Bushmasters). He not only remembers the combat there, but also the honey voice of the infamous "Tokyo Rose":

Left: American and Australian troops inspect two wrecked Japanese Type 95 tanks. The Type 95 was a diminutive vehicle with a three-man crew and armed with an underpowered 37mm gun.

"We must have ridden back across that range at least 15–20 miles [24–32km] I would say. We went back in there and we had our artillery with us. We started opening up on them [the Japanese]. They weren't in strength; they weren't as big a group. I think they gave up because of the artillery barrage we poured down on them. Then we called in an airplane strike and the Air Force got in on it. With our artillery barrage and the Air Force strike, they decided to turn back. It was an area that was so desolate and dangerous that it was even dangerous to be in there under normal conditions, but when you were trying to put up a defense or a fight, you had all the odds against you, and they pulled out. They pulled back. We put a company there. We left a company there for about three weeks anyway to make sure they didn't move back in when our unit moved out.

"Tokyo Rose came on at night and she would inform us of what was going on. She was harassing the troops continually. She told us, 'You boys stopped our soldiers from going over the ridge and coming in behind you, but we will get you out in the open up along the coast and we are going to annihilate you and all your girlfriends and wives back at home are running around with the 4Fs.' Then she would play music for us. They were going to try her for criminal activities. I don't know who went to bat for her, but the troops said that she was entertaining to us. She was the only music that we got that kept us in touch with what was going on back in the country. She didn't do us any harm because everybody loved her show. They exonerated her. I think she died just recently."

Above: Australian troops take shelter behind a tank around Semini Creek on New Guinea, December 5, 1942.

Left: Australian soldiers are at maximum alert in their water-filled position on New Guinea. Japanese positions are just 30yds (27m) away, so the threat of sudden attack is continual.

Left: Australian infantry take advantage of the cover afforded by an M3 Stuart tank. Most of the armor used in New Guinea was of the light variety.

Louis Gordon, US Army, deployed to New Guinea in early 1943 with the 41st Division. He remembers his first contact with the Japanese on the island:

"We went to a place when we landed—I think it was called Santananda—and the Japanese were already there. All they had living over there was these natives, and they took over the island and we knew their intention was to take over the island We relieved the 32nd Division and they got hit very hard by the Japanese. They had a cemetery with the monuments of the fellows that got killed. We accidentally ran into a fellow who wasn't in our outfit, actually he got kicked out of our outfit for something, and he wound up in the 32nd Division. A lot of the men knew him and he came over and started talking to us and telling us what was going on over there. . . . Our battalion started moving in and we were in combat as soon as we met fire from the Japanese. Sure enough, I was in a squad with twelve men. Right away we ran into them. We got ambushed by a Japanese machine gun and I mean we hit the dirt . All we had to do was stay quiet and it was as hot as the devil. . . . Actually, my squad leader wanted to throw a grenade and I was right by him. I said "Don't throw it. Once you pull the pin you're gonna have to throw it, you can't put the pin back in.' In the meantime, bullets were just spraying all around us. . . . The Australians were fighting along with us, but they were in a little different section of the wood. Our whole company got ambushed by this machine gun and I think my squad was the first one. They knew that we were there, but they were firing over our heads. If they had shot lower. . . . You know when you have a machine gun, a machine gun is set one way. It will rotate back and forth, but they were in one position. Finally they contacted an Australian plane. The plane was not a fighter plane, it was a reconnaissance plane. They called it, they had guns on there, and they were the ones [who solved the problem]. I don't know if they got the machine guns out altogether, but I'm sure they got some. There was more than one machine gun, but this reconnaissance plane caused the machine guns to move. We finally got to what we considered was a little safer territory, we moved back. Then we found out that five or six men got killed. The Japanese were firing right over our heads and they were hitting the troops that were behind us."

By the mid months of 1944, New Guinea had essentially been conquered, the surviving Japanese soldiers either killed or driven into miserable hiding in ineffective outposts.

The flying cap and goggles of Saburo Sakai, a Japanese ace fighter ace who was shot through the eye (notice the damaged goggles) over the Solomons in August 1942.

Bougainville

Bougainville was the largest of the Solomons, and in mid 1943 was heavily reinforced by the Japanese 17th Army in an attempt to stop the steady US advance from the south. The 3rd US Marine Division landed at Empress Augusta Bay on November 1, 1943, away from the main concentration of Japanese forces, and set up a strong perimeter. Artilleryman Orrin W. Johnson was a Marine within the 3rd Division:

"Then we were ordered to capture a part of the island of Bougainville. It was the biggest of the Solomon Islands. It is a big island. We went up and made a landing on the Empress Augusta side of Bougainville. We were there for probably 3 to 3½ months doing this. We got two airfields built for fighters to protect our bombers going over to New Guinea and also had bombers going out of there also for the battle for New Britain. It was a good trip. It was miserable in the jungle because it rained all the time. The climate wasn't too agreeable. I didn't get too sick. I got dysentery a few times. I got rid of that. We had some pretty good battles there. . .

"We landed on the Empress Augusta side near a little river called Piva River. There was a small island there. . . . There is a peninsula that goes

Above: US Marines on Bougainville in 1943. Note the P42 "frogskin" camouflage pattern of their uniforms; these uniforms were reversible.

to the island. We set up our 105[mm] howitzers on that peninsula. There were some Japanese platoons defending that area, but they got killed in the first wave. I got sent up immediately upon landing to try to locate the 3rd Raider Battalion. It wasn't their fault, they didn't communicate back. You can't use the radios we had in the jungle. They wouldn't carry. You had to lay a [field telephone] line. That's what I did. I had the forward observer crew unrolling W-10 wire all the way up there.

"There was a trail called the Piva Trail. I walked up there and ran in to where they had the firefight. The 3rd Marine Raider Battalion had encountered a Japanese battalion coming down this trail the other way. There was a big firefight up there and [the Raiders] killed all of their officers, the Jap officers. All of the others took off on foot and they moved on up ahead. They had a battle up ahead in a coconut grove. I was in that. Then the Japs stopped at a crossing on Piva where the trail divided and

Above: A US Marine artillery crew ready their 75mm howitzer for engaging targets on Torokina, Bougainville.

Right: The insignia of the US Army, Pacific (USARPAC).

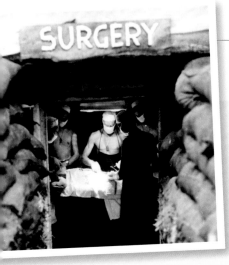

entered an east/west trail. We were all pretty green at that time but the infantry was having some problem. Headquarters ordered me personally to fire the largest barrage I could. I fired four Marine battalions of artillery and three Army battalions in one big concentration. It blew the jungle apart. There wasn't much left of those trees there by the time we got through firing. We were trying to get to a higher ground which was called Hill 1000. I had gone up the hill called Cibik's Ridge. That was how I got the chance to shoot my gun. I was on Hill 1000 most of the time after that. We finally got orders to go back home to Guadalcanal."

Major General Carey Randall was a battalion commander with the 1st Battalion, 9th Marines, sent to Bougainville in 1943. He remembers how, in the violent land warfare that convulsed Bougainville until nearly the very end of the war, an attack might be planned and delivered:

Above: Marine Raiders used canines not only for security, but also for scouting duties and even running messages.

Top left: A US military surgeon operates in tough conditions on Bougainville.

Left: US Marines gather around an LVT-1 amphibious tractor, which appears to be having a difficult time making progress in the mud.

Below: A US shoulder patch representing Command Headquarters (CHQ).

"We had an organized plan of attack that would depend on the nature of the terrain and the size of the opposition. Frequently we would have two rifle companies in the front line. They might have one third of their troops back a little bit in reserve in case they were needed to back up one or the other. We would have some machine-gun units go along with them. We would have artillery observers with radios with them and a Navy Liaison Officer for ship air support. I would be a few hundred yards behind them, just far enough back that I could keep a close eye on what was going on. If you got too close you couldn't communicate. . . The Japanese frequently attacked at night with these banzai attacks. They would make these banzai attacks and run, piling through yelling and shouting and shooting. Sometimes they would go right on by you. It was very difficult to kill them all. We didn't get too much of that. We had some very hard fighting just before Christmas. I remember Thanksgiving Day when one of the ships sent in a bunch of whole cooked turkeys. We had turkey drumsticks when we moved up this hill to attack these Japs. The hill was later on nicknamed Hand Grenade Hill. A Marine with a turkey drumstick in one hand, and a rifle in the other. That was a sight to see." **Bougainville remained a tough nut to crack for both the Americans and the Australians, but the Japanese forces there were at least strategically contained.**

The War in New Britain

On December 26, 1943, the US 1st Marine Division was landed at Cape Gloucester, in the northwest corner of New Britain, part of the Bismarck Archipelago. Occupying the western parts of New Britain would, for MacArthur, not only further isolate Rabaul, it would also quash Japanese attempts to build an airfield in the area, and would improve the US ability to move supplies along the Solomons and north to the Philippines.

Charles Allen was part of the HQ company, 1st Battalion. The fighting in New Britain wasn't always as intense as that on other islands, and could produce some unusual encounters: "My first induction into the war was went we landed on New Britain. This was the southern tip of New Britain and our group was walking along the trail to go up to the front lines when all at once the earth started shaking and it just scattered the hell out of us. A whole bunch of us. We started diving and they said, 'No.

Above: *The rocket from a Rocket Launcher, M1, better known as the "Bazooka." The M1 was a useful bunker-buster.*

That's just the air raid. The bombs are coming down from our planes.' Well, we were having quite a time on New Britain and we had put up our tents and such and such. In the mornings we would be all flooded out. We had quite a time moving through the trees and along the trails. We got up to Hill 660; I believe it was, 600, or 660. Our lieutenant was a man that had been an English teacher in Chicago University. We were up at the top of the hill. I had been placed into an observation post. . . . We were right at the top. Our lines were halfway down the hill. At the

Above: *US firepower here includes an M1A1 Thompson SMG, a Browning M1917 .30-cal machine gun, and (at the back) an M1 carbine.*
Left: *US Marines wade ashore through the surf of Cape Gloucester on December 26, 1943, having just left their LST.*

foot of the hill was the Japanese. They had got us cornered there for a while. Lieutenant heard one of the Americans holler out and said. 'Go to hell, Tojo.' The Japanese, one or two of them, that could speak English, hollered back and said, 'To hell with Roosevelt.' The lieutenant jumped up and said, 'Don't shoot that Jap. He's a fellow Republican.' From there on we had quite a good time. But, it took us about four months to go through New Britain."

Above: *A Marine mortar team in action on Cape Gloucester. The high angle of fire provided by mortars made them excellent weapons for jungle warfare.*

A "good time" was not had by all, however. **Martin L. Clayton was with the 5th Marine Regiment, 1st Marine Division:** " . . . you start moving across the island, you're digging foxholes. Every single night you're digging a foxhole, you haven't bathed. You may go three weeks without ever getting in a stream where you can bathe. I know on Cape Garten, New Britain, it was almost a month and when I took off my shoes, I couldn't even get them back on. You know, your feet would swell and you're dirty, you're hungry, you're scared. If you had one fire fight you're scared from then on. Don't let anybody tell you that when you've been in a firefight and your buddies are laying next to you all blown to bits that you're not scared from then on. I don't know of anybody that just didn't have knots in their stomach. . . . You're hungry, you're dirty, you're tired, you're scared, and that's part of an infantryman's life."

The New Guinea operation was extended with landings further east by the 1st Marine Division on March 6, around Talasea. With these operations, plus US takeover of the St Matthias Group, Rabaul and New Ireland would remain ineffective and isolated Japanese outposts.

Douglas MacArthur

General Douglas MacArthur was a towering figure of the Pacific War, his reputation matched equally by his character. Born in 1880 into a military family, MacArthur joined the Army and graduated from West Point in 1903. His subsequent career path was nothing short of meteoric. He rose through the ranks rapidly, and gained invaluable combat experience at brigade and divisional levels during World War I. By 1925 he was a full general, and in 1930 he became the Army Chief of Staff. He actually retired from the Army in 1937, but in was recalled to duty in July 1941. With the onset of war in December 1941, MacArthur's strategic and personal talents were put to work in the Pacific, as commander of the Southwest Pacific Theater. In this capacity, he led the US forces up through New Guinea, the Solomons and the Philippines (the latter from where he had been ejected in 1942). MacArthur was egotistical, autocratic, and amibitious, but he channeled all these qualities into powerful leadership. He doubtedly helped the Allies to victory in the Pacific, although his costly campaign to retake the Philippines remains controversial.

Above right: *One of the distinctive corn cob pipes made for and used by Douglas MacArthur.*

Left: *US combat boots. The corrosive climate of the Pacific was hard on footwear, and improved jungle boots were developed.*

American Firepower

Once the full might of the American industrial complex swung behind the war effort, the frontline American soldiers and sailors attained one undeniable advantage over their Japanese opponents—sheer firepower. Japanese survivors of the Pacific War have recounted their experience of US firepower with near awe, on account of its intensity, its coordination between different weapon systems, and the apparently limitless supply of ammunition. Japanese tacticians came to realize that if a US unit or formation was to be defeated, it had to be done early, before the firepower could be brought to bear, or from hidden or protected positions that limited the firepower effect.

The US superiority in firepower reached down to the small-unit level, and even down to the individual. US soldiers armed with the semi-automatic M1 Garand rifle, for example, could fire about twenty-five aimed shots per minute; a Japanese soldier with a bolt-action Arisaka Type 38 or 99 rifle, by contrast, would be skilled to squeeze out twelve aimed shots in the same period of time. Multiply the Garand firepower to fire team or platoon size, then add the firepower of supporting BAR and

Left: The Grumman F6F Hellcat was fast, tough, and maneuverable. This type claimed more than 5,000 Japanese aircraft in the Pacific Theater.

.30-cal Browning M1919 machine guns (which were both superior to and more numerous than Japanese machine guns), and it is appreciable how the American troops on the frontline could easily win the battle for fire supremacy.

Beyond small arms, the US forces also brought a vast range of heavier support weaponry to the table. Mortars were in effect medium-range support artillery for the infantry. In the Marine Corps, each company had a section of three 60mm mortars, firing high-explosive, white phosphorous, or obscuration rounds. Powerful support could also come from light antiaircraft artillery repurposed against ground targets. A quad .50-caliber mount, for example, could have a devastating effect on a Japanese position.

Below: US logistics ensured the superior volume of US firepower in the Pacific conflict. Here we see a Landing Ship, Dock (LSD) with its shipments of vehicles and supplied destined for Morotai, September 1944.

The Garand Rifle

The .30-cal M1 Garand rifle was history's first standard-issue semi-automatic rifle, and was a weapon that frequently tipped the balance in favor of US troops during small-unit engagements. It was developed by French Canadian-born John Garand during the 1920s and 1930s, and after numerous complicated trials and revisions, it was adopted for service as the "Semi-Automatic Rifle, Caliber 30, M1" in 1936, and it went on to arm the majority of US soldiers during World War II and the Korean War. While most of the world's armies used bolt-action rifles, the M1 was a self-loading design, the loading, extraction, and ejection cycle delivered via a gas-operated system. It was fed from an eight-round en bloc clip, inserted down into the internal magazine with the bolt held back. The Garand was durable, accurate, had a powerful cartridge and, most importantly, could be fired as quickly as the soldier could pull the trigger, and without the operator having to take his eye off the sights or cheek off the stock. Its one downside was that the entire clip had to be fired through before reloading; it couldn't be "topped up" in situ.

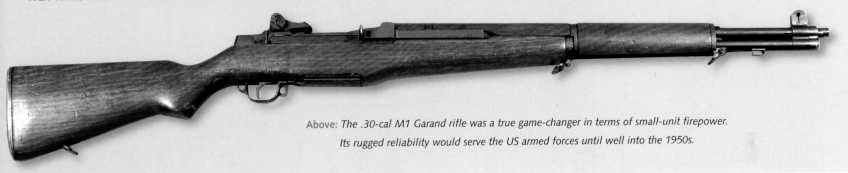

Above: The .30-cal M1 Garand rifle was a true game-changer in terms of small-unit firepower. Its rugged reliability would serve the US armed forces until well into the 1950s.

Above: A US Sherman flame-thrower tank puts down gallons of blazing oil onto a Japanese position on Iwo Jima.

Above right: The awesome array of 20mm and 40mm antiaircraft firepower on a US battleship, stationed off Peleliu in September 1944.

At the heavier end of the scale, American frontline troops enjoyed an undoubted supremacy in artillery support, both onshore and offshore. Infantry battalions could call upon firepower from field guns ranging from 75mm pack howitzers to 155mm howitzers. Where applicable, the soldiers could also call in heavy gunfire from naval warships offshore. To designate targets, the forward observers would use the Tactical Area Designation (TAD) system, with each area of the battlefield divided up into 1,000yd (914m) grids, each grid subdivided into twenty-five 200yd (183m) lettered squares. This system enabled spotters to call in coordinated fire from multiple directions. Adding to the US firepower superiority was the presence of close air support (CAS), although if an aircraft was not already present overhead, it could take up to an hour from the request for support until the moment napalm, rockets, or high-explosive bombs were delivered onto the target.

The War in Burma

The British soldiers who fought in Burma often regarded themselves as part of a "forgotten army," operating in a theater that seemed obscure and distant to the general public. Yet it was a hard-fought theater, punishing to all those who served in it. In the central parts of the country, from the spring of 1943, were the British "Chindit" forces commanded by Brigadier Orde Wingate, fighting as independent columns effectively behind enemy lines. In the north were US and Chinese forces under General Joseph "Vinegar Joe" Stillwell, the US troops including the infamous 5307th Composite Unit (Provisional), a special forces unit led by Brigadier-General Frank Merrill, hence the unit was subsequently known as "Merrill's Marauders."

Left: Orde Wingate was one of the pioneers in the tactics of guerrilla warfare. His thinking in long-range deep-penetration missions is still studied in military colleges today.

Life for the Allies in Burma was rough, with hard living punctuated by moments of intense violence. Vincent Moreno was a US Army scout with the **124th Cavalry Regiment, 5332nd Brigade (the Mars Task Force)**: "We had a couple of skirmishes and we slept in our foxholes every day. We could hear the Japanese across from us because we were up on a hill, and then there was a big gully and then another hill. They were across [from us], but they dug on the other side of the hill, not like we did. We dug in front, they dug on the opposite side so when we shot, we couldn't hit nobody. We could hear them talking at night and we could hear the tanks going on the Burma Road and the artillery would open up and we could hear the Japanese talking again. Then they would move again and then they opened up again and that's the way they'd move out at night. But it was, you know, kind of rough. We lost my best

commanding officer I ever had. He always wore a fatigue hat and you'd ask him, 'Why?', and he'd say, 'I won't be hit in the head, I'm going to be hit in the heart or the body.' And the last skirmish we had, he got it right through the heart. He was a great guy . . . Lieutenant Hobbie Kabell. Hobert but we called him Hobbie, and he was first in front. He was a great man . . . he was the Merrill's Marauders so he had been in action a lot of times."

One of the greatest challenges of operating in the Burma Theater was logistical movement in the jungle-covered, often mountainous interior. Hardy mules were the ideal mode of carrying supplies, but they could be in short supply, as US soldier James E.T. Hopkins remembers: "Instead of having six hundred mules, we would enter Burma with three hundred

Above: A group of "Merrill's Marauders" cross an improvised river bridge in Burma with their logistical livestock.
Left: Orde Wingate conducts a briefing of his "Chindits" before an aerial deployment operation in Burma.

Top of page: *The infamous Gurkha kukri was the ultimate jungle utility and combat knife, being good for slashing vegetation as well as close-quarters fighting.*
Above left: *A US soldier shows a Chinese infantryman how to load a clip into the M1 Garand rifle.*
Above right: *The Chindits were masters of sabotage and ambush. Here we see a group of the British soldiers laying demolition charges on a railroad line.*

wonderful mules and approximately one hundred horses, most of which were in poor shape. The saddle problems were made worse by [the] lack of metal pack saddle hangers. These had to be ordered and fabricated to carry fixed loads. They had to accommodate fixed ammunition, radio equipment, medical supplies, machine guns, mortars, and other equipment. The mules could each carry approximately 200lb [90kg] and most of the horses somewhat less. The horses were said to require 12lb [5.5kg] of oats per day. If bamboo leaves were available, the mules would eat this vegetation and get by on 10lb [4.5kg] of oats per day. Proper care, feeding, and mechanical ingenuity soon produced a brighter outlook for the run-down and weakened horses."

Life in the China–Burma–India (CBI) Theater was not just perilous and tough for those on the ground. Allied pilots risked their lives on a daily basis flying supplies between India and China, crossing the eastern end of the Himalayas in the process, terrain known as "The Hump." Ed Carseth was a pilot with the Army Transport Command, Ferrying

Division, flying the Hump, a journey that took: "About four to four and a half hours, each way. The C-46 [aircraft] was a little faster than the [C-]47... The C-47 only had 1,200 horsepower engines, and the C-46 had 2,000 horsepower engines. That's a big difference. We hauled just about everything you could think out of Myitkyina over to China, but it was primarily gas; that was the big deal, to keep Chennault [Lee Chennault, commander of US air units in China] going. Aviation fuel. Once I hauled a C-47 full of bugles over to China. They were little plastic bugles, they looked like a little toy. The Chinese used the bugles, like we did in the old cavalry, to sound charge, and that's what they were using those bugles for. A lot of time, ammunition. Just whatever they might have that was critical to them over there and they needed right away, that's what we would do, we'd bring it over there. Then of course, the horses, they were for artillery. We'd take four to five horses and these horses were primarily Australian horses, these were I'd say semi-draft horses, that's what they were, really. Kind of big and heavy. We'd take the pack saddle—they weighed 90lb [45kg]—and then we'd take 90lb [45kg] of feed and five Chinamen, and when a Chinaman travels he travels with all his pots, pans, his rations of rice, around his neck, in a big sock. Machine guns, whatever weapons they had, they would go along. We were loaded. The natives would put straw on the bottom of the airplane to absorb the moisture, but they never took the wet stuff out, they would just put dry stuff on top of the wet."

Kohima and Imphal

On March 7/8, 1944, the Japanese 15th Army in northern Burma launched Operation *Ichi-Go*, an invasion designed to blunt future British offensives into Burma. The initially strong advance pushed back British and Indian forces and besieged them at Imphal and Kohima, on the Indian-Burmese border, in the first week of April. The British forces there were cut off, but through air supply and tenacious defence, they hung on.

Company Quartermaster Sergeant (CMQS) Frederick Weedman was a British soldier at Kohima. Here he explains the strategy of the British counterattack in early May: "The Battle of Kohima was a bloody one. General Slim's plan was for 4th Brigade on the right to capture G.P.T. Ridge, advance to Jail Hill, and link up with 6th Brigade in the center. 5th Brigade, with 'C' Company 7th Battalion, the Worcestershire Regiment on the left would occupy Naga Village and dominate the Treasury area. The attack was to be supported by tanks and all available guns, supporting each brigade in turn. The attack began on the early morning of the May 4,1944. Major Burrell briefed 'C' Company platoons 13, 14 and 15 about the impending action. 4th Brigade delayed by

Left: A Japanese propaganda poster aimed at fostering a violent Indian independence movement. There was indeed a strong nationalist movement in India during the war years, but it never undermined the British war effort.

Japanese bunkers, reached G.P.T. Ridge, but was unable to secure the whole of it, or to approach Jail Hill. By nightfall in this part of the territory, the enemy positions and ours were inexplicably mixed. 6th Brigade failed to take 'Kiki Piquet' and although our tanks reached F.S.D. Ridge, the infantry were subjected to devastating fire from other enemy positions, and could not dig in or remain. A portion of the ridge was captured by nightfall and here again our forces and the Japanese were mixed up together.

"'C' Company entered Naga Village during the night of May 4/5. A counterattack by the Japanese pushed them back to the western edge of the village, which they managed to hold. 'C' Company dug in on Church Knoll which consisted of a ridge which overlooked 'Treasury,' where the Japanese had constructed bunkers. Each one provided cover for another and so made it very difficult for such a position to be assaulted.

Above: Garrison Hill was a focal point for the fighting at Kohima, and the intensity of the action is indicated by the blasted trees dotting the hillside.

Right: The District Commissioner's bungalow at Kohima lays in ruins. Such diminutive landmarks were the scene of vigorous close-quarters fighting. The ridge seen here was finally cleared by men of the Dorsetshire Regiment.

Top right: A British officer issues commands via field radio during the battle for Imphal and Kohima. Radio communications in hilly jungle terrain could be problematic, the landscape frequently breaking the connection.

Lower right: At Kohima, British ambulance trucks take the wounded for medical treatment. The British took more than 4,000 casualties at Kohima.

"During four days of bitter fighting, the gallant Lieutenant J. Woodward lost his life as he led an unsuccessful assault with a flame thrower. The enemy were fanatically stubborn defenders. Artillery attacks and 'Hurricane' and 'Vengeance' bombers had little positive effect. The British and Japanese were hopelessly intermingled. One side would attack, the other counterattack—neither would give way. During daylight they fought ferociously 10 or 15yds [9 or 13m] apart, and at night they crept even closer attacking with grenades and bayonets. The battle of Naga Village and Church Knoll continued remorselessly during May 8, 9, and 10. It was on the May 11 that under the cover of dense smoke bombs, an attack was launched, but was only partially successful, as next day, the enemy still held several bunkers.

"A War Correspondent from the *Daily Telegraph* was in the same trench as myself, overlooking the Japanese. He helped me to act as Observation Point for the battalion mortars. We were very apprehensive as we were opposite 'Arandura Spur,' from where a Japanese 75mm gun was shelling our position. 'A' Company, on our left received several hits, one of which was directly on their cooks preparing a meal.

"On May 23 the rains came. We were drenched to the skin, slipping and slithering, as we floundered in water-logged trenches, like the army of a generation before. On the steep hillsides, the tracks were turned into treacherous mudslides. There were four brigadiers in the 2nd Division,

one commanding each infantry brigade and another in charge of the artillery. The fact that in this battle two brigadiers were killed and two seriously wounded is an indication that everyone was involved in the close fighting.

"The only effective weapon was after the 'Sappers' had winched a tank through liquid mud, up to the high ground and dug it in so that it was able to bombard each Japanese bunker below it, with 'solid shot' at point-blank range by the tank's 75mm gun. The few remaining bunkers were demolished by thrusting pole charges through the loopholes. And so ended the battle of Naga Village. The casualties in this type of fighting were heavy. Infantry as usual, suffered most and endured most, for this was an infantry battle. Hand-to-hand, man against man, and no quarter given. On June 2 the Japanese abandoned Naga Village, and large numbers of dead were taken from the bunkers and foxholes. The northern part of Kohima was at last ours."

British reinforcements, moved in to stem the tide of the Japanese effort, meant that ultimately the 15th Army faced more than 100,000 troops, who broke the siege of Imphal (the longest of the sieges) after eighty-eight days of resistance there. By the end of June, the Japanese were in retreat back into Burma, having taken more than 65,000 casualties.

Striking at Rabaul

Rabaul, located at the eastern tip of New Britain, was one of the most important Japanese air and naval bases in the Pacific, following its capture in February 1942. As such it was extremely heavily defended from ground attack. In response the Allies avoided attempting to take the base by a land assault, but instead opted to isolate it, both through wider actions in the Solomons and via submarine interdiction of shipping, but also by destroying its viability through heavy air strikes.

Richard (Dick) Bennett, USAAF, participated in these raids, flying B-17s from New Guinea: "Our primary missions were the Japanese bases on the north coast of New Guinea. We were at Port Moresby, New Guinea, which is on the south coast. North of us, running down the center of New Guinea, are the Owen Stanley Mountains, which run up to 16,000–18,000ft [4,876–5,486m]. We would take off from the south coast of New Guinea, fly over the mountains, and then on the north coast of New Guinea were Japanese airfields. They had places like Lae, Wewak, Medanga—a whole string of Japanese airfields. Then, you had a lot of Pacific Ocean north of New Guinea, and then an island north of that was New Britain Island. On New Britain Island was Rabaul, which was the primary Japanese naval base in that part of the Pacific. Rabaul was a huge harbor that probably on an average day had a

Above: Admiral Kincaid (left) and General MacArthur stand on the USS Phoenix, prior to the invasion of Los Negros.

Below left: A raid over Rabaul, showing the confines of the harbor. More than 360 antiaircraft guns defended the Japanese base.

Below right: A Japanese merchant vessels sinks at Rabaul.

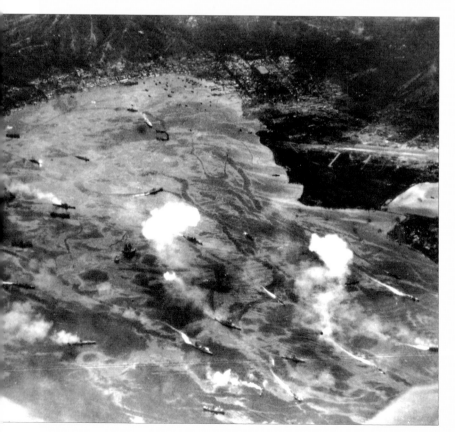

hundred Japanese ships in it of different kinds—merchant ships and naval ships. The whole South Pacific Navy was headquartered there.

"Rabaul was really our primary target. They had three airdromes around the harbor. The harbor was created by a volcano and it had these tall mountains all around ringing it. Because it was so far over the water to get there, we had no fighter cover at all. Also, we had very few airplanes. We received no replacement airplanes because Mr.

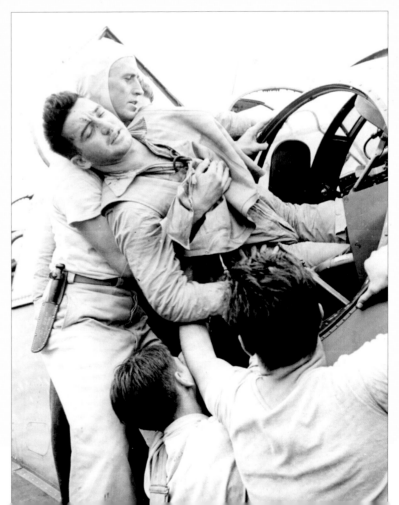

Right: *The US Navy Mark 8 Mod 8 reflector gunsight. The reflector sights had the advantage that the pilot's head did not need to be precisely aligned with the sight.*

Roosevelt and Mr. Churchill decided that the war had to be won in Europe first. . . .

" . . . if you had any kind of moonlight at all, and weren't flying in total clouds, you could discern the shorelines and you knew where the docks were. Rabaul was a big harbor and it had docks and warehouses. You knew approximately where ammunition dumps and fuel dumps were in the jungle. All of these islands are total jungle except for the parts that have been cleared for runways, and a few little towns. We would fly across the harbor and we would get about to where we thought we could hit something. The bombardier in the front would release one bomb. You would fly out to sea for 10–15 minutes, or whatever pleased you, and you might drop from 10,000ft [3,048m] down to 7,000ft [2,133m] and you would come in from a different direction and fly across the harbor again. Then you would drop another bomb. You might do this three or four times, if you were crazy. Most of

wasn't uncommon to get an engine shot out. If you were really unlucky you might get two engines shot out. Of course if you were totally unlucky, you got shot down over Rabaul. We often came back from there and the hard part of it was that if you got an engine shot out, chances are that wasn't the only damage to the airplane because the same antiaircraft fire that knocked out an engine probably also knocked out part of the rudder, or part of the other controls. So flying back those long distances across the ocean, there was only one place to go and that was Port Moresby because the Japanese held everything else. There was only one place for us to go so a lot of our flights were very 'iffy,' 'chancy,' [and] 'scarey'—coming back with a plane that didn't fly too well."

The Allied air forces dropped 20,584 tons of bombs on Rabaul, and by March 1944 it had effectively ceased to function as a military base.

Below left: *US phosphorus bombs explode amongst Japanese Mitsubishi G4M Betty and Mitsubishi A6M Zeke aircraft.*
Below right: *A wounded crewman is lifted out of his TBF aircraft aboard USS Saratoga, following a raid on Rabaul in November 1943.*

the time you tried to just make two passes across the harbor. That was to get everybody awake, excited. We only had one plane load of nine people who were keeping them awake. There were probably 2,000 people down below that we were keeping awake . . . .

" . . . you never came back without some damage to your plane. The antiaircraft fire was awesome, very intensive, very heavy, and an awful lot of planes got shot down over Rabaul. It wasn't a 'piece of cake.' It

Central Pacific Island Hopping

"We couldn't see the blood . . . we knew what was happening. These men were being picked off by the machine guns . . . we could see the machine-gun bullets hitting the water like rain."

—Charles Pace, USMC, on the landing at Tarawa, November 20, 1943

The Central Pacific "island-hopping" campaign was unique in its scope and scale. Across literally thousands of miles of Pacific Ocean, US forces worked step by step closer to the Japanese mainland, battling their way across ferociously defended outcrops of land, some of them just hundreds of yards long. As they did so, the noose closed around the Japanese homeland.

The main objectives of the US campaign were, in order, the Gilbert and Marshall Islands, the Palau Islands and the Carolines, then swinging northwards to the Marianas and the Bonin Islands, by which time the US advance would be eating directly into Japanese home territory. To accomplish this massive advance was a formidable challenge in two principal regards: logistics and amphibious assault tactics. To meet the logistical needs, the Americans relied on a unprecendented Fleet Train of merchant ships. These vessels would pick up huge quantities of supplies from ports on the peripheries of the Pacific war zone, then ship them into the combat areas direct to the naval task forces and land armies. It was relentless and dangerous work, yet it was mastered with such efficiency that the American soldier and sailor on the frontline rarely wanted for anything, particularly once the United States had taken

control of the seas from 1944. The US armed forces also became the world's unrivaled exponents of amphibious warfare, the tactics of which were especially pioneered by the US Marine Corps, with their constant innovation in littoral tactics. A typical amphibious action was preceded by artillery fire of crushing intensity, delivered by a specialized bombardment fleet of battleships, cruisers, and destroyers, supplemented by air strikes from escort carriers. The larger fleet carriers "sealed" the invasion zone off from enemy aircraft and Japanese resupply, isolating the enemy for the kill. Once the landing zones had been heavily "prepped," the troops were actually put ashore via a highly efficient amphibious process, coordinated (from early 1944) by a HQ ship to ensure the beach assault ran like clockwork. The Americans also became masters of "combat loading," i.e. loading the assault boats with the required weapons and supplies in the order in which they would need unloading at the beachhead. They also had the advantage of developing numerous specialist assault craft, such as the shallow-draft Landing Craft, Vehicle, Personnel (LCVP), or "Higgins boat," and the Landing Vehicle Tracked (LVT, or "Amtrac,") a kind of amphibious APC that could literally drive right up on the beach.

Yet despite the polish the Americans brought to amphibious warfare, the island-hopping campaign remained violent in the extreme. Technology could put men ashore, but only men could secure the islands.

Left: A shot-up Japanese Zero fighter sits on an equally devastated airbase on the island of Kwajalein, hit by US carrier air strikes in December 1943.

Taking Tarawa

The first major objective of the island-hopping campaign was for Nimitz's forces to take the Gilbert Islands, in which the principal sub-objectives were the atolls of Tarawa and Makin. The preparatory bombardment of the islands began on November 13, 1943, and the Marine assaults went in on November 20.

Makin proved to be an uncomplicated target, and was cleared within three days. Tarawa, in absolute contrast, was an utter nightmare, despite the fact that the main center for Japanese resistance was the island of Betio, less than 4,000yds (3,656m) long and 500yds (415m)

across at its widest point. Some 4,700 Japanese defenders fought to the death, and in the first day alone 5,000 men of the 2nd Marine Dvision were taken casualty. Olian Perry was a demolitions expert with the 18th Marines, 1st Battalion, Company "C": "We walked into a hornets' nest at Tarawa. No, they didn't tell us where we were going. I remember going in on the pier [a long pier constructed for merchant vessels] in a Higgins boat; the Japanese had machine guns set up under the pier and it was just murder. Higgins boats are big and the person driving it stands up in the back. You just went over the side, and the only problem was that you didn't know if you were going to land in a hole in the coral and sink from the weight of the back pack. We were pretty close to the shore when we went over the side; it was about waist deep."

Charles Pace was a Marine observing this assault, which ran into severe complications, as the inner coral reed around Tarawa meant the water was actually too shallow to allow the boats to approach close to the landing zone: "I think sometime around 9 or 10 o'clock in the morning all of the infantry got into the Higgins boats and amphibious tractors, and moved off to a line of departure and tried to get into the beach. Of course the story is well known, that they were unable to cross the reef with most of the boats, and the men had to walk from the outer reef, 300, 400, or 500yds [274, 366, or 457m] unprotected, completely unprotected in the face of Japanese machine-gun fire, to the beach. We lay offshore there. There was a Japanese naval gun that tried to reach us and they dropped several shells close by our troop ship and frightened the captain little bit so he picked up his anchor and moved back up about another half mile out to sea. One thing he didn't want was 600 Marines trying to swim around from a ship that just went down in the lagoon.

"We were still close enough that with our field glasses we could see what was going on and it was a very sickening thing. We'd watched these lines of Marines climb out of the Higgins Boats as they worked up on to the reef, and then try to walk ashore, and occasionally we'd see a man disappear. Then, maybe two or three men away, another man would disappear, and they would just drop into the water. We couldn't see the blood, of course, but we knew what was happening. These men were being picked off by the machine guns because we could see the machine-gun bullets hitting the water like rain drops. We could see it kind of working along. It made us pretty sick because all of a sudden it became abundantly clear that the Navy had not been able to stop all of that. We were going to go against a contested beach with absolutely no cover whatsoever. It made us think of what the fellows must have faced at Belleau Wood and Château-Thierry, you know, during the war some twenty-five years before, in France. So we knew we had all kinds of problems."

Top: *Soldiers of V Amphibious Corps storm ashore the island of Makin, against a minimal resistance from Japanese occupiers.*
Above: *Wounded US soldiers are evacuated from the Tarawa beaches on inflatable rubber boats to ships waiting offshore.*

"The beach was very small. They did not call us ashore that first, or even the second day. The afternoon of the second day we got the word we were to go ashore, but we were not going to land on Betio. 'Helen' was the code name for the main island that the Japs were defending. Instead we were to land at Bairiki, I think that was the name of the small atoll facing Helen, and we were to set up our machine guns there and stop any attempt at retreat of the Japanese down the chain."

Despite the horror of the landing, the Marines nevertheless established a foothold on Tarawa. An official situation report on the first day read:

Above left: *Sand-packed palm log defenses were superb at stopping small-arms fire, as these Marines on Tarawa appreciate as they conduct an airstrip attack.*
Above right: *A US Marine radio operator aboard the USS* Maryland *engages in ship-to-shore communications around Tarawa.*

"Situation at 1600; Our line runs generally from the Burns-Philp pier across the east end of the triangle formed by the airfield to the south coast and along the coast intermittently to a place opposite the west end of the triangle; then from the revetments north of the west end of the main air strip on to the north; another line from west of the center of RED 1 across the end of the island to the south coast west of the end of the main strip. Some troops in 227 (gunnery target-area designation) dishing out hell and catching hell. Pack howitzers in position and registered for shooting on tail (of Betio). Casualties many; percentage dead not known; combat efficiency: We are winning."

The Marines were indeed winning, although that must have been hard to see for many on the beach. Like Makin, it took three days to clear Tarawa, but the cost was very different—just under 1,000 Marines dead and 2,000 wounded. Of the 4,700 Japanese defenders, only one hundred of them surrendered.

Left: *Marine reinforcements wade ashore on Tarawa. The in-water phase of any landing was acutely vulnerable to Japanese counter-fire, although the apparent leisurely attitude here shows that the beach has been secured.*

Kwajalein Atoll

To the northwest of the Gilbert Islands were the next stepping stone in the Americans' Pacific advance, the Marshall Islands. Like the Gilberts, the Marshalls consisted of small, rugged scraps of land, and the key objectives were Kwajalein Atoll and, further north, Eniwetok Atoll.

The assault on Kwajalein was launched by the 4th Marine Division and the 7th Infantry Division on February 1, 1944, with the Marines landing at Roi and Namur at the northern end of the atoll's central lagoon, while the infantry assaulted Kwajalein itself. **Richard Sorenson was a member of a machine-gun squad in the 3rd Battalion, 24th Marines:** We finally headed into the beach at 1100hrs. We landed at 12 noon right on the dot, just left of the pier, Yokahama pier, which is still there. We were the right flank of Landing Team 3. . . . We received opposition on the beach from the very moment we landed. One of our landing craft was destroyed. We moved

Left: Marines surround a Japanese pillbox on Roi-Namur. Satchel charges and flamethrowers were usually the best weapons against such positions.

in off the beach as fast as we could and set up our guns to support the 1st Platoon. Opposition was light for the 1st Battalion landing but it increased the farther in we got. We were knocking out some of the pillboxes that had not been knocked out by artillery.

"About an hour after we hit the beach, a mortar shell hit the gun emplacement and killed the gunner and knocked our gun out. It badly wounded the assistant gunner and a third man in the squad. I was just behind him with two boxes of ammo, but we still had a light machine gun. Shortly after that, at 1305 or 1310hrs, a tremendous explosion occurred off to our right and the whole island turned black. I pulled out a handkerchief and put it over my mouth because we couldn't breathe. We didn't know what had happened. At first I thought a volcano was erupting. You couldn't see. The debris was coming down, just huge chunks of concrete. Another fellow and I [thought we] had run into the 16in shell and were on the right side of the explosion. Debris went as far out as the landing craft and the ships sitting out in the lagoon. It killed some of the men on the beach and injured some of the sailors. What had happened was F and G Companies of the 1st Battalion had come across this large block house that had not been destroyed. They put a sensor charge against the wall and blew a hole in it. Then a bunch of Japanese ran out the other end and they stuck another sensor charge in there while it was loaded with torpedo warheads and bombs. Thousands of tons of TNT and the smoke and cloud and debris went up 1,000ft [305m] in the air. It covered the whole island.

"After that cleared we continued to move forward. It decimated both companies. They [1st Battalion] lost over 100 men, close to 200 killed and wounded. So they had to bring in the 2nd Battalion to support them. B Company came in on our side, but they were reserves and they were supposed to support us. We advanced to what they called Sycamore Street and went across the island east to west and west to east. We regrouped at that time to allow the 1st and 2nd Battalions to move up on our flank before we advanced. At 1600hrs we were told to go ahead and we started advancing. Well the Japanese had reorganized and we did not know at that time that all of their high-ranking officers had been killed. The team that I was with moved forward. By 1730hrs, we had gone almost to the end of the island. . .

Above: A huge pall of smoke hangs over Roi Island, February 1, 1944, after US Marines unwittingly set off a torpedo warhead magazine. Twenty Marines were killed in the explosion.

Right: *The basic USMC herringbone twill (HBT) utility uniform was primarily intended as a fatigue uniform, but its comfort and durability meant it was frequently worn in combat.*

"The next morning as the sun came up, we found ourselves completely surrounded by Japanese, about 250 attacking our side of the island. We wondered where the rest of our troops were. Our own troops didn't know where we were. We were catching mortar fire and machine-gun fire from our own troops who were behind us. We were fighting as best we could and doing a pretty good job. I went through a bandolier of ammunition in that rifle. I think we were under attack the first hour. I got wounded. My rifle had no stock left on it. I had three grenades left and gave them to a guy. I crawled off into a depression and I thought if they broke through I would get my throat slit. They weren't taking any prisoners and we weren't either. As an assault unit, you cannot afford to take prisoners. We killed everyone that we could see. I lay there and a corpsman came over and he tied off two arteries. He actually saved my life, because I would have bled to death."

Kwajalein proved as stubborn in defence as Tarawa; of the 8,000 Japanese troops on the atoll, only 130 survived the battle. Yet the Marine casualties were lighter—just 372 dead. This was largely due to US refinements in amphibious warfare tactics, particularly in the intensity of bombardments delivered on Japanese shoreline defenses. One US Army soldier observed that "the entire island looked as if it had been picked up 20,000 feet and then dropped."

Below: *A group of Marines hunker down on Kwajalein Atoll. The blasted landscape was partly due to heavy B-24 preparatory raids on the island.*

The US Submarine War

The hidden nature of operations performed by submarines means that in Pacific War histories US naval submarine operations haven't always been given the prominence they deserve. In fact, the US Navy's submarines were a critical factor in the final Allied victory in the Pacific. Once a policy of unrestricted submarine warfare against Japanese merchant shipping was adopted in December 1941, the submariners began a campaign that rose to a devastating crescendo of Japanese merchant and military losses. A total of 1,178 merchant ships were sunk by submarines (55 percent of the total Japanese losses), plus more than 200 combat vessels—including eight aircraft carriers and eleven cruisers. Such losses put a logistical stranglehold on Japan from which it never escaped, dramatically curtailing its resupply of occupied territories and its industrial outputs at home.

The early phases of the US submarine war were not encouraging. The US Navy lacked experience in submarine operations, and until 1943 its submarine arm was plagued by a series of problems, including: lack of good commanders and replacement personnel; defective Mk 14 torpedoes; issues in sourcing and supplying spare parts; no radar to guide them to target; and a lack of coherent submarine warfare doctrine. By late 1943, however, these problems were steadily being resolved. A clear doctrine had been developed, focused on severing key Japanese maritime supply lines, and this had filtered down to a new generation of aggressive commanders and increasingly experienced crews. Improved radar equipment was allied to better intelligence, meaning that interception rates went up dramatically. Torpedoes were improved, swapping magnetic influence detonation for

Above right: *The conning tower of a US submarine. Surfacing was a submarine's most vulnerable moment, but was essential for recharging the storage batteries, charged by air-breathing diesel engines.*

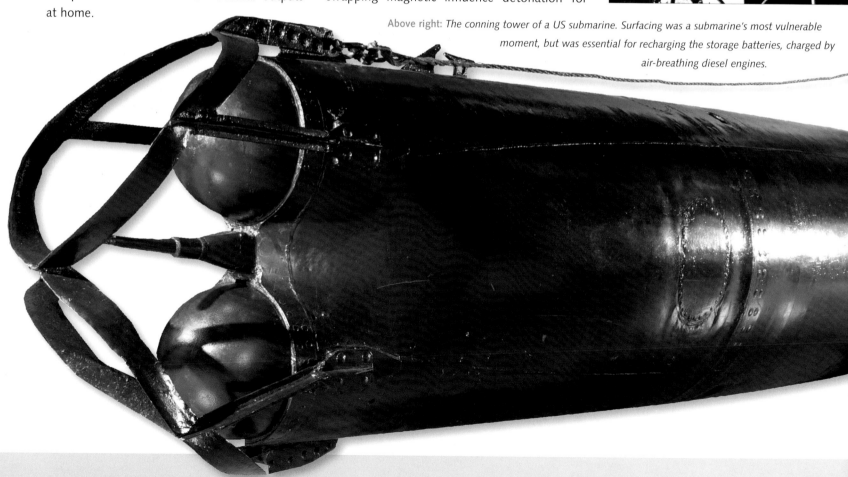

contact detonation. Moreover, the steady depletions of the Japanese escort vessels meant that US submarines increasingly operated in a reduced-threat environment.

Eventually it reached the stage where individual US submarines would often enjoy multiple kills on single voyages. Joseph Base was a submariner aboard the USS *Redfin*, and laconically remembers just one patrol: "On the second patrol we left on March 19, 1944 and went to Darwin again to refuel. Then we went up into the Celebes Sea. There we had a little bit better success. We had a convoy of six ships and plotted them during the day and then at night we made a run at them from the surface. We had radar back then at the time and they apparently didn't have any. We could see them at night but they couldn't see us. So we went in and fired torpedoes and sank two of the ships. Then we shot around to the other side and hit the other two and sank those. Then we got chased into a bay somewhere. It really wasn't much of a bay but we didn't want to go in too far. We were running up there just to get away and the guy turned his searchlight on us and he spotted us. So then we dove and he dropped some depth charges, but nothing too serious. We also sank another destroyer that time too."

The American submarine crews came to expect such high kill ratios, but the nature of their operations meant that they could never adopt a complacent attitude. On the surface, and sub could be surprised and shot up by a Japanese fighter or destroyer, and underwater depth charges threatened to implode the hull. In total fifty-two US submarines were lost in action, from a force numbering 288.

Left: The HA.19 Japanese midget submarine, which participated unsuccessfully in the attack on Pearl Harbor in December 1941. The submarine failed to enter the harbor, and was grounded and captured.

Below: The US Navy's officer submarine qualification badge. A silver version was produced for enlisted men.

Life on the Subs

Submarine service required a special breed of man. There were few perks. Submarine crews were often treated to superior food, and indeed the hearty fare of the submariner was something used in US Navy recruiting campaigns. Yet the length of submarine patrols (one crewman's very first patrol lasted fifty-two days), and the paucity of refrigeration, meant that fresh food would quickly deteroriate, leaving the crew with frequently unimaginative tinned goods or the often unfamiliar delicacies picked up in Pacific ports. The interior of a submarine was hot, noisy, sweaty, and claustrophobic, although recruits to the submarine service were thoroughly tested for any claustrophic tendencies. The air became laden with human body odor and the smell of diesel fumes, and it only really became refreshed when the submarine was able to surface and throw open its hatches for a decent period of time. Moreover, in dangerous operational areas the crew might rarely see daylight, the submarine staying underwater during the vulnerable daytime hours and only surfacing at night. All told, the life of the American submariner was a test of endurance and good humor.

Above: A chief petty officer of a US submarine stands beside an access ladder. He is manning the submarine control station, and to his left are the diving controls. Submarines demanded a high degree of technical knowledge to man.

Clearing the Marshalls

knock out everything. Would you believe that happened? Golly, it knocked the whole thing out. I had already dug a foxhole for myself, you know; just in case. They [Japanese aircraft] came over and they knocked the radar out; and they bombed us for two-and-a-half hours on a moonlit night, and we didn't have a thing that we could hit back with. . . .

Left: *Eniwetok Atoll smoulders from the effects of battle. The atoll iself was comprised of some forty individual islands.*
Below: *A Marine advance on Eniwetok receives some welcome cover from armor.*
Bottom: *A typical scene at a beachhead, choked with supplies of every kind.*

With Kwajalein secured, the rest of the Marshalls remained to be cleared. The final major piece in the Marshall jigsaw puzzle was Eniwetok Atoll, with initial landings beginning on February 17, 1944, at Engebi. The operation was to be carried out by the 22nd Marine Regiment plus the 106th Infantry Regiment.

John Karl Rankin, USMC, was a radar specialist, tasked with establishing radar cover on the atoll. "Well, of course, they bombed that island like crazy, to start with, before they went in, and then they secured that; and so then we were able to move in with our radar. We were in Marine Air Warning Squadron 1. . . . They told us before we even left the United States that if one particular spot in that radar was hit, it would

"I realized that everything was being bombed. They were destroying our ammunition dump, our gasoline dump, and they were bombing big holes in the company's street, enough to drop a jeep into, and the shrapnel was whistling over your head, right through those tents. Oh, I'm telling you, and our radioman got it. He stepped outside his tent to see what was going on and he lost the top of his head and his scrotum. The shrapnel just killed him instantly. Quite of few of the guys had broken arms; and one fellow in the ammunition dump, got burned bad, and it was terrible to see him. He looked like he was burned all over. He didn't make it. It was bad news.

"I didn't have duty one particular night. See, we had three shifts. Three eights are twenty-four, yeah. Eight hour shifts. . . . After two-and-a-half hours a big, old Betty, bomber, a Japanese bomber, came over. . . . He just looked like he was moving so slowly, and I looked up and saw that thing move over me. I had my rifle, but I wasn't about to shoot at him because if I did, their gunner would have riddled us to pieces. That's one thing; you didn't give away your spot. You had little carbines and they had machine guns and those things . . . could just tear you up.

"Then they finally left, so we came out and started looking, trying to assess what damage was done and everything. I had hurt my knee but it was just bumped, you know, and I had torn a cartilage and it was sore. But, golly, guys were killed and hurt, broken bones and everything. I didn't even report it. It happened about the middle of March, I'm pretty sure. So we got real busy and we relocated our radar thing and repaired what was broken and bombed and moved it up to another part of that little, old island. We sandbagged that one in. Man, I mean, we had that sandbagged in great.

"Then, April 14, here they come again. Well, my crew was on duty . . . . They started coming in and we could see them; and so there were four Betty bombers coming in at us. So, we alerted our planes, scrambled our F4U fighter planes, which had .50-caliber guns. That old workhorse was something else. They scrambled those and got them up there, and I was dead reckoning four flights coming in, four flights going out. I never could do that before when I was in training, and I never did do it after that. But I did it that night and I got every bit of the information they needed. We stopped them. I thought that was a pretty good birthday present. I think I was twenty-three [that day], yeah. That's right."

Eniwetok, and the nearby Parry Islands, were cleared over the course of a tortuous five-day battle, in which the 2,000 of the Japanese defenders were winkled out from the landscape and killed. Indeed, securing the Gilberts and Marshalls had been an especially sobering experience for Nimitz's forces in the Central Pacific, illustrating just how stubbornly the Japanese would attempt to hold onto every scrap of land,

Top: *Victorious US Marines raises a bullet-riddled Japanese battle flag following the victory on Eniwetok Atoll.*

Above: *Marines, their youthfulness covered in grime, attempt to unwind after a period of forty-eight hours in combat.*

no matter how geographically barren or apparently worthless it appeared. Nevertheless, taking these islands meant that Nimitz now had a stepping-off point for the invasion of the Marianas, plus a useful forward operating base for actions against the important Japanese naval base at Truk.

Battle for Saipan

While the invasion and clearance of the individual Gilbert and Marshall islands had taken a matter of days, the battle for Saipan was to take more than three weeks of horrific fighting. The Mariana Islands consisted of Saipan, Tinian, and Guam, which were physically much larger prospects than previous island conquests, but again very well defended.

The attack on the largest of the Marianas, Saipan, was delivered by Admiral Turner's 5th Amphibious Force, with landings by troops of the 2nd and 4th Marine Divisions, V Amphibious Corps, beginning on June 15, 1944. The Japanese resistance, however, was astonishing, so much so that the reserve 27th Infantry Division had to be landed two days later. Artillery officer 1st Lieutenant Arnold C. Hofstetter, of the 3rd Battalion, 10th Marines, was still fighting for the island in the first week of July, as noted in this after-action report: "Small-arms and machine-gun fire was

heard to the front and right front at considerable distance at about 0300, July 7, 1944. No information as to source could be obtained. Later, the fire appeared to come closer and, since it appeared that the position might be attacked, the gunners were told to cut time fuzes to ⁴⁄₁₀ second in preparation for close-in fire.

"About 0515, just as it was getting light, a group of men seen advancing on the battery position from the right front at about 600yds [548m]. It was thought that Army troops were somewhere to the front, so fire on this group was held until they were definitely identified as Japs at about 400yds [366m]. We knew that our men manning the listening post were somewhere to the front, so the firing battery was ordered to open fire with time and ricochet fire on the group to the right. Firing was also heard from the machine guns on the left.

"After the howitzers started firing, it sounded to me like numbers 3 and 4 were not firing enough, so I went to these pieces to get them firing more. I got them squared away and stayed with number 4 until Japs broke through the wooded ravine to the left, and I heard that word had been passed to withdraw. The firing battery fired time fuze

Right: A Japanese Type 3 land mine, its body made from brown terracotta material.

Below: Marines on Saipan run for cover after setting off an explosive charge in a Japanese dugout. The typical satchel charge was the M37 Demolition Kit, which contained eight blocks of high explosive.

Above: Gas drums are offloaded from Landing Craft, Vehicle, Personnel (LCVP) on Saipan. Admiral King stated about the Pacific conflict: "Whatever else it is, so far as the United States is concerned, it is a war of logistics."

Above: *Marines battle through Garapan on Saipan's west cost. The village was destroyed in the fighting, with thousands of civilians killed in the crossfire.*
Lower right: *P-38 Lightnings seen on Isley Field on Saipan. The first US air unit to begin operating from Isley was the 498th Bombardment Group.*

was when we pushed everybody down to the end of the island. Some of the civilians were down there with them and there was a cliff there. I remember these ladies setting out there and they would comb their hair and fix themselves. We were calling to them with bullhorns to come in. We wouldn't hurt them, but the Japs had told them what we were going to do to them. One [woman] would get up and throw her baby off the cliff and then she would jump. That was one of the things that sticks with me pretty good. A lot of other things I don't remember. I must have shut out a lot of things. I see movies where people are hollering all this. I don't remember that. If we did that, I don't recall it. The only things I remember are some body hollering, 'Corpsman.' When a man got shot, he wanted a corpsman. If you was with a man that got shot, you wanted a corpsman. I can remember hollering, 'Corpsman.' But, I don't remember. Somebody must have given me some orders during that time, but I don't recall those orders. I guess that's, maybe that's the reason, that when I got back, I was pretty well adjusted. I never had to have any kind of treatment, or anything, for it. I probably shut some of those things out that I didn't want to remember."

and percussion fuze so as to get a close ricochet. Some smoke shell was fired. Cannoneers were shot from their posts by machine guns and small arms . . . which interrupted the howitzer fire and finally made it impossible to service the piece.

"The remainder of the firing battery fell back about 150yds [137m] from the howitzers, across a road, and set up a perimeter defense in a Japanese machinery dump. This was about 0700. We held out there with carbines, one BAR, one pistol, and eight captured Jap rifles, Japs got behind us and around us in considerable strength. They set up a strongpoint in a point of woods to our rear. . . . About 1500, an Army tank came in from the right and got the strongpoint and Army troops relieved us. I estimate that 400–500 Japs attacked the position. They used machine guns, rifles, grenades, and tanks."

The terrifying fact emerging from the battle for Saipan was that almost all the defenders on the island appeared committed to fighting to the death, despite that fact that there were some 27,000 Japanese troops on the island. Saipan was finally secured on July 9, with more than 13,000 American casualties. One grim addition to the death toll on the island was more than 1,000 civilians who committed suicide, believing Japanese propaganda about US atrocities. Marine Ray Harrison remembers one tragic occurence:

"Well, I guess, it took us about thirty days to secure the island and one of the things I was really impressed on

Above: *Talismanic items of Japanese dress were no protection against American weaponry, yet a strong belief in the afterlife also prompted Japanese troops to adopt suicidal tactics.*

Follow-up at Tinian

The action against Tinian followed quickly on the heels of the taking of Saipan. Again, the duty of taking the island fell to the 2nd and 4th Marines, who were pitted against 9,000 men of the Japanese 31st Army. The US Navy began their preparatory bombardment of the island on July 16, and the 4th Marines went ashore on July 24, with the 2nd Marines following the next day.

Jack Gilbreath, 4th Marine Division, had already participated in the capture of Saipan: "So then, in about a couple of weeks we went to board LSTs and went from Saipan and over to Tinian. The big importance of Tinian was, naturally, for the big airbase there that the Americans wanted. And they wanted the airbase on Saipan. So they were both good bases.

"We were on Tinian only about two weeks. Tinian wasn't too tough. Thank goodness that our brass in the Navy and the Marines had figured out a landing space that was very small instead of where the Japanese expected us to land in the town of Tinian. There was a town there and it was called Tinian Town. And [US forces] had done the raid on it, with firing and everything, so the Japanese were defending it; but we landed on the other side of the island and during the whole landing thing, the whole division had to go in and the beach was about 200yds [183m] wide. So we were in there a good mile before they knew we were landing over there. . . . They [the Japanese] wanted to knock our mortars out and we did our best to knock all of theirs out. If you've read much about Iwo Jima you'll discover that mortars were a very deadly thing. People [are] wounded by mortars more than artillery. They're a wicked weapon. But we had quite a few firing there, and the Japanese that were on Tinian were veterans of the China war so they were a tough bunch. But we got the upper hand in a hurry and it went along

Right: A Japanese artillery bunker on Tinian, hit by American gunfire. Although US preparatory bombardments never crushed all opposition prior to landings, they inflicted heavy casualties and degraded Japanese command and control.

Below: American LVTs pull off the Tinian beach to return to the ships offshore. The LVT could maintain 7.5mph (12km/h) on water.

Above left: *A Japanese position on the streets of Tinian Town. The position is crudely but robustly constructed, leaving a firing port at the front. Such positions would be difficult to spot by attackers during the confusion of battle.*

Above right: *Tinian Town was virtually obliterated in the fighting, but on July 30 the 4th Marine Division occupied the urban zone.*

Left: *Japanese bodies lie strewn across the Tinian battlefield, killed during a fruitless attack. Few surrendered. In fact, one Japanese soldier, Murata Susumu, remained holed up on Tinian until 1953, when he was finally captured.*

and it was all over within about ten days. So actually we were there only about two weeks, then back aboard ship and went back to Hawaii then."

The commander of a Marine reconnaissance platoon, Lieutenant Victor Maghakian, remembers launching an ambush: "After getting the men in position . . . near the road junction . . . I went on a reconnaissance. . . . I spotted a large enemy patrol coming down the road with a scout out in front. After seeing that they moved into position in a cane field about 50ft [15m] from my platoon, I crawled back and told Captain Key [commanding the division reconnaissance company] what I planned to do. In the meantime the Japs were digging in and were making a lot of noise talking and did not suspect that we were so close. . . . I passed the word down the line to open up and fire rapid fire into the cane field, knee-high grazing fire, upon my signal. . . . we opened up and let them have it as fast as we could pull our triggers. They began screaming . . . and making awful noises. Then after a few minutes I ordered my platoon

to fall back to the division lines because I was afraid that maybe our own division might fire on us. . . . Next morning I took my platoon back to the road junction and the cane field and found between thirty-five and forty dead Japs in that area. I did not lose a man."

A notable incident occurred a few days after the 4th Battalion's arrival at Tinian. In the words of the battalion executive officer: "An air spotter reported that a Japanese tank had stopped on a crossroads on the southern plateau. This crossroads was the base point on which the battalion had registered. 4/10 fired one volley of eight howitzers and scored one direct hit on the tank. This tank was thus destroyed by one volley at a range exceeding 6,500yds [5,941m]."

Guam

Guam was the last of the Marianas that remained to be invaded and captured. Responsibility for this job fell to the 3rd Marine Division (with additional troops provided by the 1st Marine Brigade) plus the 77th Infantry Division, which faced around 18,000 troops of the Japanese 31st Army. Ralph H. Ketchum, an engineer with the 19th Marines, was in the first wave on Guam, which landed on July 21 on the north-western coast:

"They got us up at four o'clock in the morning. Got dressed and got all your stuff together and put it on topside of the ship. Then they had a church service if anybody wanted to attend, and everybody was there. Then they went down and fed us breakfast. Then they got us, put us in the ships—put us in the Higgins boats at 0530. We went out there and circled around and around and around until 8 o'clock. Then at 8 o'clock, the Navy raised the shelling off of the beach, so then we started in for the beach. About twenty of them Higgins boats in a straight line. When we got there, there was big coral reef and that's far as they'd go. We had to

walk across a coral reef for 600yds [548m]. The Japs started shelling that coral reef, but we made it to the beach . . . in our outfit everybody made it, but from the 23rd Marines ahead of us we found about eight or ten of them dead. . . .

"Well, we got on the beach and got organized. We were supposed just to hold the beach to unload supplies and the infantry, and all them was going up to the mountain [Mt. Chechao]. They got caught in a trap, about three or four of them [with] Jap machine guns behind them. . . . Then they called artillery from the Navy in there and the Navy put them big shells right down amongst them. That ended that.

"That night, we stayed on the beach and unloaded food and supplies and ammunition and gasoline. They would drop gasoline in barrels off the ship, and we'd go out there and get them and shove them into the shore for the trucks and tanks. Then, the next day we got the artillery in so the artillery would start pestering them Japs. . . . Well, we just stayed there unloading stuff and loading trucks out to take them up behind where the frontline was. We moved up behind the frontlines then. Then the next day, the next night, the Japs broke through our lines and got in behind us. . . . We were fighting behind us and in front of us, too. Practically killed

Above: US Marine soldiers are deployed to Guam aboard a US Coast Guard Landing Craft Mechanized (LCM).

Left: A 5in gun crew aboard the battleship USS New Mexico (BB-40) pump shells rapidly through the weapon during a bombardment of Guam. The 5in/51-caliber gun had a range of more than 15,000yds (13,716m).

Above: *Marines advance across Guam, with armor in support. Guam included some very difficult terrain, including dense jungle.*
Right: *A sobering insight into the precarious nature of life in a war zone—a US helmet punctured through with a bullet hole.*
Lower right: *A brave American proceeds with utmost care up the stairs of a ruined house, to tackle a Japanese sniper within.*

every one of them. Something odd, three guys at dark one night were coming down a road behind us, and they were singing 'Yankee Doodle' and the Sergeant said, 'Kill 'em, they're Japs, Kill 'em.' The guys were ahead of them 'cause they thought they was Marines. He said, 'I said kill them, damn it.' So, they finally killed them and they was three Japs singing Yankee Doodle. Ain't that something?"

The physical conditions on Guam deteriorated during the operation, adding their own contribution to the ordeal of the American troops:

"It rained night and day up there then. We was in mud up 'til all the way, you know. Then we started carrying ammunition up to the frontlines every day. We'd carry a truckload of machine-gun [ammunition] and we'd carry rifle ammunition. We didn't need to carry the artillery because the big guns was down where we were. Those 155mm howitzers could shoot 12 miles [19km] away. They had the ammunition right there beside them. One day we were running on a big hill and the truck stopped. They were working on the truck, and I noticed this Jap laying over there about 20ft [6m] [away], and it was fresh mud sliding off of his shoes. I said, 'That Jap just walked up here. He's alive.' The guy jumped out, went over there, and kicked him in the gut, and he's, 'No, he's not alive, he's dead.' Then when he got back to the truck it was about that time [the Japanese soldier] raised up with a hand grenade, throwing a hand grenade. A man named Stockwell shot that hand grenade out of his hands and it went off, but we didn't get hurt. . . . It rained every day on that Guam invasion. We slept in foxholes half full of water and all that kind of stuff."

The ordeal on Guam paid off when Japanese resistance was effectively quashed by August 10. The United States now had the Marianas chain in its possession, a significant outcome being that it now had bases for long-range B-29 actions against the Japanese homelands, and that Japanese supply lines across the Pacific were now severed.

Peleliu

One historical outcome of the Pacific War is that small Pacific islands that might have remained unknown to the vast majority of people in the West have achieved notoriety for being bloody battlegrounds of World War II. A case in point is the island of Peleliu in the Palau Islands chain, which was fought over by US Marines and 10,600 Japanese defenders between September 15 and November 24, 1944.

Peleliu's physical characteristics were a primary ingredient in the high casualty count of the battle, as a regimental narrative from the 1st Marines explained: "The ground of Peleliu's western peninsula was the worst ever encountered by the regiment in three Pacific campaigns. Along its center, the rocky spine was heaved up in a contorted mass of decayed coral, strewn with rubble, crags, ridges and gulches thrown together in a confusing maze. There were no roads, scarcely any trails. The pock-marked surface offered no secure footing

Left: A US Marine gives his wounded comrade a drink. Some 8,450 American soldiers were wounded on Peleliu.

shell. Into this the enemy dug and tunneled like moles; and they stayed to fight to the death."

In an attempt to suppress the defenders, the US air units and naval gunnery subjected the small island to a massive preparatory bombardment, before the soldiers of the 1st Marines went into the landing beaches. Wayburn Hall was a mortar man with the 1st Marines, and he remembers watching the pounding of the island as the Marines cut through the waves:

"You knew that we were going to lose some people. He [the CO] said that we are going in there and in seventy-two hours we ought to be headed back to Gavatu in our tents. We knew it was going to be fast and furious. . . . Everybody had his job to do and the plans were laid out with the Amtracs landing in their proper order and the wave of boats out there circling to bring that wave in. The Amtracs went in and came back, reload, and go back in...

"We were maybe 2,000yds [1,828m] from the beach. As it got more light you could see smoke plumes coming down. The Navy was strafing it and the crescendo picked up as ours approached for a landing. I think H-Hour was 8 o'clock for the first wave. I was in the first wave. Corsairs came over and bombed and strafed. We were still in the water. . . . We could see that they were really pounding the beach there. They were just tearing it up. Nothing could live on that"

Once ashore, however, he quickly understood that a large number of defenders were very much alive, as the Marines took heavy fire. He received an injury to the mouth from an exploding mortar round that killed another man. Here he describes the shock of being wounded, and the chaos of the landing beach: "It [the wound] was bleeding a lot. I was crawling and trying to get up there. There was a shell hole, good-sized shell hole. They said 'Get in that shell hole and stay in there.' I don't know who, but someone hollered at me. I crawled over to that thing and sat down. Most of the firing was going overhead anyhow by that time. The troops, the first waves, had cleared out. The Japs had machine guns firing right at the base. The air strip was pretty close . . . and not that far from the beach. I crawled up there and the rest of the platoon moved on. . . . The tractor backed out and more were coming in. The beach was piling up and it was shell holes and mortars in there on the beach..."

Above: In a violent preparation for the assault on Peleliu, 8,000lb (3,628kg) of high explosive is detonated on the shoreline.

even in the few level places. It was impossible to dig in: the best the men could do was pile a little coral or wood debris around their positions. The jagged rock slashed their shoes and clothes, and tore their bodies every time they hit the deck for safety. Casualties were higher for the simple reason it was impossible to get under the ground away from the Japanese mortar barrages. Each blast hurled chunks of coral in all directions, multiplying many times the fragmentation effect of every

Above: *The US Willys MB Jeep was a superb light utility vehicle, both dependable and tough with good off-road performance.*

Above, center: *A US Corsair of the 2nd Marine Aviation Wing drops napalm on Japanese hillside position.*

Above, far right: *Wounded are evacuated on Peleliu. Some of the US divisions suffered 70 percent casualties in the fighting.*

Right: *A soldier of the 1st Marine Division uses a manportable flamethrower to take out a Japanese bunker.*

On September 28, the Marines extended the operation with a landing at Ngesebus Island. A 5th Marines after-action report from that day noted that: "The landing was highly successful. Some fifty of the enemy were killed or captured in the pill boxes on the beach without having so much as a chance to fire a shot at our approaching waves. The fighter planes did a remarkable job of strafing the beach up to the time our leading wave was 30yds [27m] from the water line. A Japanese officer captured in the beach positions stated that the strafing was the most terrifying experience he had been through and that they had been allowed no opportunity to defend the beach. . . ."

The battle of Peleliu has been described by the USMC as "the bitterest battle of the war for the Marines." The claim can be justified. By the end of the action, the Marines had taken just over 6,500 casualties, of whom 1,252 were killed. In a now wearily familiar experience, just a fraction of the defenders—202 men—surrendered.

The Seabees

The contribution of the Naval Construction Battalions (NCBs) to the Pacific War was inestimable. Without their mechanical ingenuity and courage under fire, the campaign against Japan would have dragged on months longer, and Allied casualties would have been profoundly higher than they were.

The NCBs, known officially as the "Seabees," were formed in January 1942. Before that time, the US forces had relied mainly upon civilian contractors to perform base construction and maintenance in the Pacific and other military zones. In late 1941, however, Rear Admiral Ben Moreell, Chief of the Bureau of Yards and Docks (BUDOCKS), made an official request to create military units that would provide combat engineering support to US Navy and Marine formations. The request was granted, and by war's end more than 325,000 men had served in the Seabees.

The range of technical skills covered by the Seabees was exhaustive, with more than sixty trades represented, including plumbers, electricians, vehicle mechanics, land surveyors, metal fabricators, carpenters, and builders. This spectrum of talents meant that the Seabees were capable of tackling all form of jobs, from laying roads and building airfields, hospitals, and port facilities, to installing barracks, powerplants, and showers.

While the Seabees were meant to be primarily technical troops, they were often at the forefront of the fighting, particularly given their supporting role in facilitating amphibious assaults (such as laying matting to allow amphibious vehicles to gain traction on beaches). This combat role is reflected in the official Seabees' motto: *Construimus, Batuimus*—"We build. We fight." Demonstrating the mixed combat/engineering role, here former Seabee Art G. Anderson describes some of the process of building airstrips on Iwo Jima:

"Then there was another fighter strip on the other end of the island, and we surveyed that one under fire. The Japanese were still on one side of it, and Marines were on the other side, and the generals and everybody wanted an airstrip between where those two were still fighting. So it was my job with our boys, the 31st Seabees, to go out and survey this. They sent an Admiral and a Commodore over there to be darn sure we did. We worked night and day. We had all kinds of schemes worked out

Above: *Seabees make rapid progress laying Torokina Airfield on Bougainville, 1943.*
Left: *Seabees man a diesel-powered generator on a Pacific base. Eighty percent of the Seabees went to serve in the Pacific, owing to the lack of existing infrastructure in that theater.*

to where we would crawl on our bellies under fire, and you would jump up with your [ranging] rod, and we would have an instrument set up over here behind a camouflaged area, and we would know on a map that at precisely two minutes to four or something this thing was going to pop and the instrument man would have his machine set up there, and he had about three seconds to zero on it because that old boy was going to be there one, two, three and he was going to hit the deck. In that time, this instrument man had to take a reading on him."

The Seabees served in every US theater in World War II, but 80 percent of them were sent to the Pacific. Some select statistics indicate their importance. They constructed housing facilities for 1.5 million men, plus 111 major airstrips, more than 2,500 ammunition magazines, 441 docking piers, and storage for 100,000,000 gallons of gasoline. They became much-valued by all other troops in the theater, both for making combat operations possible but also often for turning a barren strip of Pacific land into something approaching home from home.

Airfield Construction in the Pacific

The Seabees constructed a total of 111 major airstrips in the Pacific, providing the physical infrastructure for US air operations across the theater. The first step in constructing an air strip was often to repair combat damage suffered in recent fighting. Using trucks preloaded with sand and gravel, the Seabees refined the art of filling shell craters to such a degree that a bomb-cratered airstrip could be transformed into level, hard-packed earth in under an hour, depending on the number of men available. Next, the surface had to be capable of taking an aircraft. Here technology came to hand. The Seabees could create a runway surface from aluminum alloy planking or long rolls of asphalt-impregnated burlap. However, the most popular surface was the Marston Mat, a perforated steel plank that could be locked onto other such mats to form a runway or road. One hundred workers could lay a 3,000ft (914m) runway using Marston Mats in just one hundred hours.

Left and Below: *As expressed by the recruitment poster to the left, the Seabees came to have an intense esprit d'corps, and an efficiency admired by all services. In the image below, Seabees quickly lay an airfield using Marston Mats.*

Philippine Sea — Japan Retaliates

The US operations against the Marianas chain precipitated what is now known as the battle of Phillipine Sea. Threatened by the US expansion, the Japanese sent a large naval force (1st Mobile Fleet and Southern Force), which consisted of seven carriers and forty-six other vessels, to interdict Allied invasion shipping in June 1944. Forewarned of this move, the US Task Force 58 sailed to meet it, vastly superior in numbers and firepower—it included fifteen carriers and ninety-seven other warships.

Left: *A Japanese officer aboard a carrier poses beside a scoreboard in the Philippine Sea, June 1944. In the final analysis, however, the battle was another profound defeat for the Japanese Navy.*

The first clashes between the two forces came on June 19, with Japanese carrier strikes, but these were virtually destroyed (see pp.130–31). In return, US aircraft attacked and sank the carriers *Taiho* and *Shokaku*, adding the *Hiyo* on the 20th. Thomas E. Dupree of the *Lexington* Air Group, was an SBD pilot during the battle:

". . . we took off and rendezvoused and headed out to the Jap fleet . . . our target was the *Hiyataka* and I don't believe they had a ship by that name, but that was what our intelligence people called it and that's what they thought it was, and that's what we thought it was when we hit it. We got several hits on that carrier. I don't think we sank it, but it was damaged severely and sunk later.

"And I know one of the carriers in that fleet was . . . either the *Shokaku* or the *Zuikaku*, one of them had already been sunk. They were sister ships that sat very low in the water and if you saw them the fleet, even at a distance, you could tell the difference in the *Shokaku* and the *Zuikaku* from the other carriers because they didn't sit up 55ft [17m] out of the water like all the other carriers. They were about no more

than about 25 or 30ft [7.6 or 9.1m] out of the water. I know that ship was in the fleet but it wasn't our target so we didn't bomb it.

"But after we hit the ship we were coming out of the dive and a lot of ships were firing at us and I was firing back at those guns; and of course when you fire back at the guns they stop firing because you won't shoot on it anymore if they're not firing and they know that. But I ended up shooting up all my ammunition. As we got on out in the western sky it was almost dusk, sunset, and it was getting kind of dark, but it was still light enough to see. We were trying to join up when I got a Zero making a run on me, and I had no way of getting out of the way of it, because he had the altitude and he had a Zero and he was a lot faster then me. So I just put the plane in a slight turn and with a little bit of a skid on it, so that when he made his point of aim he missed me about 20 or 30ft [6 or 9m] to the right. So he pulled up and made another run on me, and this time I took it and put it in a left turn with a skid in the opposite direction. This time he missed me twice because he tried to correct and of course he over-corrected and he missed me, and then he flew straight at me. Of course with a bullet proof

Below: *The USS* Indiana *fires its big guns against the Japanese coastline, 1945. At the battle of Philippine Sea, however, she served primarily in an antiaircraft role.*

the right and flew down under him and finally caught up with him and flew a formation on him. I was right on his tail, but I couldn't shoot him because I didn't have any ammunition. And he began to lean over and look to try to see my airplane and I flew back away from him on the other side and he looked. So he turned several times and I realized that he wasn't going to keep looking so I just moved off and waved to him, and he waved back and I got back in formation behind him and I called the fighters. I never knew whether it was accidental or if they got my call, but anyway I saw a couple of F6s over us and getting ready to make a run and when they started their run I just pulled out of formation and turned my wings up so they could tell that I was an SBD and they shot him down. And I could always brag that I was the only SBD pilot that ever beat a Zero in a dogfight and got him shot down without any ammunition. It was a rather exciting experience for me. Of course, he didn't shoot me down."

windshield and a bulletproof bulkhead that was the safest place I could be just flying straight at him, because I had protection against his bullets if he flew straight at me and I flew straight at him, but if I turned away from him, he'd have a direct shot into my cockpit. So I just flew straight at him and he pulled up right over my head and I said, 'Dan, I don't think we missed him over five or ten feet'. Dan said, 'We didn't miss him over six inches'. He said, 'I could have touched him.' He said, 'That was a close call!' But anyway I saw as he was making that second pass he was going right toward the water so I just turned sharply to

Right: Two US carriers come under Japanese air attack in the Philippine Sea. The carrier in the foreground is the USS Bunker Hill.
Below: The battleship USS South Dakota *dodges Japanese bombs and responds with heavy antiaircraft fire.*

The destruction of three carriers was a loss that the already weakened Imperial Japanese Navy could not sustain, and the commander of the force, Admiral Ozawa, steered his units away from further contact on the 20th. It was now evident that the IJN was becoming an impotent force against the sheer might of the US Navy as it manifested itself in 1944.

Marianas "Turkey Shoot"

The air combat during the battle of Philippine Sea was so utterly one-sided that it was eventually labeled the "Great Marianas Turkey Shoot." In a tangled swirl of epic dogfights, the Japanese lost more than 600 aircraft, as opposed to losses of 123 for the Americans. F6F fighter pilot Alex Vraciu achieved multiple kills during the action, taking his personal tally up to nineteen aircraft. He remembers a string of those victories, over a clearly outclassed enemy:

"By this time, we were in a perfect position for a high-side run. Giving a slight rock to my wings, I began a run on the nearest inboard straggler, a Judy dive-bomber. However, peripherally, I was conscious of another Hellcat that seemed to have designs on that Jap, also. He was too close for comfort, almost blindsided me, so I aborted my run. There were enough cookies on this plate for everyone, I was thinking. I streaked underneath the formation, getting a good look at their planes for the first time. They were Judys, Jills, and Zeros. I radioed an amplified report.

"After pulling up and over, I picked out another Judy on the edge of the formation. It was doing some wild maneuvering, and the rear gunner was squirting [firing] away as I came down from the stern. I worked in close and gave him a burst. He caught fire quickly and headed down to the sea, trailing a long plume of smoke. I pulled up again and found two more Judys flying as loose wing. I came in from

the rear, sending one down burning. Dipping my Hellcat's wing, I slid over on the one slightly ahead and got it on the same pass. It caught fire, also, and I could see the rear gunner still peppering away at me as he disappeared in an increasingly sharp arc downward. For a split-second, I almost felt sorry for the little bastard. That made three down, and now we were getting close to our fleet. The enemy planes had been pretty well chopped down, but a substantial number of them still remained. It didn't look like we would score a grand slam. I reported this information back to base.

"The sky appeared to be full of smoke and pieces of planes, and we were trying to ride herd on the remaining attacking planes to keep them from scattering. Another 'meatball' broke formation up ahead, and I slid over onto his tail, again working in close because of my oil-smeared windshield. I gave him a short burst, but it was enough; it went right into the sweet spot at the root of his wing tanks. The pilot or control cables must have been hit, also, because the burning plane twisted crazily, out of control. In spite of our efforts, the Jills were now beginning to descend to begin their torpedo runs, and the remaining Judys were at the point of peeling off to go down with their bombs. I headed for a group of three Judys in a long column. By the time I had

Left: *Crew members of the light cruiser USS* Birmingham *stand and watch the contrails of fighters slugging it out overhead, June 19, 1944.*
Below: *The pilot of an SBD-5 from the USS* Lexington *looks to camera during a flight in April 1944. Behind him sits the gunner in his open cockpit, armed with twin .30-cal. Browning machine guns, set in flexible mounts to provide rearward-facing defense.*

Right: *At the battle of Philippine Sea, on June 19, 1944, an F6F Hellcat returns to the USS Lexington. Although Japanese propaganda declared the carrier sunk, in fact it survived the battle largely unscathed.*

reached the tail-ender [last one in the group], we were almost over our outer screen of ships, but still fairly high. The first Judy was about to begin his dive, and, as he started to nose over, I noticed black puffs beside him in the sky. Our 5-inchers were beginning to open up. Foolishly, maybe, I overtook the nearest one. It seemed that I barely touched the trigger, and his engine started coming to pieces. The Judy started smoking, then torching alternately, off and on, as it disappeared below.

"The next one was about one-fifth of the way down in his dive—appearing to be trying for one of the destroyers—before I caught up with him. This time a short burst produced astonishing results. Number six blew up with a tremendous explosion right in front of my face. I must have hit his bomb, I guess. I have seen planes blow up before, but never like this! I yanked the stick up sharply to avoid the scattered pieces and flying hot stuff, then radioed, 'Splash number six! There's one more ahead, and he's headed for a BB [battleship], but I don't think he'll make it!' Hardly had the words left my mouth than the Judy caught a direct hit that removed it immediately as a factor to be worried about in the war. He had run into a solid curtain of steel from the battlewagon.

"Looking around at that point, only Hellcats seemed to be remaining in the sky. Glancing backward to where we had begun, in a pattern 35 miles [56km] long, there were flaming oil slicks in the water and smoke still hanging in the air. It didn't seem like just eight minutes—it seemed longer. But that's all it was—an eight-minute opportunity for the flight of a lifetime.

"In my satisfaction with the day's events, I felt that I had contributed my personal payback to the Japanese for Pearl Harbor. However, this feeling began to dissipate in a hurry when some of our own tried to shoot me down as I was returning to the *Lexington*. Although my IFF was on, and my approach was from the right direction and I was making the required two 360-degree right turns, it didn't seen to matter to some of the trigger-happy gun crews in the heat of this fleet battle. I would like to think that the choice words I uttered on the radio stopped all that nonsense, but I know better. So I came down and landed aboard, and I flashed my 'six' [six fingers raised] at the bridge as I was taxiing up the deck. As can be expected, there was a great deal of excitement later in the ready room—including the liberal use of hands to punctuate the aerial victories."

As was evident by such victories, Japan was now struggling to crew its aircraft with experienced and competent pilots, with training times dramatically reduced.

Above right: *A military compass, a simple device that nevertheless could save a pilot's life in the expanses of the Pacific Ocean.*

Left: *A Japanese fighter goes does in flames under the guns of an American opponent. By late 1944, many of the Japanese aviators were woefully undertrained.*

Reclaiming the Philippines

"At 0910 we had taken a hit which knocked out one forward gun and damaged the other. Fires had broken out. One of our 40mm ready-lockers was hit and the exploding shells were causing as much damage as the Japs."

—Doy Duncan, US Wildcat fighter pilot, battle of the Philippines, 1944

In July 1944, the Allied high command began a new debate about how to inflict the final defeat upon the Japanese homelands, now that victory was clearly in sight. From the leading US force commanders, two propositions emerged and were put forward to President Roosevelt, each advocated by a strong personality.

Admiral Ernest King, the Chief of Naval Operations, argued that the correct course of action was to strike toward the island of Formosa (Taiwan), bypassing the heavily defended Philippines. By taking Formosa, it was reasoned, the United States could conduct a more effective bombing campaign against the Japanese homeland, sever Japanese communications with the southern and eastern parts of its empire, and gain a proximate foothold for a subsequent invasion of Japan itself. It should also be noted, however, that some commanders even recommended that the United States bypass both the Philippines and Formosa, and go straight for an invasion of Kyushu, mainland Japan.

General Douglas MacArthur's strategic viewpoint was radically different to that of King. He argued vigorously for an invasion of Luzon, and the reconquest of the Philippines, rather than moving to the more northerly

point of Formosa. He reasoned that taking the Philippines would be far more effective in cutting off Japan from its southern conquests, and that Luzon would be a better platform for providing air support for operations further north. Furthermore, MacArthur argued that if the Philippines were taken, then Formosa could actually be bypassed in the advance towards Japan.

This intense debate ultimately resolved itself in MacArthur's favor. In fact, the majority of the US military leadership preferred MacArthur's plan. From Luzon, the US forces could then push direct into the Japanese home islands by striking at Okinawa, with the possibility of future attacks into the main Japanese islands from three directions: the southern, central, and northern Pacific.

The plan sounded clean on paper, but the dire reality of the Philippines campaign was another matter altogether. Ultimately the Philippines would be defended by nearly half a million men from the the Japanese 14th Area Army. Against this opposition would be the US 6th and 8th Armies, heavily reinforced by indigenous regular and guerrilla forces, who were encouraged to rise up once the American landings began. The outcome was a campaign of absolute brutality, wrestled as hard in the sky and on the sea as on the land. It would be fought into the very last days of the war, with fighting rumbling on until August 15 in places, although MacArthur himself declared the Philippines liberated in July 1945.

Left: The devastated remains of Manila's walled city, destroyed in five days of fighting from February 23, 1945. The last Japanese resistance in the city was crushed on March 3.

Landings at Leyte

The opening phase of MacArthur's reclamation of the Philippines was an invasion of Leyte, one of the major islands in the center of the Philippines chain. The invasion took place on October 20, 1944, and was conducted by the US 6th Army under General Walter Kruger, the army consisting of X Corps and XXIV Corps.

The landings took place on eastern Leyte, and unlike the traumas of the island-hopping campaign, they were largely uncontested. Ken Wiley was with the US Coast Guard during the landings, and remarked upon the lack of Japanese land resistance plus the reception of the locals:

"We surprised the Japanese in the Philippines by landing on Leyte. They didn't know where we were going. They had 7,010 islands so we went to a place really that they weren't expecting us to be. Yeah, they had aircraft that came down and tried to bomb us and everything. But it was too late, when we turned into Leyte, for them to get all their troops down there to meet us. That was the difference [from previous landings] . . . We bombed the beach and everything. We had a lot of our fire going, but I don't remember a single shot being fired at

Below left: Logistical support ships and troop transporters steam towards Leyte on October 20, 1944, the first day of the invasion.
Below right: An aerial view shows the multiple amphibious landing craft, in close-arrayed ranks, taking troops ashore to Leyte during the invasion.

Left: A brass naval artillery case. Intensive offshore bombardment preceded amphibious landings by days or even weeks.

us in the boats. We took them completely by surprise as far as any land movement against us.

"They sent airplanes in to shoot us and bomb us—they could [at least] do that. We didn't have any beach fire. . . . We were shooting the airplanes down fast, but some still got through. They were constantly over us. When the airplanes break through and get over you, then our planes can't do anything about it. They are right there. That's when the antiaircraft tries to get them. . . .

"They would come over one to five at a time. . . .Because I was in the boat crew, the boat crew in general quarters, we were supposed to be out in the boats. But, if we are under way then we would stay up in the officer's area where we could see everything that was going on. I liked that. Consequently, we got to see the airplanes. We got to see the ships that got hit and so forth. The suicide planes began in earnest there in the Philippines.

"When we landed on the beach, we had Filipinos in outrigger canoes that came out almost immediately. They knew we were coming. They were there to greet us. They were the happiest people I have ever seen alive. They would come out in those outrigger canoes and they were so happy. One of them that I was able to sit and talk to for a long time was a young school teacher. She told us what the Japanese had done to them

Below: *A triple-mount Japanese 25mm antiaircraft cannon, used for both AA fire and for ground defense work.*

Above: *Dulag beachhead on Leyte. The vessels are Landing Ship, Tank (LST). Depending on the vehicle types, an LST could carry more than thirty vehicles.*
Below right: *US troops get low for cover during the invasion of Leyte. In most sectors, the initial landing sites were secure in under an hour.*

and how cruel they had been. She told us that the girls—young girls—they would tape their breasts and [make] them look like boys. I don't think anyone today can realize how vicious the Japanese were to everybody. They looked down on us as less-than-human people.

"The people that came out got everything we had—clothing, bed clothes, and everything else we gave it to them. Everybody just stripped themselves of everything, and they in turn had brought gifts out to give to us. The one gift that they gave me was this knife that was made out of an old file, but it was in a cane scabbard. I wouldn't take anything for it. It is a real treasure for me to have it."

The principal opposition to the Americans on Leyte was the Japanese 16th Division, under the command of General Tomoyuki Yamashita. At first the land resistance to the American invasion was relatively light, but as the two American corps spread out into the interior, the defenders pushed back more tenaciously, making some localized counterattacks in the central part of the island. Yet the American forces were consistently outmaneuvering their opponents, spreading out across the Leyte and also making another amphibious landing of the 7th Infantry Division around Ormoc Bay on December 7. By the end of the month, Leyte was securely in American hands.

Naval Battles at Leyte Gulf

The battle of Leyte Gulf was one of the largest, most decisive, and most complicated naval clashes in history. In essence, the "battle" was actually multiple engagements around the Philippine Islands, as the IJN deployed its combined fleet in an attempt to prevent the United States securing and developing its foothold in the Philippines. The Japanese plan was for a Carrier Decoy Force in the north to draw away the protective cover of the US Task Force 38 (the carrier component of the US Third Fleet, which was commanded by Admiral William Halsey), then for two major warship Striking Forces to make incursions against the landings in the central Philippines.

The naval clashes began in earnest on October 23, when US submarines sank two heavy cruisers (*Atago* and *Maya*) from the First Striking Force. The engagement then intensified massively over the next two days, the principal battlegrounds being the San Bernadino Strait and the Surigao Strait, and the seas off Cape Engano further north, where the Japanese and US carriers came to blows.

John W. Underwood was a Grumman TBM Avenger gunner/radio operator with VT-19 aboard the USS *Lexington* (CV-16), part of Task Force 38 dealing with the Japanese carriers in the north of the battleground:

"We were out on a rim and we were the farthest north. Our dive-bombers also acted as scout bombers. They could fly and carry more gasoline and fly longer distances. They were out scouting and they picked up that Japanese fleet coming down from the north. Which it turned out, they intended for us to pick it up. They had four carriers in it, [plus] two of those battleships that were half battleship and half carrier and a bunch of cruisers coming down from the north. . . . The other ships were coming through the Surigao Strait to try to free up that invasion with all of the invasion forces, but Halsey took us all. . . .

"On the dawn of the 25th, we launched everything. But on seven of our torpedo planes they had not been able to load the torpedoes. Everything went and we were stuck with some other aircraft and a couple of dive-bombers that didn't get off. By the time they got us loaded and everything, we took off with what they called the second wave. . . . We had seven torpedo bombers and I think two dive-bombers. I'm not sure about the dive-bombers.

Left: *The gunner of a US Patrol Torpedo (PT) boat, a torpedo-armed fast-attack craft, mans his twin Browning .50-cal. machine guns.*

"We flew to that [Japanese] fleet. The first group had a crippled cruiser and the air group commander instructed us to finish off that cruiser, but our flight leader argued with him. 'We are off the *Lexington* and that's the old *Zuikako* [a *Shokaku*-class aircraft carrier]. Planes from that ship sank the *Lexington* [CV-2]. We are out here to get revenge.' Finally he said, 'I can't give you any fighter cover. I can't give you any lead dive-bombers, but if you want to go in and commit suicide, that's your job.' So that's what we did.

"That *Zuikako*, we got three hits on it and our plane got one of them. It had already been hit I guess, but it was still afloat. You can't really describe what something like that is like. The pilot came on and he said they were shooting at us. I was looking at the radar screen and I said, 'Mr.

Left: *The eagle, globe, and anchor formed the three core elements of the Marine Corps insignia.*

Below: *The Japanese cruiser* Kumano *is hit by bombs from US Helldiver aircraft, seen circling overhead, on October 26, 1944.*

dropped us right down on the water, as low as he could get. He told me [later] when he came to visit me that he was trying to keep it 15ft [4.5m] off the water. We shot right past that aircraft carrier. I got a good shot at it anyway. I could see those Japanese gunners as plain as anything, dressed in white. So I unloaded at it. We got down between the ships and they were shooting at each other. It sounded like we were hit a hundred times, but when I got back I didn't find a single hole in that airplane but I would have sworn that we got hit a hundred times. Of the seven of us, six of us came back."

Above: *A Japanese carrier circles to avoid US air attacks at the battle of Cape Engano, October 25, 1944. By the end of this day, the Japanese had lost another three carriers to US air strikes.*

Right: *The rank chevron for a US Navy 3rd class petty officer gunner's mate.*

Meyers, they are 20 miles [32km] out.' He said, 'Take a look out the window.' I looked out the window and they had red, blue, and green ammunition floating all over the sky and we were 20 miles [32km] away.

"When we made the run . . . you had to get at 1,500yds [1,371m]. We started this run and I switched to the short range and I was giving him the range. I remember very well calling, '1,600, 1,500, 'Drop it', 1,400, 1,200' and he dropped it. He wanted to get in closer, which he did. We hit that thing amidships. When I swung around and grabbed the gun handles and looked out the window, the water looked like it was boiling with shells. He

Above: *In the Surigao Strait, Leyte Gulf, the crew of a US PT boat pick up Japanese survivors from sunken ships. In total, the Japanese Navy lost about 12,500 men during the battles around the Philippines, plus nearly thirty warships, including a fleet carrier.*

Left: *The IJNS* Chokai, *a Takao-class heavy cruiser, fires its main 8in (20cm) guns. During the battle off Samar on October 25, 1944, a hit from a US 5in shell caused the sympathetic detonation of torpedoes, leading to the ship's eventual scuttling.*

The battle of Cape Engano was a stunning victory for Halsey's Task Force 38 over the Japanese carrier force, demonstrating the clear superiority of American air power at this late stage of the war. The *Zuikaku* was sunk, as were the light carriers *Chitose* and *Zuiho*, plus and the destroyer *Akizuki*. The light carrier *Chiyoda* and the cruiser *Tama* were seriously damaged.

Yet further south, other elements of the IJN had closed in on the Philippines, intent on destruction.

Color Photography

The Pacific Theater was brought to life by color photography like no other theater in World War II, courtesy of US press and military reporters. Rudimentary color photography had developed during the early years of the 20th century, but during both World War I and World War II black-and-white images were dominant, primarily on account of both film availability and the developing costs. Yet in the 1930s, improved types of color film emerged, in particular the Agfacolor film from Germany and, in 1935, the Kodachrome film in the United States.

Kodachrome was available, from 1936, for 35mm and 828 still-camera formats. Even to today's image-overdosed eyes, the quality of the photos, with their heavily saturated colors, is striking. The Pacific Theater was particularly suited to such film, which responded well to the excellent light conditions and the deeply contrasting hues of the Pacific

Left: A war correspondent's patch. Press accreditation was, in the early years of the war, indicated by a green "WC" armband, but this became the patch seen here. War correspondents did not display rank on their uniforms.

Ocean and tropical landscapes. Yet the cost implications of using the film were such that it was generally confined to use in the hands of those photographers who were officially employed by the military or another government agency. In fact, the US armed services recruited dozens of photographers to record the war; the US Navy even gave photographers a separate military rating. Great names amongst this group were Ed Steichen, Wayne Miller, Horace Bristol, and George Strock. Color photographs were shown only selectively to the American public, partly because of their potential intelligence sensitivity, but also because the color carried more emotional impact.

Above: *Photographed in beautiful color, US sailors pay a visually poetic tribute to victims of the Pearl Harbor attack.*

Right: *War photography gave a new insight into combat conditions, as in this shot of a flamethrower team in action in the Solomons, April 1944.*

This page: American correspondents in particular invested in color photography, especially in the Pacific Theater. The drama of what they photographed ranged from the quotidian to the horrific, and they provided a unique documentation of a war very distant from the American homeland.

Death at Leyte Gulf

The naval gun battles around Leyte were, ultimately, US victories, but they were no one-sided affairs. The clashes began promisingly on October 24 in the Sibuyan Sea, where US aircraft hit and damaged the battleships *Nagato*, *Yamato*, and *Musashi*, the latter eventually capsizing and sinking.

Doy Duncan was a US Navy Wildcat pilot, and participated in the attacks on the giant Japanese warships, specifically *Yamato*:

"I never saw so much ack ack in my life. They really put it on. When we were coming down part of the time you couldn't even see your target. But those tracers go down there and hit the deck and it looked like a giant sparkler. You were just seeing every fifth round. We made three coordinated attacks and we got a couple of torpedoes off but it didn't slow them down. That big rascal is huge. It was funny, on the second round I got so interested in shooting at him that I somehow felt that something was awfully strange and I jerked back on my stick and looked at my altimeter and it said 200ft [60m]. I was right down on top of him. So I went as straight up as I could and ducked into a cloud at about 3,000ft [914m]. I came out the other side of the cloud and I almost had another heart attack because there were planes coming out of a cloud and I don't know how close we came. . . .

"We didn't do much damage the first run. But as we get down toward the bottom of the run they could reach you with the other ships. So all heck would break loose and we would get out of there and we'd come back and regroup, and go at him again. We'd come back and the second time we got him burning pretty good. That would encourage us so we'd come back and line up for a third run. It was all machine-gun fire—.50-caliber bullets—and he exploded from one end to the other and we knew we had him. The Japanese fleet was running off and leaving him. So we decided to make one more run. We were out of ammunition and we were going to have to leave. On the third run I got a 20mm through my left wing."

Greater victories were to come. The next day the US Task Force 77 caught and surprised a force of two battleships, four destroyers, and one cruiser sailing up the Surigao Strait. In a deft forty-minute attack

Above: The USS Birmingham *pulls alongside the USS* Princeton *to assist with fire-fighting aboard the carrier.*

Below: The great Japanese battleship Musashi *takes hits during the battle of Leyte Gulf. It took a prodigious amount of punishment to sink the ship: about nineteen torpedo hits and seventeen bomb strikes.*

in the early hours of October 25, the US Task Force destroyed all but one of the Japanese ships, and sank another Japanese cruiser the next day. This victory, however, convinced Halsey to go out to pursue the northern Japanese carrier force, leaving Rear-Admiral Thomas Sprague's heavily outnumbered Task Group 77.4.3, an escort carrier group, to face the full power of Admiral Kurita's First Striking Force in what is known as the battle off Samar. The battle was a bloodbath for the Americans, a two-hour action that saw

Above: An ingeniously crafted model of a US destroyer. Life aboard a warship occasionally yielded time for creative activities.

Below center: A set of Japanese naval binoculars from the battleship Nagato.

Below left: The Zuikaku is hit by bombs. A total of seven torpedo and nine bomb strikes would finish the carrier.

Below right: In a final act of martial spirit, the crew of the Zuikaku saluted and cheered the ship's ensign as it was lowered, even as the great vessel heeled over and began to sink.

them lose an escort carrier and three destroyers. A Lieutenant Hagen remembers the loss of one of those ships, the destroyer USS *Johnston*:

"At 0910 we had taken a hit which knocked out one forward gun and damaged the other. Fires had broken out. One of our 40mm ready-lockers was hit and the exploding shells were causing as much damage as the Japs. The bridge was rendered untenable by the fires and explosions, and Commander Evans had been forced at 0920 to shift his command to the fantail, where he yelled his steering orders through an open hatch at the men who were turning the rudder by hand.

"... We were now in a position where all the gallantry and guts in the world couldn't save us. There were two cruisers on our port, another dead ahead of us, and several destroyers on the starboard side; the battleships, well ahead of us, had fortunately turned coy [were retiring from the battle]. We desperately traded shots first with

one group then with the other. Shortly after this an avalanche of shells knocked out her remaining engine room and fireroom. . . . At 0945, five minutes after the ship went dead in the water, the captain gave the order 'Abandon Ship'."

The battle off Samar was a brutal clash for the Americans, and also included heavy Japanese kamikaze attacks on October 25, which sank the carrier *St. Lo.* but at the critical moment the Japanese withdrew, fearful of retaliatory US carrier aircraft attacks. The fighting went on into the 26th, especially among the opposing carrier forces. Yet by the time the Japanese broke off in retreat, they had lost four aircraft carriers, three battleships, ten cruisers, eleven destroyers, and one submarine, plus about 500 aircraft and 10,000 men. This level of loss, for a navy already suffering from earlier battles, was in effect the final nail in the coffin of the IJN.

Air War over the Philippines

The air war over the Philippines made one point clear—the Japanese air forces were now simply no match for US airpower. This was partly attributable to US production of combat aircraft massively outstripping that of Japan; from 1939–45, the United States manufactured 99,950 fighter aircraft, compared to 30,477 by Japan. But the Americans were also turning out far more well-trained pilots. In 1943 alone, the United States trained 89,714 pilots, compared to just 5,400 in Japan, an astonishing disparity. It was such an inequality that led to the Japanese resorting to increasingly desperate measures, such as the wasteful kamikaze attacks over the Philippines.

The air battle during the Philippines campaign was far from just a matter of aircraft-vs.-aircraft combat. In fact, just as many enemy aircraft were shot from the skies by the banks of antiaircraft guns mounted aboard offshore US ships. Melvin Bice was a gunner aboard the escort carrier USS *Ommaney Bay* (CVE-79) in the Leyte Gulf:

"That was like shooting fish in a barrel. They sent these kamikazes out. The sky was full of them. Then this one came in on us from the rear and

Left: A silver Air Attack on the Philippines medal, struck in 1942 to commemorate Japanese attacks on the islands.

Below right: The P-47 Thunderbolt proved to be excellent in both fighter roles and ground-attack capability.

back then the radar wasn't much good. On radar, if the Japs got down close to the water, which they did, you couldn't pick them up. And if they got too high you couldn't pick them up. There was just an area in there where you could get them. Anyway, this guy—it was another light bomber, a Betty bomber—came in from the rear and we saw him there. He was coming in low and that was alright . . . in thirteen seconds we put sixty-four rounds into him. Those darn things, the way it was explained to me, they were built out of balsa wood and treated canvas. The only way that you could knock them down, the easiest way, was to get your shells into the motors. It had to hit metal. The 40mm was one of the best antiaircraft guns that they had in World War II. Since then they have a hundred things that are better, but back then it was top dog. We had no

Above: The light cruiser USS Columbia *is attacked by a Japanese kamikaze aircraft off Lingayen Gulf on January 6, 1945. The aircraft hit home, the resulting explosion killing fourteen men and wounding forty-four others.*

problem. We shot him down." **It should be pointed out, however, that** *Ommaney Bay* **was eventually sunk by a Japanese kamikaze, having been attacked by a two-engine suicide aircraft on January 4, 1945, while the ship was in the Sulu Sea.**

Up above, the US fighter pilots also continued to inflict deep cuts on the Japanese aviation. Joe M. Sassman was a Grumman F6F Hellcat pilot aboard the USS *Lexington* **during the Philippines campaign:**

". . .there had been reports of more Japanese aircraft flying around, so anyway we were assigned, eight of us, to divisions on a fighter sweep. This was when Lindsey was leading it, he was also our Skipper by that

time. We had lost our first Skipper. . . . We lost another Skipper then by antiaircraft fire. So, Lindsey, Lieutenant Lindsey, was our Skipper and he was leading two divisions of us as a fighter sweep. On proceeding to Manila, or to that area, one of the aircraft developed an oil leak and had to return to ship, so Lindsey assigned a wingman there to go with him, so we were down to six.

"So, we were on a search, and all of the sudden we were around Clark Field, I think, and one of the guys said, 'Tallyho, one o'clock high!' So, the next thing . . . we were full power going after them. We went through them, and . . . it become a dogfight. We were twisting and turning and shooting. We said there were eighteen of the Zeros all there on that flight, and we got seventeen of them. One of them got away. The last thing I remember on that after the dogfight, my flight leader was chasing one and we were diving down low and this Jap plane was... and I was having trouble keeping up with him because I had everything on and it seemed like I was losing a little. Seckel fired into this Zero and the next thing, we saw the guy bail out, and he was so low that he hit a tree. But then his plane crashed right there."

What is striking about what must have been a relatively commonplace encounter is that the six US fighters take on eighteen Zeros, and destroy almost all of them, demonstrating US air superiority.

Above: A kamikaze is shot from the sky in a blaze of fire. If US fighters could not intercept the suicide aircraft, the only defense for the American ships was to throw up a dense wall of antiaircraft fire.

Below: The tailplane of a Yokosuka D4Y, a type of dive-bomber, litters the deck of a US carrier following a kamikaze attack.

War in China

Of all the theaters of combat in World War II, one of the largest is actually one of the most ignored in Western histories of the conflict. The war between China and Japan began in 1937 and continued until 1945. It consumed huge amounts of manpower on both sides, and generated dizzying casualty lists. Japan's death toll in China is unclear, but certainly it numbered more than one million. Of China's military forces, approximately 1.4 million died in combat, plus 8–9 million civilians. All told, nearly a quarter of all combat casualties in World War II were inflicted in the Sino-Japanese War.

Japan invaded China on July 7, 1937, following a long history of growing tensions and localized conflicts between the two nations. The Japanese were able to take advantage of the fact that China was already a split nation, fighting its own bitter civil war between the communist forces of Mao Tse-Tung and the governing nationalists of Chiang Kai-shek. Although the warring Chinese parties eventually (in 1944) came to an expedient agreement to stop fighting themselves and face the greater threat of the Japanese, the fact remained that the Chinese forces were diverse and divided, and generally poorly equipped and trained. The Japanese thus made a victorious advance, taking cities such as Shanghai and Nanking and pushing deep into the Chinese interior.

By the end of 1939, Japan occupied most of western China, apart from the territories south of Changsha, but now the offensive was running out of steam. As the Germans experienced in the Soviet Union, the Japanese found their logistics chains overstretched, so the war devolved into a stalemate. Furthermore, once the United States entered the war at the end of 1941, the Chinese forces benefited from Allied supplies being flown to them over the Himalayan "Hump" or driven to them along the Burma Road. By this time, US air units were also operating from China from mid 1941, and from 1942 to 1944, American air power was established at several major air bases in the southern parts of the country, from which operated units of the 14th Air Force. The Japanese eyed these air bases with menace, especially once long-range US bombers started to hit Formosa.

Above: Chinese pilots pose against a Republic P-43 Lancer fighter, provided courtesy of US aid, before they take off on a mission over Kunming, 1942.
Below: A Boeing B-29 Superfortress sits at a base in China. From the Chinese bases, the US bombers could hit the Japanese home islands.

On the ground, 1942 was a relatively quiet year, but in both 1943 and 1944 Japan went on the offensive once again. American air power proved critical in helping to stem the tide of the 1943 advances, but Operation *Ichi-Go* in April–December 1944 succeeded in the occupation of Changsha and southern China and the loss of the 14th Air Force bases. Although this situation was clearly serious, the offensive nevertheless stretched already overcommitted and weakened Japanese forces, who were now suffering a string of defeats in the Pacific Theater against American ground forces.

The Japanese in China largely held onto their gains until the end of the war. But ultimately the deployment in China did not help the Japanese fight its wider war, keeping hundreds of thousands of men pinned down in a vast theater when they could have been used to better effect elsewhere. Some of the last acts of the war, however, were played out in the China territories, when the Soviet Union invaded Manchuria on August 9, 1945. This opening of a new front was another factor in the final Japanese surrender.

Above left: *A Japanese armored train passes over a bridge around Shuangtaitzu, China. Logistics remained an insurmountable challenge for the Japanese in the China Theater, on account of the sheer distances involved.*

Above right: *A Japanese mortar team on the Chinese frontline. They are armed with what appears to be a Type 97 81mm mortar, a common infantry support weapon.*

Left: *Defeat in China. Japanese troops in Shanghai in late September, 1945, prepare to hand over authority of the city to an advancing US-Chinese force, following the final Japanese surrender.*

The Battle for Luzon

Leyte had been secured by the end of December 1944, but there still remained the challenge of Luzon, the biggest of the Philippine islands and one heavily defended by the Japanese 14th Area Army. Following an intensive US air campaign against Japanese aviation on Luzon and Formosa, the initial landing took place on January 9, 1945, in the Lingayen Gulf. The landing, by soldiers of the US 6th Army, was not significantly contested. US Army soldier Wesley Visel was an LVT driver during the landings, which now reflected the amphibious warfare efficiency of the US forces: "We came off the LST combat-loaded. . . . There were seven waves of us that hit the beach. . . . Then on topside there would be trucks and stuff that were lashed to the deck. The Seabees would be onboard. On the sides of the LSTs they'd have fastened these long thousand-gallon square tanks fastened together to form a long line. The last one would have the motor in it."

Although the landings were straightforward, the resistance the US troops experienced as they advanced inland was ferocious. While XI

Patriots of the Philippines :—

American and Philippine forces are liberating your country from Japanese oppression. Enemy air, land and sea forces have already suffered heavy reverses in the Leyte area.

As our landings continue, it is essential that our bombers and fleet prepare the way.

We do not want to injure a single Filipino. During the period from the 15th of December to the 8th of January follow these instructions carefully: —

Stay away from the Japanese troops and any place where they are gathered together.

Avoid all buildings, dumps, airstrips, and bridges used by the Japanese.

And most important of all, at the first sign of our landing, move away from the beaches. Move inland as far as possible.

For your own safety comply with this request.

Left: An American leaflet provides warnings and guidance to Filipino citizens, offering advice about how to survive the fighting around the beaches and inland.

Corps drove towards Manila, Bataan, and the Bicol Peninsula, the I and XIV Corps attempted to clear the central and northern parts of the island. The following excerpt from an after-action report by 6th Infantry Division, entitled "Final Phase of Luzon Campaign, 1 July to 21 August, 1945," illustrates the daily brutality of the fighting, even as the war was being brought to a conclusion elsewhere:

"Battle for Lane's Ridge, 1–8 July:

Operations along Highway 4 on 1 July were limited by landslides and heavy rains to reconnaissance and security patrols, forward and to the flanks of leading elements of the 63d Infantry. A few enemy stragglers were encountered. A landslide on New Highway, 4,500yds [4,115m] north of BOLOG, it was estimated by the Engineers, would take three days to clear. A temporary dry weather by-pass around

Left: A US Sherman tank blasts Japanese positions during the advance across the Philippines. Shermans were also used heavily in the battle for Manila.
Right: American troops make a river crossing on Luzon. Luzon was heavily contested over the course of a two-month battle.

this for 1/4 ton trucks and tractors was made impassable by the end of the day by heavy rains.

"The following day a reconnaissance in force by a reinforced platoon of the 1st Battalion, 63d Infantry, encountered an estimated 50 riflemen and 4 MGs about 900yds [823m] northeast of HUCAB on New Highway 4. At the same time the 2d Battalion, 63d Infantry, advancing 700yds [640m] along Old Highway 4, overrunning a small delaying position, but later being held up by an unknown number of Japs with automatic weapons, defending from astride the highway. The finding of 29 dead Japs during the day testified to the effectiveness of our artillery and air strikes, while 20 rounds of enemy 47mm or 75mm which landed in the 62d zone caused no damage.

only 200yds [183m], meeting determined resistance from rifles and an estimated 5 MGs. The Company held the ground gained while enemy positions were pounded by artillery fire, and other elements of the battalion hacked their way through heavy bamboo thickets and underbrush, seeking flanking routes of approach. Tanks could not be brought forward to support the attack, because of a large bomb crater blocking the road at the junction of the Jap cut-off and Old Highway 4. On 6 July, a reinforced platoon of Company 'G' sought to envelop the enemy's west flank, cutting their way through dense bamboo and up precipitous ridges only to be stopped by 6 MGs and numerous riflemen covering the western approach to the Jap strongpoint. The platoon pulled back while artillery concentrations were laid on the enemy replacements. An attempt by Company 'F' to make a flanking approach to the east was blocked by deep gorges. In an all-out effort on 7 July, following napalm and demolition bomb air strikes by all available supporting weapons, the 2d Battalion, 63d Infantry, assaulted and took the forward slope of LANE'S RIDGE."

The battle for Luzon ran until the end of the war, by which time the Americans had taken nearly 8,000 dead and 32,732 wounded; the Japanese had lost 192,000 dead.

Above: By the end of the Luzon campaign, 36,550 American soldiers had been wounded. Here we see casualty treatment during the first wave of landings on Panay Island.

Right: A wounded US soldier is given a drink of water before air evacuation courtesy of a PB4Y-3 flying boat.

"On 3 July, elements of Company 'G,' 63d Infantry, pushed up Old Highway 4, killing 16 enemy and capturing an LMG, to a point 2,500yds [2,285m] northwest of HUCAB, where stiff resistance developed along high ground later named 'LANE'S RIDGE.' A defensive position including 5 caves was cleaned out, at a cost to the enemy of 45 lives. MG fire from adjacent enemy positions forced the leading platoon to withdraw for the night.

"Company 'G' contined the attack next morning, following an air strike, and set the stage for the four-day battle of LANE'S RIDGE, which later proved to be the Japs' final position guarding the approaches to KIANGAN. Company 'G' secured a position 400yds [366m] south of the ridge, preparatory to an attack on 5 July. This attack was launched at 0800, following an air bombardment and artillery and mortar preparations. Company 'F,' in the assault, advanced

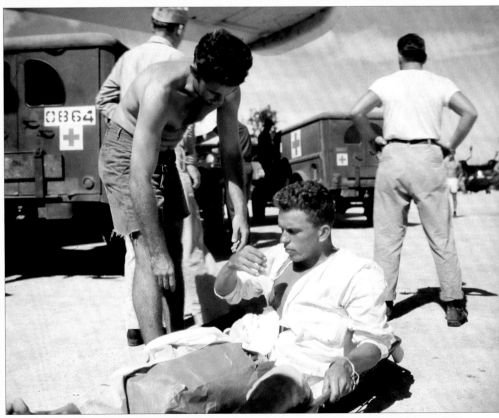

Bloodbath in Manila

The battle of Manila was a grim centerpiece to the overall struggle to secure Luzon. The advance on the city by the US forces was essentially two-pronged, with the 1st Cavalry Division and 37th Infantry Division descending from the north, and the 11th Airborne Divison from the south. They faced a well-prepared enemy, entrenched in a city of more than one million inhabitants.

The month-long battle, which lasted from February 3 to March 3, was appallingly destructive, with large areas of city reduced to wasteland as the Americans fought for every street and building. The Japanese in the city, being effectively surrounded by the Americans, fought with utter commitment. An indication of the battle that lay ahead came from one US officer of the 3/148th Infantry (37th Infantry Division), crossing the city's Pasig River in assault boats:

Above: US troops take cover behing a wall in Manila and pour on fire, three of the men using Browning Automatic Rifles (BARs).

Top right: LST-942 sets out for the Visaya Islands in the Philippines. The Visayas campaign began on March 19, 1945, with landings on Panay.

Lower right: US troops disembark small craft after making a river crossing in Manila. Manila was one of the few city battles the Americans fought in the Pacific.

"Leaving the near bank, the I Company boats were making good progress, moving in a ragged crescent, when the Jap fire stormed through them—machine guns and cannon. This fire, coming from the west, ripped through the formation, scattering boats, turning the move into a mad dash for the cover of the far bank. It was spellbinding to watch pieces of paddles and splintered chunks of boat plywood fly through the air while men paddled with shattered oars and rifles. On reaching the far bank, the men jumped out of their boats and scrambled up the bank taking their dead and wounded comrades with them. What seemed to last for hours was over in ten minutes."

The destruction unleashed upon the city was profound, and in the course of the fighting more than 100,000 civilians were killed. Monty Guidry was a US Navy radio man, but he visited the city shortly after the fighting, and saw the consequences first hand:

"Different parts of the city were less damaged than others . . . but the worse damage was in what they called the Old City, the walled city of

Manila . . . the government buildings were just shot, oh I mean destroyed . . . holes and destruction all over. We'd go inside and try to walk up the stairs and there wouldn't be any stairs some places and you'd walk around and have maybe [a little] room to go around. But finally we went to the roof of one of these big beautiful Washington-type buildings, and we'd go up the roof you know and we'd have to go the bathroom real bad—and course there were Jap bodies all over on top and we'd just squat down beside the body and do our thing."

Joe Rackley was a combat radio operator with the 37th Infantry Division, 145th Infantry Regiment, who was also a witness to the destruction within the city: "We got on a ship and we went from Bougainville around New Guinea into the Lingayen Gulf on the back side of Luzon. After we started landing, we knew where we were going. We were going to go take MacArthur's [former] house first. That was our first objective. We didn't have any opposition. We got on the landing craft and we got off. We were walking, no hostility whatsoever. All that day we walked. Then we started taking MacArthur's house, which we put on the radio, no heavy artillery, all small-arms fire. That's what we put on the radio. We had to take his house by small-arms fire and some more got killed. I mean lots of them. Anyway when we got through taking his house, we were ordered to take . . . one of the fifteen prisons down close to the University. That was through town.

"It was hard going there, lots of fighting. What I remember, we had a lot of boys from Washington, Oregon; lumberjacks. To me they were old men, because they were in their thirties, middle thirties and late thirties. Myself; I was only eighteen. . . . We went into the University, then from the University, we went right through town and we came up onto this old brewery, and that stuck in my mind. We come on to this brewery and the Japs had already made beer. These boys from Washington, lumberjacks, got in there and started drinking that old green beer. They got all drunk, drinking, and there were two snipers across the street in a hotel, on the second floor. The boys would walk out of that brewery and they would pop them off—I'm not lying, I'm not kidding, there was boys stacked up there four or five feet high. Just because of their foolishness."

The Japanese were blasted out of their defensive positions, and often took out their frustration on Manila's citizens. Thousands were killed in deliberate mass executions, and rape of the women was commonplace. By early March, however, the survivors were free.

Top: *Manila was almost razed to the ground by the fighting in 1945, with an estimated 100,000 civilians killed.*
Above: *Filipino civilians rejoice at the news of the final Japanese surrender. The fighting in the Philippines continued until the very end of the war.*
Left: *A soldier's personal grooming kit. Doubtless chances for improving appearance were few during combat operations.*

MacArthur's Victory

The battle for Luzon was just one element of the final acts of US victory in the Philippines. In the far south, the US 8th Army commanded by General Eichelberger was battling its way across the island of Mindanao, plus the numerous smaller islands to its north. In the course of these complicated operations against the Japanese 35th Army, the 8th Army made more than fifty amphibious landings at various locations. The islands were secured with difficulty, with the Japanese being predictably unwilling to surrender. Yet through the US ability to maneuver at will, many Japanese units were simply isolated and fixed in place, later to surrender on conclusion fn the war.

MacArthur ultimately made good on his promise of "I will return" to the Philippines, although the sheer cost left a question mark over the

value of the campaign that remains to this day. The man himself stepped onto the Philippines on October 20, 1944, at Leyte. 1st Cavalry Division officer Cesar Forezan, Jr. witnessed this event, plus the reality of the fighting for the Philippines, as he himself went ashore on Leyte:

"I climbed a net up side of the ship to the LCI. . . . as we debarked on shore with the enemy firing at us and the battleships firing their weapons at the enemy, the first thing I saw was [a] dead sergeant with a bullet hole through the head and helmet . . . and yellow because of Atropine that we had to take to keep from getting malaria and all those diseases. . . . General Chase who was a commander at that point asked me if I'd had something to eat. I said, 'No.' So he said, 'Go ahead and eat something and then come and see me.' So I did this . . . after I'd finished eating I came back, 'Sir, I'm finished.' He said, 'Well, okay. Lieutenant I want you to go along the shore at White Beach and see if

you can find a jeep; we have lost a jeep and we think it's somewhere in the water. And if you find it, let us know.' So I walked along White Beach from headquarters and sure enough I spotted a jeep in the ocean with the windshield sticking up out of the water . . . close to shore, but nevertheless in the water. As I was standing there looking at this jeep, I see this beautiful launch coming into shore and I just kept an eye on it. And lo and behold it was General MacArthur himself. And he stepped off the little boat . . . into the water with President Osmena with him; General Kenny his Air Force Chief of Staff . . . Army Chief of Staff . . . General Willoughby [MacArthur's Chief of Intelligence]. He walked ashore with four six-foot MPs with Thompson submachine guns, [each] with a round ammunition drum, surrounding him. He picked up the microphone and his words were, 'People of the Philippines, I have returned.' I was planning to salute the General because I recognized who it was immediately because of his uniform and his height, but I decided I better not . . . there might be snipers around and then I could get him in trouble."

This historically poignant event passed quickly, and Forezan returned to the realities of the war around him, moving to Luzon:

Left: An LCI(R) rocket ship unleashes a battery of sixty 5in rockets during the invasion of Polloc Harbor, April 17, 1945.

Below: Crewmen on the bridge of a vessel assisting a burning LST scan the sky nervously for Japanese aircraft.

Left: *A Japanese Army mess tin, used to store food.*

"And we landed on Luzon in the dark after the Merchant Marine people took us there. And as I landed on shore a Japanese 8in gun started firing from the mountains not too far from the Lingayen Gulf where we landed. As I reached the shore of the ocean, I noticed that there was a dead dog there and she had had puppies. And I immediately grabbed one of the puppies; put it under my jacket . . . I found out the puppy was full of sand fleas, and I was full of sand fleas. I had a little Freon bomb; I took the puppy out; I bathed him in Freon bomb; that took care of the fleas and then I did that to myself.

Below: *A US issue individual battle dressing.*

SMALL BATTLE DRESSING
CAMOUFLAGED STERILIZED
CARLISLE MODEL   STOCK No. 2-396
RED COLOR INDICATES BACK OF DRESSING
PUT OTHER SIDE NEXT TO WOUND
GUILD FOUNDATIONS NEW YORK, N. Y.
1997.567.25.2
SMALL BATTLE DRESSING
SMALL BATTLE DRESSING

U.S. ARMY FIELD RATION K DINNER UNIT

Above: *US K rations were provided in three individual boxed meals for complete daily sustenance: breakfast, dinner, and supper.*

Above left: *Jungle casualty evacuation often took mechanical ingenuity and, in this case, strong nerves on the part of the casualty.*

Above right: *October 23, 1944, and soldiers of the US 1st Signal Company on the Philippines display captured Japanese flags.*

"Our headquarters was in the little town of San Fabian with a church right across the street where we were located. And every morning when I would get up, I would go by the church and always I'd see a small baby coughing as children died. And we also fed the children of the village . . . we gave each little child a bucket and we told 'em when to come by and they would come by in the afternoon and we'd give 'em a bucketful of food. And the medics would also take care of them. . . . The next thing that I can recall was that we baptized 300 children of the Philippines who were not allowed to be baptized during the Japanese occupation."

Such acts of humanity were profound counterpoints to the wider horror of the Philippines campaign, which in the final accounting cost the Americans nearly 80,000 casualties.

Iwo Jima and Okinawa

"I got in right beside a casualty. I don't know where he had been hit. . . . The first words he said to me, 'Have you said your prayers?' I said, 'Yes.' He had a morphine mark on his forehead, so when the fire lightened up I got up and started to run again down the beach. . . ."

—George Raffield, attached to the 3rd Battalion, 28th Marines, 5th Marine Division, Iwo Jima

By the beginning of 1945, it was apparent to all that Japan was destined for defeat. The big remaining question was the manner in which Japan would collapse. The battles of Iwo Jima and Okinawa provided salutary evidence to support the view that Japan would continue to prosecute a campaign of unrelenting resistance.

Although Iwo Jima and Okinawa were the culmination of a long "island-hopping" campaign by the US forces, they nevertheless occupied a unique position in both the strategic context of the war and the psychology of the Japanese nation. The net was clearly tightening around the Japanese homeland, with the Marianas already under US control and MacArthur steadily clawing back the Philippines following the US landings on Leyte in October 1944. It was evident to the Japanese high command that the next logical stepping stones would be the Japanese home islands themselves.

Iwo Jima was a small, strange scrap of volcanic land that lay 650 miles (1,045km) south-east of Tokyo, part of the Japanese Bonin Island chain. Its importance lay in the fact that if it could be captured by the US forces, it was sufficiently proximate to Japan to allow long-range fighters to reach Japan and back. This in turn would mean

Left: Members of an M5A1 tank go to the assistance of an M4 Sherman crew on Okinawa, the medium tank having been flipped over by an antitank mine.

that the US strategic bombing campaign against Japan, made viable by B-29 missions from the Marianas, could now enjoy over-target fighter cover. Okinawa, just 340 miles (550km) from mainland Japan, offered an even more tempting prize for the Americans. Not only would it be a direct acquisition in the Japanese islands themselves, but it would also provide the platform for viable ground-support fighter-bomber missions, an essential ingredient of any mainland Japan campaign.

The strategic importance of these two islands naturally led the Japanese to invest heavily in their defense. Utilizing the complex natural landscape, the Japanese created fortress islands, studded with hundreds of concealed and reinforced positions, and laced with cave networks and tunnels. Iwo Jima—despite being just 5 miles (8km) long—had a garrison of 22,000 troops, commanded by General Tadamichi Kuribayashi. On Okinawa, which measured 60 miles (96km) long, Lieutenant-General Ushijima Mitsuru was the leader of 77,000 Japanese troops plus 20,000 Okinawan militia. All the defenders were left in no doubt that the success of their defense was integral to the survival of their homes and families.

It was this unique combination of limited physical space, defensive structures, and highly motivated defenders that made the battles for Iwo Jima and Okinawa some of the bloodiest in US history. The cost of claiming the islands fed directly into the eventual application of the atomic bomb.

Going in... the Landings on Iwo Jima

Despite its small scale, Iwo Jima was destined to receive one of the most punishing preparatory bombardments of the entire war, courtesy of the big guns of the US Navy and the aerial firepower of the US Army Air Forces. The pummeling began in earnest on June 15, 1944, months before the planned invasion in early 1945. However, the fortified nature of the island, which demonstrated Japanese ingenuity in defensive structures, meant that the results often fell short of the hoped-for complete destruction. As one intelligence officer for Task Force 56 reported in late January 1945:

Above: *A pre-invasion briefing before the assault on Iwo Jima. A critical element of the planning stage was the sequencing between the assault troops and the logistics.*
Right: *Landing craft push their nose up onto the beach at Iwo Jima, during the first day of landings on the island.*

"Photographic coverage of Iwo Jima to 24 January 1945, indicates that damage to installations resulting from bombing strikes between 3 December 1944, and 24 January 1945, was, on the whole, negligible. These strikes have apparently not prevented the enemy from improving his defensive position and, as of 24 January 1945, his installations of all categories had notably increased in number. The island is now far more heavily defended by gun positions and field fortifications than it was on 15 October 1944, when initial heavy bombing strikes were initiated."

The bombardment went ahead with unrelenting persistence, however. Then, during the early hours of February 19, 1945, the 4th and 5th Marine Divisions rolled in on their Amtracs and landing craft to make the initial assault and to establish a beachhead. What they found there

was not only a blistering Japanese defense on the shore line, but also a sulfurous, crumbling, or rocky landscape that defied the traction of both feet and vehicle tracks. Marine George Raffield was a machine-gunner with the 31st Replacement Draft Detachment, attached to the 3rd Battalion, 28th Marines, 5th Marine Division, and went in on the fourth wave. He here captures some of the confusion and intensity of those first hours:

"Well, while we were at the line of departure, there were a lot of naval aircraft that were strafing the beaches, strafing Suribachi [the extinct volcano in the far south of the island], and bombing Suribachi. There were aircraft that were coming down from the north of the island, B-24s bombing. The volcanic ash and smoke had risen to about the height of Suribachi, maybe 500+ feet [152+ m] in the air. You could see the fringe around that at the water's edge. When we left the line of departure, the flag came down and we proceeded to go for the shore. I landed in the fourth wave. When we hit the beach there was a tank just to the right of where the Higgins boat dropped the ramp and it was under artillery fire. That was the wrong place to be, so we went up, across and over the first terrace into the tank trap, and across the tank trap and went up to the next terrace, the second terrace. When we got there, there was a lot of heavy stuff that was coming in: artillery, mortars, and rockets. My platoon leader, Lieutenant Conley motioned for me to come to him. I went to him and he said to me, 'George we

are on the wrong beach. We are on Red One. What I want you to do, I want you to go down the beach toward Green Beach, and find out where the 31st CP [command post] is and come back and tell me.' So I shed my pack and left it with him. [I] Kept my cartridge belt and rifle, and I started down the beach. As I was going down the beach, the fire would get so hot, the artillery, rockets, and mortars, etc., until I would stop and try to get below the surface of the ash. I would use my knees, hands, elbows, feet, to try to get below the surface. The first time that this happened I got in right beside a casualty. I don't know where he had been hit, but he had his canteen in his left hand and he was shaking that canteen and I could tell that there was no water in it. The first words he said to me, 'Have you said your prayers?' I said, 'Yes.' He had a morphine mark on his forehead, so when the fire lightened up I got up and started to run again down the beach. I went on down to Green Beach and found the CP. That was the Battalion CP, or the Beach Master CP. I don't know which, but that is where my platoon was supposed to be, the 4th Platoon of the 31st Replacement. So I turned around and went right back up the beach and followed the same route that I took to go down to Green Beach. I got back to where Lt. Conley and the 4th Platoon were dug in. I led them down the beach then, heading toward Suribachi, to Green Beach. As we were going along, the pioneers had come in and they had ribboned off a parcel

of real estate that was mined and they were in there searching for mines with knives and bayonets, and they were finding personnel mines. I had run through that twice going to Green Beach and going back."

Through mounting levels of casualties (2,500 Marine casualties on the first day), a priority was to consolidate the beachhead and push supplies to the troops at the frontline, a role in which Raffield subsequently found himself: "During the night, an LST would come in and open her bow doors, put her ramp down, and would be adjacent to this airfield matting and they would back trucks right into the deck where they carried the tanks and vehicles. We would go in and start loading these Six Bys with everything—food, water, ammunition. It was carried right to the frontline troops from the vessel."

Although the landing was heavily contested, the Marines had firmly established themselves on the island by the end of the day, and began the long haul of clearing it.

Left: *A wounded Marine is helped to the rear by a comrade. The Marines took 2,400 casualties on the first day of the Iwo Jima battle.*

Taking Mount Suribachi

As the highest point on Iwo Jima, Mount Suribachi was a natural objective for the first phase of Marine operations on the island. A fascinating account of the stateside training preparations for tackling this feature comes from Marine infantryman Fred Haynes, 28th Regiment, 5th Marines: "We trained there in the Parker Range for about 2½ months. We went through the same routine that we had gone through at Pendleton so that by the time that we got word to go to Iwo the regiment was probably the best-trained regiment the Marine Corps has ever turned out for that mission. Because on the side of Mauna Kea,

Left: The M2 flamethrower was a manportable weapon with a burn time of seven seconds.

have them walk up to where they hit the beach, in the case of most of them in amphibian tractors. The first battalion was to cut the island off. It was to cut the narrow neck, about 700yds [640m] wide, cut that off and the 2nd Battalion, which would follow the 1st [Battalion], was to turn left and

Above: A Marine artillery gun team fire their 37mm gun toward targets on the slopes of Mount Suribachi, towering up in the background.

Right: A unit of Marines arrive at the top of Mount Suribachi. Although the US flag was planted atop the volcano on February 23, much hard fighting remained ahead.

which is where we were training on the Parker Range, there are a number of volcanic bubbles that stand out at various heights off of Mauna Kea slopes. We found one that was about as high as Mount Suribachi, 550ft [168m] or so, and we outlined the island with white tape around the tip of Suribachi, and then the length of the beach that we were going to land on. Our planning was far enough along then that we had assigned all the Marines in the first two battalions to boat teams, so every man knew which boat team he was in and we would form them up near this Suribachi thing. We would form them up in boat teams about 500yds [457m] off of that 'make believe' beach and

commence the assault on Mount Suribachi. So the men of the 1st and 2nd Battalions knew what they were supposed to do, knew what it would be like, as well as you can make it in a make-believe world, and because of that training they were so good that when we hit the beach at Iwo, we landed on the left flank over Beach Green."

The rest of Haynes' account explains the reality of the operation against Surbachi, plus the story behind the legendary flag raising:

"It was a 500yds [457m] wide beach, right underneath Mount Suribachi, so our early casualties came primarily from Suribachi, but a

Left: *US Marines find a moment of solemnity and peace atop Mount Suribachi, as they take battlefield communion. In was not uncommon for military chaplains to be killed in action.*

operation. Forestall and Smith, saw that flag go up and Forestall is reported to have said to Smith, 'This makes the Marine Corps good for another five hundred years.' He also said that he, in his capacity of Secretary of the Navy, would like to have that flag, the first one. So that word came down to us, to the commander of the second battalion who had put up the first flag."

As history now knows, the raising of the second flag, the replacement to the first, was a moment captured in a Pulitzer Prize-winning photograph by Joe Rosenthal. Jim Humphries was serving in a Marine Pioneer Battalion during the battle for Iwo Jima, helping to run in supplies from the beachheads to the frontlines. He also witnessed the flag raising over Suribachi. Although the battle was by no means over, the flag raising had an electrifying effect on the soldiers: "We blew our whistle until it was ruined. We just went crazy. You can't believe how good that flag looked. We were right there at the base of Suribachi and we knew how ferocious the fighting was on Suribachi. Actually, it was in doubt. The outcome was very much in doubt in our minds anyway, until we saw that flag. That did it. We knew we got it. The flag actually came off an LST, the second one. The bigger one. And it was about a hundred yards from us. I think it was Renny Gagon, one of the flag raisers, came down to the beach sent by Lieutenant Shower. And he came to my ship first because we were nearer to the base of Suribachi. Our O.D. officer of the deck sent him down to the LST because the flag would be bigger."

number of artillery pieces hit us quite frequently. So, anyhow, the first battalion to land got across the island in very, very short order. They were over by about an hour and fifteen minutes after we landed. The reason that they moved so fast was that we had carefully planned—we had a good naval gunfire officer, and we had carefully planned a rolling barrage of destroyer and cruiser fire. That fire formed a kind of an angle; it was aimed to silence Suribachi if it could. So it was in front of the 2nd Battalion. In front of the 1st Battalion we had a regular rolling barrage, and while we suffered some casualties from our own fire, there weren't many, but that is the reason our troops were able to get across the island.

"So we isolated Mount Suribachi by about 1030 or so on D-Day. We then focused on Suribachi and on the 23rd of February one of the patrols from the 2nd Battalion, carrying a small flag, [a] US Flag [in] American colors, went to the top of Suribachi. There was little fighting once you got above the level of the caves. So they made it to the top fairly quickly and at 1020 they raised the first flag and that sent happiness and jubilation through everybody because a lot of people looked at it as if the war was won. Well, of course, it wasn't, but it happened that on the command ship, Acting Secretary of the Navy, James Forestall, was there with Hal 'Mad' Smith, who was the Marine overall commander for that

Left: *The legendary American flag at the top of Mount Suribachi. Of the six men in the immortal photograph by Joe Rosenthal, three of them were subsequently killed in action.*

Clearing Iwo Jima

Daybreak over Iwo Jima on the second day of the battle revealed something of the generalized horror and cost of the first day. One Marine described the scene with a sense of shock:

"The wreckage was indescribable. For 2 miles [3.2km] the debris was so thick that there were only a few places where landing craft could still get in. The wrecked hulls of scores of landing boats testified to one price we had to pay to put our troops ashore. Tanks and half-tracks lay crippled where they had bogged down in the coarse sand. Amphibian tractors, victims of mines and well-aimed shells, lay flopped on their backs. Cranes, brought ashore to unload cargo, tilted at insane angles, and bulldozers were smashed in their own roadways."

For those inland, the engagement was a grinding affair, with literally thousands of deeply entrenched Japanese positions having to be extinguished in small-unit actions utilizing flamethrowers and explosives. Peter N. Karegeannes was a corpsman with 5th Marine Division, 26th Regiment, 2nd Battalion, serving with Headquarters Company and later with Fox Company.

"You had high casualties, more casualties than [you] could ever experience, and the Japs were entrenched so deeply, none of them hardly ever came out. I saw one Jap, he came out from where he was sitting in the cave, and he ran about five yards and some Marine sniper blasted him, got him, and killed him deader than a doornail fifty yards away." Karegeannes also noted that the Japanese "were entrenched in deeply." He explained that the only way to tackle deep positions was often to go right into the mouth of the position, and hurl dynamite satchel charges in there. This was a risky proposition. "A lot of guys never made it, they got killed before they got there with the dynamite and blew his damned cave all to hell. That's how we could advance forward, otherwise you had to stand down for a while. Never a dull moment, believe me."

For Marine Gilberto Mendez, who landed on the island six days after the initial invasion, the experience degenerated into a relentless

waking nightmare. In addition to machine-gun fire and periodic banzai charges, snipers were a nagging concern: "Casualties with wounds on their heads [were] all over the place. And I didn't sleep because of the stink of the blown-up bodies. Bodies torn to pieces." Sometimes, however, the hidden enemy became highly visible: "...there were about twenty of us pinned down (three squads). [It was] about 7 o'clock in the morning, when I saw something shine maybe about a hundred yards in front of me. As the sun was coming this way . . . I saw something shine. And I thought it was a mirror, it was somebody in front of us, some of our troops with a mirror, because they also had showed us in line camp how to communicate with a mirror, like the Native Americans did. I don't know whether it was a Morse code or a special code or whatever. But that's what I thought, somebody's trying to communicate with us. But it didn't turn out that way. It was an officer, a Japanese officer's sword, and they were coming from one of the caves. And you could hear them. 'Banzai! banzai!' And we found out later, during the mopping-up operations, that there was an incline going upwards . . . and I couldn't see 'em. We could hear 'em, but we couldn't see 'em. And as they went up then they exposed themselves, you could see their helmets and then you could see the head, and then you could see part

Right: US Marines maneuver around a Japanese bunker, steering their way around potential fields of fire.

my rifle on that part of the rock, and I was holding with my left hand, I was pulling down on the sling. You know how the sling goes from the forward stock to the bottom. I was holding the front of the sling and so I started seeing a helmet and then further up, and it kept on walking. When I saw below his neck I pulled the trigger, Pow!"

Left: *An M3 Stuart Light Tank. M3s were used extensively around the Pacific Theater, as they were small and relatively easy to transport*
Below: *Flamethrowers killed the occupants of bunkers as much by axphyxiation as by flame.*

of the torso. These are not our troops. And the bullets were flying already. but they couldn't see me because the rock was big enough to protect me, [my] whole body, and I could be in any position, in a kneeling position or a prone position or a standing position... Anyway, I was shooting until I ran out of ammunition. So I debated whether to go back to our line, because I had people on my left and I had people on my right of our troops, so I decided to crawl. This is where I found myself talking to myself. 'Don't get up.' Because I knew, I had seen the bodies with shots in the head. Well, they got up and they exposed themselves and they were gone. I said 'Don't get up, Gilberto. Don't get up.' So I crawled like a lizard and went over to my left and a guy gave me one bandolier, took it off of his neck and he gave me a bandolier, then I went further up and another guy threw me another one. That was two more bandoliers, I went back to my rock. And here, they kept on, the Japanese, kept on coming up out of the cave. So I put myself in a position, I was kneeling, but I had

Right: *Lieutenant General Holland Smith congratulates Major General Graves Erskine, commander of the 3rd Marine Division, for the victory on Iwo Jima.*

In this one action Mendez claimed twenty enemy soldiers, a visceral example of how the casualty count spiralled for both sides across the island. Such scenes were repeated hundreds of times across the island, before Iwo Jima was finally cleared by March 26. The final cost of the battle was sobering—6,821 Marines dead, 20,000 wounded, and virtually all of the 22,000-strong Japanese garrison slain, almost literally fighting to the last man.

Operation Ten-Go

Above: *The battleship* Yamato *is here seen at Kure Naval Yard, during its final fitting out in September 1941. It was finally commissioned for service on December 16, 1941, just days after the Pearl Harbor attack.*

[6,096m] and going over toward the ships and we went on up to 21,000ft [6,400m], which was about our maximum altitude. We noticed it was a pretty big ship. We asked permission to go in and attack her and we did. There were eight of us. We all dropped on her and we all missed her. Came close, but we missed her. There was a lot of antiaircraft fire. In fact they claim that it was about as heavy as any time during the war by the Japanese. An observer said there was so much antiaircraft fire that he couldn't even see us, it just blocked us out. I was hit on that hop. There was an explosion and I thought it probably was one of the 18in [46cm] shells that came up from the *Yamato*, about 100ft [32m] below my wing. It spun my plane clear around and I recovered and took shrapnel in my left wing. I was losing oil from the concussion of it. I did go ahead and go down and dropped my bombs, but I'm sure I missed. I was the third one in on the dive and the plane following me flew through the burst area and he was shot down. He went down. He was able to land and he landed in the bay. He was taken prisoner of war."

One of the features of *Yamato* was that it could fire huge shotgun-like "beehive" rounds from its main guns as an antiaircraft response, and

Below: *The USS* Lexington *(CV-16) was part of the Task Force 58 that sank the* Yamato. *The* Lexington *was an Essex-class aircraft carrier, and it was capable of carrying more than one hundred combat aircraft.*

Operation *Ten-Go* was, quite literally, a naval kamikaze mission. As American forces began preparatory bombardments against Okinawa in late March 1945, the Japanese high command refined their defense plans for the island. In a controversial decision, but one backed by the Emperor and commander-in-chief of the Combined Fleet, Admiral Toyoda Soemu (Yamamoto had been killed), it was decided to send a suicide fleet of navy ships to Okinawa. The intention was for the *Yamato*, the world's biggest battleship, plus the light cruiser *Yahagi* and eight destroyers, to punch their way through the Allied fleet, beach at Okinawa, and there sit as a static defense until destroyed.

Yamato was the formidable centerpiece of this operation. Displacing 70,000 long tons, it bristled with a total of 187 guns, including nine 18in (46cm) main guns and 162 antiaircraft guns. One man who had already experienced the force of *Yamato*'s defenses was Francis R. Ferry, flying an SB2C Helldiver from USS *Bennington* as part of VB-82: "On March 19th we were assigned to bomb Kuri Harbor. We flew to Kuri and were in a holding pattern waiting for our assignment to attack when we noticed that some ships were out in the bay west of Kuri. Our skipper asked for permission to go over and investigate. We were flying about 20,000ft

Straight Down: Dive-bombing techniques

Dive-bombing was a centerpiece of US Navy anti-ship aviation tactics during the Pacific War. As a form of bombing it was both intellectually and physically demanding, with a high risk to the aircrew. The advantage of dive-bombing over conventional level bombing was that the gravitational acceleration of the bomb, the effects of wind resistance on the bomb's trajectory (known as "trail"), plus the forward motion of the aircraft could be aligned vertically with the attack path of the aircraft and the intended strike point of the bomb. In essence, the aircraft became a gun, and where it was "aimed" would be the point of impact. Furthermore, by attacking in a steep rather than a shallow dive, the pilot could reduce the angle of error around the target, with relatively minor adjustments required to keep on target and a reduced requirement for predicting the forward flight of the bomb to the impact point. A release angle of 65–70 degrees was considered optimal. The pilot also had to allow for deflection, especially on a moving target like a ship, rotating the aircraft during the dive to ensure that the light of sight was maintained and the direction of the dive was parallel with the axis of the ship's movement.

Right: An American bomb explodes just off the starboard bow. The multiple bombs strikes on Yamato's *superstructure served to knock out much of the ship's antiaircraft capability, while torpedoes fatally holed her beneath the waterline.*

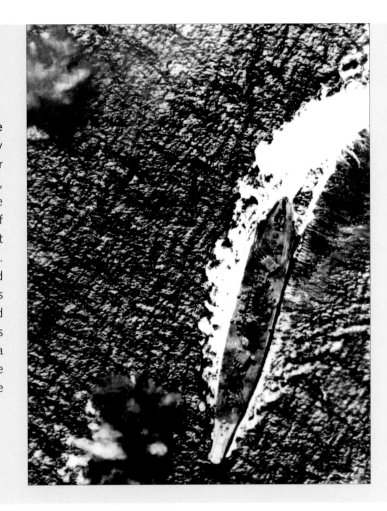

one of these might have been responsible for the damage to Ferry's wing.

Ten-Go was launched on April 6, 1945, but was almost immediately spotted by American submarines, and its position and bearing reported to Vice-Admiral Marc Mitscher's Task Force 58, with its eleven carriers. At around 1000hrs on April 7, the carriers began to launch strike missions against *Ten-Go*, the attacks going in at 1230hrs. Yamato was naturally the concerted point of attack, with torpedo bombers concentrating on the port side to increase the chances of a capsize. In total, the great ship took eight torpedo and fifteen bomb strikes during the course of the afternoon, before capsizing at 1420hrs and being blown apart in a massive magazine explosion. Eight destroyers were also sunk in an action that embodied the impotence of the late-war IJN.

Left: The Yamato's *extraordinary naval journey ends at 1423hrs on April 7, 1945, after a catastrophic magazine explosion. The smoke rose more than 3 miles (5km) into the sky.*

Horror at Okinawa

The US preparatory bombardments on Okinawa began in earnest on March 23, 1945, although US and British carrier aircraft attacks on supporting Japanese air bases on Formosa and nearby islands had already been running a week by this point. Operation *Iceberg*, the invasion itself, was unleashed on April 1, the initial landing force consisting of the 1st and 6th Marine Divisions of III Marine Amphibious Corps, and the 7th and 96th Infantry Divisions of the US Army's XXIV Corps. A characteristic

Below: A Japanese Type 38 rifle, chambered in the underpowered 7.7 x 50mm Arisaka.

Right: "PATEXIA" sign hung on a tent at Machinato Airfield, Okinawa. The tent was occupied by men of the 319th Bomb Group, 439th Bomb Squadron.

PATEXIA
OKINAWA
BRUMBACH, G.E.
DANIELS, T.W.
GUETZLAFF, H.E.

Above: Streams of 5in rockets ripple out from US LSI(R) vessels during the preparatory bombardment of Okinawa. The rockets were individually inaccurate, but collectively they were a powerful area weapon.
Right: US soldiers move quickly from their landing craft up onto the Okinawa beaches. Initial resistance was limited, but intensified terribly inland.

experience of those men who made the initial landing was that there was initially little in the way of shoreline resistance. There was, in the words of Clarence E. Shockey, 1st Marine Division: "A little. Not much. But there was a little. Because we went in on the north end of the island and, oh yeah, it was April the first, the day of love. We hit there and, as I said, we move in and got very little fire, enemy fire, very sparse. There were one or two guys that had been shot and were in the water. We go on in and we all got on the beach and then we were told to dig in and into a foxhole for the night."

That situation changed horrifically as the US forces began to press inland, against the pre-prepared Japanese positions, which often had interlocking fields of fire. On many occasions, it was difficult for the US troops to identify where the fire was coming from. The

following account, from Thomas R. Dunham of the 1st Marine Division, illustrates the intensity and brutality of the fighting that emerged on the island:

"So I'm looking on the left, that's where all the grenades were coming from, afraid to call out for my partner 'cause I didn't know what had happened to him. I didn't want them to locate him or locate me and didn't want him hollering and yelling, so [I] just kept quiet and kept [my] eyes open. I had a big clump of Johnson grass right in front of my foxhole between me and the rest of the top of the hill. . . . I hear footsteps on the right front. Now there's a trail out there that's at least

40yds [37m] clear shooting, but here comes a Jap with a rifle and a bayonet. He's steadily coming toward me. I reached over for my BAR and the slide wouldn't go all the way back. . . . I was tugging on it and tugging on it and that Jap made it up to the edge of the foxhole and he planted his feet and swung that bayonet around. I don't know why he didn't shoot, he had a clear shot. He just loved that knife, I guess, or he didn't have any ammunition. I don't know what it was. Anyhow he's not going to tell us 'cause when Dideo . . . saw him he screamed real loud and that Jap turned and took about three steps toward him. I saw what happened, I dropped the gun strap, loaded up the [BAR] rifle, and I cut him down. And here's more footsteps and here's the second one coming down this trail and he's got that rifle and that bayonet. I give him five or six. He went down face forward. Hollywood wouldn't do this, but, lo and behold, there's a third helmet back there and he's going down too. I was using half ball ammunition and half armor-piercing. Every other load was the armor-piercing."

"He was directly behind him, I didn't even see him until he started falling. He got everything the second one got. So I left my BAR over to the right front, still I didn't know where my partner was. [There were] Two wounded guys over here and didn't move my head, but I was moving my eyes, constantly moving, and looked over and this third Jap fell. . . . His right hand was just an inch at a time inching back toward his hand grenades. So I had to give him a few more and put in a fresh twenty rounds. I'd used probably fourteen or fifteen. I got reloaded. I don't know how long I sat there, time just kind of froze. I was so scared I probably wouldn't have looked at a watch if I had had one. Everything just stood still and off to the left front here comes a head, chest, and a belt and he's looking right at me but he doesn't see me. That is, his vision is right toward me. I had to move my BAR back to the left and down he went. We'd been trained not to do this; if you go down, roll, move, don't come up at the same place, and I don't think he'd been trained. I lined up the BAR, got it all settled out. It wasn't but about maybe three minutes here he comes like he was on a hydraulic lift of some kind. I waited until his belt buckle got in sight and I touched off four or five. I saw the dust coming off of his chest when it was hitting him, so I didn't hear any more from him. In another few minutes the rest of the platoon got up there. Seven or eight of them made it up, they were standing up. They had taken care of all these snipers on the left, machine guns, and Nambu automatic rifles. They wanted to set the

Above: *The well-concealed entrance to the headquarters of the Japanese 32nd Army on Okinawa. Cave complexes could extend hundreds of yards underground.*

machine gun up on this flat spot where I was. They asked me to move so they could set up the machine gun. The platoon leader got up there, Lt. Bosworth, and he looked at my hand and 'How does it feel?' 'I don't feel anything.' The feeling was all across my thigh where the hot slug passed by." **Through thousands of small clashes such as these described, the Marines and Army soldiers managed to spread across the island, although they paid for every foot gained.**

Kamikaze

As part of Operation *Ten-Go*, the Japanese launched unprecendented waves of kamikaze attacks against the US shipping around Okinawa. In fact, between April 6 and June 22, total kamikaze sorties numbered 1,900, often delivered in mass attacks called *kikusui* (floating chrysanthemum), designed to overwhelm the American defenses.

One man who experienced the effects of the kamikaze attacks first hand was Doug Aitken aboard the destroyer USS *Hugh W. Hadley* (DD-774). On May 11, the destroyer was one of many US vessels that came under a nearly two-hour kamikaze attack involving more than 150 aircraft:

"We were at General Quarters at least at dawn and at dusk and frequently all night long. At dawn we secured from General Quarters and went to the normal watch, which is a four-hour watch. I happened to have the four to eight watch that day in CIC, the Combat Information Center. I had gotten off of watch at about 0745 and went down to the ward room, which is the officers' dining area. . . . I was starting to eat my hard-boiled egg breakfast and all of a sudden the heavy sounding bell was again heard throughout the ship, 'Gong, gong, gong, gong. General Quarters, General Quarters. All hands man your battle stations.'

Both left: Japanese kamikaze pilots ready themselves for death. Sometimes pilots were even welded into their cockpits to ensure their commitment. Each suicide pilot carried the flag.

Normally, that's all you hear. This time was different. Immediately following 'General Quarters, General Quarters. All hands man your battle stations,' the word was heard, 'Commence firing! Commence firing! Starboard side!' There was something very close. . . . A seaplane was approaching low over the water. [It] Didn't get picked up by the radar. [It] Came in low on the water and they started firing right away and they got it before it hit us obviously. That was a sign that, 'Hey, we gotta watch it. There's something out there.'

"This battle lasted an hour and forty minutes. During that time, we got twenty-three shot down confirmed, including the three that hit us. The *Evans*, which was another destroyer which was with us (we were the senior of the two ships), they got nineteen. They were put out of action before we were. They were an older destroyer. Not much, but they were a previous class. They were put out of action in about an hour. We had another forty minutes before we got clobbered. . . . I have to tell you I did not see, personally, any single kamikaze. Neither did the executive officer. Neither did any of the people in CIC see any single kamikaze

Above: *The Royal Navy aircraft carrier HMS* Formidable *was hit by a kamikaze off the coast on Okinawa on May 4, 1945.*

Above: *A huge cloud of smoke billows from the USS* Bunker Hill *following hits by two kamikaze aircraft, which killed more than 300 men.*

. . . except on the screen. We saw piles of them there. It got to a point where this expert team of air controllers were helpless because the fighter pilots don't want to be bothered with somebody telling them, 'Hey, look here's a fly over here! There's one over here!' They can see them all. They're within visual range of all these guys and they had to do their own tactics to take them out one by one."

During the engagement, the destroyer was hit by one bomb, a Yokosuka MXY-7 *Okha* jet-powered suicide aircraft, and two further kamikaze planes. Aitken remembers the impact: "Oh, we felt it. There wasn't any question about when we got hit because a ship our size, 375ft [114m] long approximately, hit by an airplane at a high speed, you know it. You can feel our ship's guns going off. The 5in [guns] have a concussion. But when an airplane hits you, you know it. One plane dropped a bomb just before he hit on the afterdeck house and completely wiped out a 40mm crew. There was nothing left of the gun and nothing left of them. They were gone. Set fires going, with ammunition exploding and gasoline exploding and so on. On the 0-1 deck, as we called it (it's on the deck just above the main deck of the ship), is where the guns were mounted; the 40mm and the 20s and the torpedoes were up there. Incidentally, my personal room was on the main deck just underneath that 40mm which I said was totally wiped out."

Above: May 5, 1945, and crewmen clear debris and repair damage aboard the escort carrier USS Sangamon *(CVE-26), after a kamikaze dropped its bomb and crashed into the deck off Kerama Retto the night before, resulting in fires, eleven crewmen dead, twenty-five missing, and twenty-one seriously injured.*

The succession of hits were now taking their toll on the ship and on its crew: "We could sense the list and first of all, power went out. All power was lost because we couldn't generate any power. We had an emergency diesel generator, but nothing to run everything on the ship. All power was lost. We sensed that and we sensed the list so we opened the doors and went out and could see all this commotion and all this smoke. We didn't know what was going to happen. Pretty soon, within a minute or two, the captain said, 'Prepare to abandon ship!' That means get all the wounded over the side. When he was informed by the engineering officer and the first lieutenant, who is the damage control officer, that the ship is in sinking condition with three engineering spaces flooded, by the book it's not supposed to stay afloat. With this list, no power, and he knew that the shafts were broken by this humping underneath and one shaft was driven back into our rudder. We couldn't steer. So, you know, you're pretty helpless."

While the majority of the crew evacuated the ship, a tenacious fifty-man damage-control party nevertheless managed to keep the ship afloat, and it was subsequently repaired. Thirty crew died in the attack.

The Japanese Soldier

There were many myths propagated about the Japanese soldiers in World War II, some of which persist to this day. One of the most pervasive was that the Japanese were experts in jungle warfare, and that they could survive on just a handful of rice a day. In reality, the jungle was just as hard on Japanese forces as on any other troops, and in some campaigns thousands of Japanese infantry starved to death as ration supplies dried up.

The origins of the "jungle warrior" myth, however, have a grain of truth in the sheer physical and mental resilience, plus the ideological motivation, of the average Japanese soldier. About 80 percent of the Japanese soldiers recruited were from the poor laboring classes, particularly farming and heavy industry, hence they arrived at basic

Right: An early version of the Japanese Nambu pistol. It fired a 7mm pistol cartridge.

Left, below: The crew of a Type 98B Medium Tank look happy in their duties as they pose for the camera.

Below right: Japanese infantry training could be physically brutal and was often conducted with an attention to realism, especially in the pre-war and early war years.

training perfectly familiar with physical hardship, and also with a limited supply of food. Japan was also an inherently deferential society at this time, so the recruit would have entered the armed services with the mental expectation of being completely subject to the wishes and whims of his commanding officers.

For those men who entered military service via conscription in the pre-war years, there was nearly a full year of training ahead, running from January to November. Within this period, January–May focused on intense physical conditioning and basic military discipline, both of which were enforced with regular lashings of corporal punishment. Those who

passed this phase moved into a two-month period of more tactical small-unit infantry training, building up to battalion-size exercises during August and September, with regular wargaming and route marches of more than 20 miles (32km) distance. October and November brought the culmination of training in vast maneuvers, sometimes performed before the eyes of the Emperor himself. It is also worth noting that during this training period the Japanese soldier would have also learned the fundamentals of night-fighting, one quality that certainly did separate the Japanese soldier from many of his Western counterparts. The training involved visual acclimatization to night conditions (including the wearing

Above: A Japanese soldier, his face etched in weariness, conducts a march while carrying a machine-gun tripod.

Japanese POWs

One quality of the Japanese soldier that particularly unnerved their opponents was their apparent unwillingness to surrender, preferring death rather than capture. During the battle of Peleliu in September–November 1944, for example, of the 10,900 defenders only 202 enemy personnel were captured, and only nineteen of these were actually soldiers (the rest were foreign laborers). To the man, the rest were killed or committed suicide as a last act. The battle of Okinawa, however, was the first instance of really large-scale surrender to the American forces. In total, 10,755 Japanese military personnel surrendered or captured, about 12 percent of the total force on the island. The reasons behind the upsurge in surrender were multiple. First, it was evident to many Japanese soldiers that the war was all but lost, and continuing to fight was an exercise in futility. Second, some Japanese troops came to understand that the garish stories of American atrocities were largely exaggerations. Finally, the late-war recruits often hadn't been hardened in the manner of previous generations.

Below: *The bottom of the barrel. A US soldier attempts to communicate with two Japanese juveniles, captured in military uniform during the last months of the war. Implausibly, they claimed they were eighteen and twenty years old.*

of dark glasses in the early evening hours before exercises), use of the peripheral vision over the central vision, maximizing the focus on silhouettes (often by conducting visual reconnaissance from a prone position), and adjusting firearms point of aim to allow for more accurate night firing.

The pre-war training of the Japanese soldier was rigorous and effective, and produced an army of resilience, courage, and an indomitable will. The realities and attrition of war soon eroded all these factors. Training times were reduced in order to rush reinforcements to the frontlines (by 1945 a soldier might experience just five weeks of basic training before being sent to fight), resulting in a drop off in combat efficiency and numerous instances of over-promotion, with the knock-on effects of poor or inexperienced leadership. Manpower losses became simply unsustainable, and the 5.5 million men that made up the Japanese armed forces in 1945 were a shadow of their 1941 counterparts.

To the last man...

The fighting for Okinawa would continue for nearly three grueling months. While the northern part of the island was secured in about two weeks, XXIV Corps battered itself against the formidable defenses of the "Shuri Line" in the south. The characteristics of this relentless fighting are here described by Charles H. Brittan, a Marine Scout and Sniper in the Headquarters Company, 1st Battalion, 5th Marines, 1st Marine Division:

"They [the Japanese] were dug in and hidden. They had fortified the south side of the island with caves. It was just a tremendous amount of caves. The terrain was ridges—valleys and ridges all away to the south.

Of course you had to take one ridge at a time or one hill at a time and they defended it. We would have lots of resistance for maybe a day, or two days. And then they would pull back to the next ridge. And then we would take that. . . And then it was just like that all the way down south."

One of the most traumatic factors in the battle for Okinawa for many was the experience of encountering civilians caught in the line of fire,

or suffering from the general depredations of war. Marine Lenly Cotton here describes both the youth of the American soldiers on Okinawa, and some of their dealings with the locals, which had some unexpected outcomes:

"Our platoon was—other than the one who could vote—they were all under twenty. Ninety per cent were nineteen or younger, there were as many below eighteen as above, five or six that were sixteen, including myself, and one that was fifteen that I know of personally. . . . I hear crying and there's a dead Japanese woman with a baby with sores all over him and so I give him some water and some K-rations and wanted to take care of the baby, and at about that time I see a head pop up out of the ground and I see that it's a woman and child and they're down this cave. Well, I'm not too happy about crawling down into a cave when there's probably a huge complex of them. At that time a tank comes round and sees that I've got a cave and I'm trying to have this

Left: *US soldiers use explosive charges to flush Japanese defenders out of their cave position on Okinawa.*

Right: *A bulldozer of the 4th Regiment, 6th Marine Division, on Okinawa in April 1945. Bulldozers were on occasions used simply to fill in Japanese bunkers, sealing the occupants inside.*

Japanese [man] talk these people out of there. Anyway, these people don't want to come up and the tank wants to throw a round down there and all. With women and children down there, there's no reason to do this, and if there are some soldiers down there let Military Police or what's coming behind take care of them. There were four of us and I don't recall whether it was five or six prisoners we'd got. They were down to their loin-cloths, they just wanted to be taken prisoner. Fortunately the word was out to try to show kindness and so we gave them all our water and whatever we could.There must have been a thousand eyes watching us, because when they seen this here comes soldiers piling out of every nook and cranny, and the next thing you know there's four of us and we have hundreds of prisoners. And a few of them, thinking about their honor, start using grenades on themselves, just committing suicide."

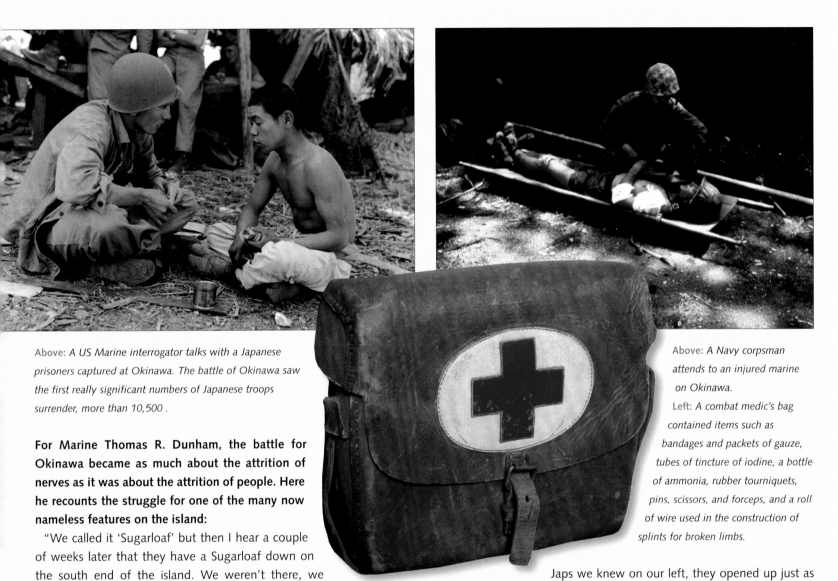

Above: *A US Marine interrogator talks with a Japanese prisoners captured at Okinawa. The battle of Okinawa saw the first really significant numbers of Japanese troops surrender, more than 10,500 .*

Above: *A Navy corpsman attends to an injured marine on Okinawa.*
Left: *A combat medic's bag contained items such as bandages and packets of gauze, tubes of tincture of iodine, a bottle of ammonia, rubber tourniquets, pins, scissors, and forceps, and a roll of wire used in the construction of splints for broken limbs.*

For Marine Thomas R. Dunham, the battle for Okinawa became as much about the attrition of nerves as it was about the attrition of people. Here he recounts the struggle for one of the many now nameless features on the island:

"We called it 'Sugarloaf' but then I hear a couple of weeks later that they have a Sugarloaf down on the south end of the island. We weren't there, we weren't even to Shuri Castle. We were headed that way, trying to get that way, but then we left this hill that had been so tough and it was about almost a half mile across this valley. We spread out single file and started across there. We had a new lieutenant by then. Our first platoon leader, Lt. Bosworth, got shot in both legs and they took him out. My buddy, Herb, who lives in Houston now and is a member of our [Veteran] Association, got shot in the butt and they took him out. They let eight of us get across. We had a fresh platoon leader, Lt. Woodward, I think, was his name. The hill was straight up, but there was a trail up beside the hill that we were going to. So we went up the trail and curled around and we were on the south side of the hill and the rest of the people were going south. Well, they had this valley patterned with their mortars, big guns, and machine guns. . . . Us eight was cut off. We had

Japs we knew on our left, they opened up just as we got up and got into cover. We had a cave full of them at the back. They shot our new lieutenant. He died that night. We had mortars and big shells coming in from the front. We didn't know what we had on the right. They shelled us with those things big as trash cans; most of them were duds but still they'd shake the ground. We were lying in the pathway. That was the lowest depression we could find. We were lying head to foot. One of those duds came in, there was a pine stump . . . around beside the trail. The shell went under and flipped that stump on top of Wheeler. The lieutenant was already on a stretcher. We had built a stretcher out of poles for him, he'd been shot in the stomach."

By the time Okinawa's defenses had been subdued, by mid June, the island had seen the deaths of more than 120,000 Japanese and more than 12,500 Americans.

Supporting the troops – Air & Naval Ops

The late-war island operations were vast combined forces enterprises. While the Army and Marine Corps slugged it out on land, the Navy and Air Force fought their own wars offshore and overhead, principally by providing support fire/close air support, logistical support, and medical evacuation.

The intensity of the fighting on Iwo Jima and Okinawa can blind us to the fact that air crews and naval personnel had to cope with the usual spectrum of environmental and engineering challenges, all within the context of an unforgiving war zone. J. Whitfield Moody was a TBM pilot with VT-260, flying off the USS *Chenago*. On one mission over Okinawa, an arrester-hook problem meant that he became more intimately acquainted with the island:

"Our tail hook ran on a little track and it was supposed to be down. [Except our] tail hook wasn't all the way down. So they said the Kadena airstrip was open. Our troops had taken it and we could go to the island and land on the airstrip there. We were already back to the carrier before they found out that my tail hook wasn't down. I landed on the strip and it was pretty well beaten up. So I landed on the edge of the strip. We got down and didn't bang up anything. The next day we looked at our ship and tried to figure out why the tail hook wasn't coming down. There was something that had prevented it from going down. We found torn metal was holding the hook so we straightened it out so the tail hook would go down. The engineers that came to repair the airstrip, they found that I was almost out of gas. They found a cave close to the airstrip there and we found what we thought was aviation gas, but it had Japanese markings and we couldn't tell. They looked for a gas can and they found one that was way back in the cave that [the Japanese] hadn't been able to shoot a hole in it before they left. They took it and pumped it into my gas tank and . . . I decided to take off. I thought I knew about where the carrier was. . . . We tested the gas and the engine seemed to be running airight so we took off. Fortunately we found the carrier and finally got home."

For the Navy crews off the islands, the crews also had to contend with the frequently violent weather that blew through the tropics with some frequency. A typhoon that struck the Okinawa fleet on June 5, 1945, sank six vessels, damaged thirty-three others, and cost six American lives. (These losses were light—another typhoon in December 1944 had sunk three destroyers and had killed 790 sailors.) Here one US Navy

Left: Phosphorus bombs are dropped over Iwo Jima by 7th Air Force Liberators in October 1944, leaving tendrils of white smoke.

crewman describes the experience of being aboard a small craft near Japan when a typhoon struck the fleet:

"Aboard LCS LL29, we are on our way to Japan. The fleet is huge, and includes every type of ship in the United States Navy. When we get near Japan the part of the fleet that we are attached to is to break away and sail toward Kure, which was the port for Hiroshima and had been a major Japanese naval base. As we near Japan the seas are getting very bad. We get word that we are heading into a typhoon. Soon the wind in the rigging was howling. It was typhoon *Louise* playing its own maniacal music. If you made the mistake of opening your mouth while facing the wind, you could not close it. The seas had become monstrous, the only time you could see another ship was if you were both on top of a wave. Our little ship would climb up one side of a wave, get to the top, and tip forward so far that the screws would

Below: The USS Idaho, *a New Mexico-class battleship, pounds shore targets on Okinawa with its 14in guns, April 1, 1945. The supremacy of carriers in open water combat meant that battleships largely become shore-bombardment platforms.*

come out of the water. Then we would slide down the other side, and when we hit the bottom of the trough, the flat bottom would hit. The sound was like being inside a huge drum, and everything on the ship would shake, including the mast. It was my turn on signal watch in the conning tower. The officer on watch with me got a message through the voice tube that we were getting into a mined area of the sea, and mines had been spotted that the storm had torn loose.

"It was not safe to be out on any part of the decks, most of the time they were under water. A seaman managed to get up the ladder to the Conning Tower to help watch for mines. I had been in a New Jersey hurricane, and storms in the Atlantic, but this was the first time I was truly afraid. I knew that if we ever got broadside to those 70ft [21m] waves it would be the end for our little ship, and in those wild seas there would be no survivors. As if all this was not bad enough, the lookout spotted a mine. As we slid down the back side of one of those huge waves we were headed right toward that ugly thing, with those horns sticking out all over it. I knew in my heart, that it was all over, but when we hit the bottom of the trough, our bow wave pushed it away. It passed down the whole length of our ship never more than six feet away. I have been told almost all of my life that I have a slightly irregular heartbeat. And I know just when it started."

The Pacific Theater was by far the most extensive theater for the US Navy in World War II. At peak US Navy strength, in July 1945, some 1.3 million men served aboard American ships in the Far East, and total Navy losses during the war were nearly 30,000 men.

Above: A leather Japanese map case, a much-prized item to capture for the US military intelligence units.

Below: To the left, we see a casualty being evacuated from the USS Bunker Hill to the USS Wilkes-Barre. The naval clashes around Okinawa produced high levels of casualties, as suggested by the wounded men (below right) in a converted LST.

Strategic and Atomic Bombing

"I pulled away over to the Jap on my right when I saw my first Oscar explode in the air. I lined up immediately on this second ship and began firing at about 30 degrees."

—Lieutenant Oscar Perdomo, 464th Fighter Squadron, Japan 1945

The atomic bombings of Hiroshima and Nagasaki in August 1945 have rather skewed the public perception of the air campaign against Japanese in the last year of the war. Although the atomic bombings were undeniably unique events from technological and human points of view, they were actually the culmination of an epic destruction that had already been unleashed against the Japanese homeland.

The strategic bombing campaign against Japan was the grim coalescence of several factors. The US capture of the Marianas Islands (Saipan, Tinian, and Guam) meant that now the USAAF had a base from which the new long-range B-29 Superfortress bombers could make return missions against the Japanese home islands. Although mechnically temperamental, the advanced and fully pressurized B-29 had an operational range of 3,250 miles (5,230km) and could carry a standard ordnance load of 20,000lb (9,090kg). Initially, the B-29s were used in high-altitude raids against Japan, but General Curtis Le May, commander of the 20th Air Force, ordered a switch in tactics, opting for low-level raids using copious volumes of incendiaries, the choice of munitions a deliberate targeting of Japan's largely paper and wood houses.

Left: *Another innovation in the B-29 Superfortress was its remotely controlled .50-cal. machine-gun turrets such as this one, whose gunner peers from the domed side window in the aft fuselage.*

With the adoption of the new fire-bombing strategy, the door opened to the most destructive air raids in history. For example, during Operation *Meetinghouse*, flown on the night of March 9–10, 1945, 334 B-29s created a firestorm of such intensity that an estimated 100,000 people died and 15.8 square miles (41 square km) of the city was destroyed.

The B-29s delivered mass devastation to the heart of Japan. Yet the American experience of attempting to capture small island outposts such as Iwo Jima and Okinawa, and apparent refusal of Japan to consider surrender, meant that more extreme options of ending the war were sought. The "Manhattan Project"—America's vast industrial effort to construct the world's first atomic bomb—had begun back in 1942, with the first successful test of a fission device conducted on July 16, 1945, in New Mexico. A month later, two similar weapons were used in earnest against Hiroshima and Nagasaki, those, along with the Soviet invasion of Manchuria, prompting the Japanese government to make an unconditional surrender.

The Pacific War officially ended on September 2, 1945, with the formal surrender ceremony aboard the deck of the USS *Missouri*. If we include all Far Eastern theaters in the final reckoning, including China, the war had cost the lives of about 26 million people. Japan, which had launched the conflict with an act of militaristic hubris, now lay almost entirely in ashes.

Hitting Japanese Shipping

Above: Bombs ripple through the waters of Kure Harbor, Japan, during an attack by US bombers on July 29, 1945. In three days of attacks here, the US aircraft sank more than ten Japanese warships, including a carrier and three battleships.

A decisive factor in the defeat of the Japanese in the Pacific was the Allied war against Japanese shipping. In total, Allied forces sank more than 10 million tons of Japanese shipping, ensuring that Japan was unable to exploit its new-found empire to fuel its relentlessly greedy war machine. In effect, Japan was being starved into submission. While US Navy submarines accounted for 55 percent of the Japanese maritime losses, predatory combat aircraft also took a huge bite out of the enemy's shipping. Not that such raids were simple, as John Jacobson, a combat pilot with the 37th Fighter Group, attests about operations over the Solomons:

" We'd usually go out sometimes at 4 in the afternoon—we were flying planes that were mostly dive-bombers; we couldn't fight with the Japanese fighters—they were very maneuverable. If you tried to turn with them, they'd just get in behind you, so we were relegated to strafing and dive-bombing. We'd go out looking-for targets and if during the night Japanese destroyers came down and were shelling up and down the coast (they would as soon as it got near daylight), they would scadaddle back to where they came from and we'd go out looking for them. On several occasions we did and we'd try dive-bombing them, but it's very difficult to dive-bomb a ship that's moving, and turning, and twisting. Once you commit to a dive you don't have the ability to twist and turn like they can so we didn't have much success ."

There were, however, as many successful missions as there were failed missions. Richard Salter was commander of the 77th Bomb Group, and a B-26 pilot, conducting operations over the Aleutians. Here he described an encounter with a Japanese ship:

"So that's getting us close to October 12, 1942, and the important thing about that date is that on that day I was leading a flight of B-26s, and there was another flight as well; and we were going out to intercept two Japanese destroyers which were northwest of Kiska. We spotted the destroyers on the horizon, and the element on my right headed for the leading destroyer, and I headed with my three airplanes for the second destroyer. They started firing their big guns, and they weren't even coming close. They were apparently doing it for psychological effect, and they did have a psychological effect because I was confused and worried about how I can make my bomb run. Here we were, carrying six 300lb [136kg] bombs with either a three- or four-second delay fuse; I can't recall exactly. I wanted to try to figure out how I could make my

Above: The cruiser IJNS Nachi is attacked by US aircraft on November 5, 1944. The attack was comprised of three waves of aircraft, and it resulted in the ship sinking from multiple torpedo, rocket, and bomb strikes.

Above: A Japanese merchant ship is wrecked by a parafrag bombs, small parachute-retarded fragmentation bombs dropped at low altitude.

Below left: This image, of wrecked and abandoned Japanese Type D midget submarines, was taken in February 1946 in Kure, the location of the Kure Naval Arsenal and numerous ports in Hiroshima Prefecture.

Below right: Another victim of the Kure bombings, in this case the aircraft carrier Amagi, rolled over on its side.

bombing run with the least exposure to their guns. So as I was approaching them, my navigator was leaning over, propped on the back of my co-pilot's seat, and he said, 'What are you going to do?' I said, 'I'm going to make a 360-degree turn, and I'm going to make up my mind while I'm making this turn.' So I came out of the turn and headed for the stern of this destroyer. In other words, I was going to pass over it from stern to bow, lengthwise. Just before we got to the destroyer, a projectile came through the plexiglass nose, through the instrument panel, and burst out most of the panel. I thought we had been hit by some big projectile. I told the co pilot—he had the switch for the bombs; he could toggle all the bombs in an emergency—I said, 'Toggle [drop] your bombs as fast as possible!' He started toggling them off, and we know that we got one hit on the destroyer's stern, one amidships, and one on the bow. At the last second, I had to pull up very abruptly because I was flying very low over the water and I needed to miss the destroyer's mast. We cannot account for the other bombs, but when we left there, the destroyer was just blowing up. . . .

"So we got out away from that run, and I looked back, and my navigator was in convulsions with blood spurting from his head. He had been hit by a fairly heavy object from the instrument panel, not the projectile. Also, on the run I lost my right wingman, so we headed back to Adak as fast as possible to try to get my navigator some medical attention. It was my understanding, and our understanding at the time, that the destroyer we attacked was definitely sunk; and it was our understanding that the other one sank, also. However, years later, it was said that the leading destroyer limped back to Japan. I don't know whether that was true or not."

Fighter Missions

The war between Allied fighters and their Japanese opponents became profoundly one-sided as the war developed. During the early phases of the Pacific conflict, the Allies were outperformed by well-trained pilots flying the Mitsubishi Zero, an aircraft with superior performance to US Wildcats. As Allied aircraft types improved, US air strength grew prodigiously, and Navy and USAAF squadrons refined tactics, however, a slaughter of Japanese aviators and aircraft began. By 1944, youthful Japanese aviators typically had a life expectancy of two or three missions, an unsustainable rate of loss.

Lieutenant Oscar Perdomo of the 464th Fighter Squadron, flying P-47 Thunderbolts, became one of the last aces of World War II, earning the Distinguished Service Cross for an ace-in-a-day mission over Japan on August 13, 1945. His account aptly illustrates the one-sided combat:

"Major Jarman dived on the closest Jap and I followed behind with my element. The number two Jap split-S'd and disappeared under the clouds, so I turned sharply to the right to go after the last three that had turned to the right but were still visible. I pushed the throttle into water injection with the prop pitch at about 2,700rpm. As I gained on the

Oscars [the Nakajima Ki-43] I placed my gyro sight on the last one and adjusted the sight diamonds on his wings. At this time the Oscars were flying a very loose vee. When I closed into firing range, I gave him a burst and saw my bullets converge on his nose and cockpit. Something exploded in his engine and fire broke out. I was still shooting as he fell to the right.

"I pulled away over to the Jap on my right when I saw my first Oscar explode in the air. I lined up immediately on this second ship and began firing at about 30 degrees. I shot at this Oscar until parts flew off and fire

Right: The P-38 Lightning was a versatile aircraft, its mission spectrum including dive-bombing, level bombing, photo-reconnaissance, and interception.

Below left: A P-51K, "Mrs. Bonnie," sits on Ie Shima in August 1945, by which time Mustang-equipped elements of the 5th Air Force had moved north to support the air raids on Japan.

Below right: Some battered Japanese fighters, including the Nakajima Ki.84 "Gale (foreground)," see at Kimpo Air Base in Korea.

Above: *A time-worn F6F Hellcat, on display in the National Museum of the Pacific War.*

broke out on the bottom cowling of his engine. I ceased firing when he rolled over slowly and dove straight into the ground and exploded. At this time, I would have gone after the Jap flight leader if either of these two first Oscars were still in the air now behind me.

"The leading Oscar had made a slow turn to the left as if to see what was going on behind when he saw me. I was closing in on him and he began a tight turn. Still to the left, gaining speed, and streamers were trailing off his wingtips. I had the advantage in that I was still out of firing range and had my throttle all the way back so that I could stay inside of his turn. Streamers were pouring off my own wings beginning at the roots. I caught him in my fixed crosshairs and led him as much as I could, firing all the way in. He continued his spiral turn about 180-degrees until he was about 100ft [30m] off the ground. Then he hit a high-speed stall, because I saw his airplane shudder and it snapped him still tighter to the left and into the ground where he exploded like a napalm bomb. I put my throttle forward and started back toward town. As I came back I could see the fires from my first Oscar and there above was a man in a parachute. I trained my sight on him until I closed in. He was a Jap in a leather flying suit or a shiny green one. I didn't press my trigger; instead I rocked my wings. I kept climbing up to 1,500ft [457m] looking for our P-47s. After a little bit, I saw two [Yokosuka K5Y] Willows flying in formation at about 800ft [244m]. I pulled back my throttle and went down after them. They saw me at the last minute and separated. . . . the P-51s joined our flight and we came out together."

Japanese aircraft were especially vulnerable to cannon fire, being generally poorly armored. Captain William Morris, 463rd Fighter Squadron, remembers firing at a Kawasaki Ki-45 "Nick":

"We made a diving left turn into him going into a string formation. We attacked from the rear making all tail shots. We all shot at him and pulled up to the right. I looked down and saw Rampy, the number four man, shoot off his right wing and right engine at about 17,000ft [5,181m]. The rest of the plane then practically fell apart in the air. The plane was a Nick apparently very new of a shiny OD color. No chutes were seen and there is no doubt that the plane was destroyed."

Above: *A Hellcat prepares for takeoff from the deck of the USS* Yorktown. *Hellcat fighters accounted for about 56 percent of the total US Navy and US Marine Corps air-to-air kills in the war.*

The B-29 Raids

The strategic bombing of Japan was made possible by one aircraft—the B-29 Superfortress. It had a longer range and heavier bomb load than any other aircraft in service, and once the Marianas were in US possession then it also had forward bases from which to operate. The first B-29 raid on Japan was conducted on June 15, 1944, against steel mills at Yawata, but this fifty-aircraft raid was a drop in the ocean compared to the massive destruction unleashed in 1945.

Garvin Kowalke was a B-29 pilot. He remembers undertaking a twenty-hour mission up to Hokkaido, to attack industrial facilities. The following account also explains much about how B-29 missions were run: "When we were on a long, high-altitude, bombing raid with the B-29s and in formation, we would fly individually to the IP [Initial Point]. We would take off individually, one right after another, and we headed for a certain point just outside of the target area. When we hit this point, here is where we would make a big circle, and as we are making this circle, all the rest of the aircraft that had taken off and flying up there with us, they are

Above: *A B-29 Superfortress, aptly titled "Special Delivery," is prepared for a raid over Japan. This aircraft was operating out of Saipan.*

Left: *Although the threat levels above Japan were not as high as they were for US air crews over Germany, the capture of Iwo Jima in 1945 enabled P-51 Mustangs to accompany the B-29s throughout the raids over Japan.*

getting into formation. We have well over a hundred aircraft that will finally get into formation and come in and then go over the target area in formation. This is what we did. Our second wing commander, his aircraft had some mechanical problems and he got delayed. So here we are, we are the lead ship. We are the command ship and we are coming in on the target. Yes there were some fighters coming up that we spotted. Hardly any antiaircraft [fire]. They just didn't anticipate that we were going to be up there at Hokkaido dropping bombs on their factory, so there was very little antiaircraft and the fighters that came up, we were tucked in pretty tight, and our gunners just opened up and the fighters didn't even come up to attack. They got the heck out of there. In fact, I want to comment, one of the wing bombers, his gunner was so excited about shooting that he hung on to his gun too long and burned the barrel out. So he was without a gun. We went ahead and made the run, and as we were coming off of the target, back out over the ocean, here came our buddy, the Wing Commander, all by himself. He makes the run and he has a perfect target set up and his was a bullseye. So we knew that we got close to 80 percent of that target wiped out. . . . "

The mission described here was a high-altitude attack against a localized target. Kowalke was also involved in low-altitude runs against

area targets, which became common from March 1945, although precision attacks continued against facilities such as aircraft and munitions factories. Here Kowalke describes the different approach, and the very different effects, of delivering one of Curtis LeMay's now infamous fire-bombing missions:

"We'll run that between 10,500ft [3,200m] and maybe 11,500ft [3,505m]. Now there are going to be at least 300 aircraft involved in the flight of this mission. We go over and we are separated only by a few minutes, only by 500ft [152m]. In other words, aircraft one will go at 11,000ft [3,352m]. Aircraft two is at 11,500ft [3,505m], two minutes

Above and right: Uniform patches for the 20th (top) and the 5th Air Forces.

behind, or three minutes behind. Aircraft three is at 10,500ft [3,200m]. So that separates them both at altitude and gives them some distance. Airspeed is all the same. They all have to be at the same airspeed going across on their mission. To set it off, there are at least three or five 29s [that] will go in at low altitude. They are going in at mission altitude. What they are going to do is put their bombs on the strategic outer limits of the city and they go clockwise so the next aircraft that comes through at 11,000ft [3,352m], he sees those fires already started by the spotting aircraft. All they do is then drop their bombs just short of those fires.

Above: The Japanese capital city of Tokyo, here reduced to a gaunt shell following a massive B-29 strike.

Left: Incendiary bombs rain down from the bomb bays of B-29s over the city of Kobe, on June 5, 1945. The switch to incendiaries as the principal munition of area bombing unleashed apocalyptic levels of destruction upon Japan's cities.

They just keep adding, and adding, and adding until the whole city has been engulfed. I commented on this when I flew my second mission after the atomic bomb dropped and I was at low enough altitude that I looked over Hiroshima. It was completely, completely destroyed, but I could recall another city that we hit that was 90 percent destroyed. I mean it was completely burned up, but it took 300 of us to do it. It is just something that you are looking at and computing."

The B-29 raids were gruesomely effective. Not only were hundreds of thousands of Japanese citizens killed, but some 8.5 million of them were left homeless. The USAAF continued to fly strategic bombing missions against Japan even after the atomic bombing, the last on August 12.

The Manhattan Project

The management of the Manhattan Project—which gave the United States fully functioning atomic weaponry by mid 1945—was characterized by two qualities: cost and speed. The costs rose to rival the budget of a small country; total expenditure was $2 billion at 1940s prices, partly through the sheer expenses of investing in facilities and technology, and partly through paying the salaries of more than 130,000 people eventually employed on the project.

The speed was to a large measure achieved by the appointment of Brigadier-General Leslie Groves, US Army, as the project director, overseeing productivity at the three main research centers: Oak Ridge, Tennessee; Los Alamos, New Mexico; and Hanford, Washington. Groves had a powerhouse personality that may have made few friends among the scientists and engineers, but certainly got things done. After the war Groves justified his approach:

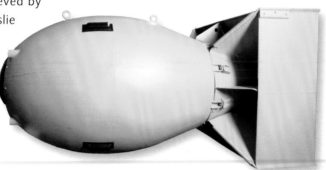

Above: A model of the 21-kiloton "Fat Man" atomic bomb that destroyed Nagasaki on August 9, 1945.

". . .decisions were made promptly. Now, that is the big difference between the way that we operated and the way that things are generally done today. If you think of all the time that is spent in the preparation of reports and studies and economic analyses and money costs and all the rest of it today in the slightest decision, that is why they cannot get anything done. Now, actually, you save money as well as time, and you get a better product if you do not hesitate so much. It is the same thing, as an illustration, in the construction of a new building such as an office building or an apartment house. If you can cut say two months off the construction time of that building, you are going to have . . . your income is going to start two months sooner. You are also going to find that it actually probably will not cost you as much to finish it, because you have two

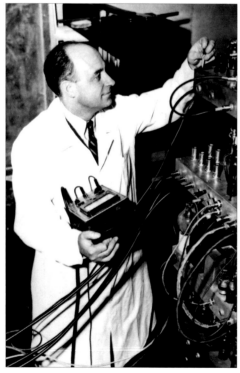

Above left: Dr. Enrico Fermi was an Italian physicist who moved to New York in 1939 and subsequently became one of the leading minds in the Manhattan Project.

Above right: The Alpha I "racetrack" at Oak Ridge, used for separating the isotopes of uranium and producing usable quantities of uranium-235.

months less of overhead." Another factor in the (eventual) rapid progress made was the galvanizing intelligence that Nazi Germany was also engaged in scientific research into the possibility of developing an atomic weapon system.

While Groves was certainly a prime-mover in taking the project to fruition, the technological discussions about weaponized nuclear fission actually began in the late 1930s, aided in the United States by the emigration of several notable European scientists, fleeing from

Above: *A newspaper announces the atomic bomb strike on Japan, over the more benign scene of a shift change at the Oak Ridge plant.*

fascism. The Manhattan Project itself essentially began in 1942 with the construction of major research facilities; the opaque project title came from the fact that the Manhattan District Corps of Engineers was given the building work, with Groves in charge from September.

The development of a working bomb was the product of several factors, including the manufacture of sufficient plutonium-239 at the Hanford Works. The first atomic weapon in history was detonated at 0530hrs on July 16, 1945, on the Alamogordo air base south of Albuquerque, New Mexico. This 20-kiloton device was proof of concept, and two air-deployable devices were subsequently produced for use against Japan, these weapons eventually taking the names "Little Boy" (destined to be dropped on Hiroshima) and "Fat Man"(Nagasaki).

Above: *Robert Oppenheimer was a complex and controversial individual, regarded as having the requisite ambition to help push the Manhattan Project to fruition.*

Robert Oppenheimer

Robert Oppenheimer was one of the intellectual and organizational forces behind the realization of the Manhattan Project. Born in New York in 1904, he went on the study physics at Harvard, graduating in 1925 before obtaining his Ph.D at the University of Göttingen. Oppenheimer's career seemed destined for high-level academia—he held positions in both the University of California, Berkeley, and the California Institute of Technology—but from late 1941 he was drawn into the nascent atomic weapon research, particularly focusing on methods of separating uranium-235 from natural uranium. In 1942, however, he became the scientific director of the Manhattan Project. Oppenheimer was the creative mind behind the creation of the Los Alamos research facility, and there is no doubt that he helped drive a team of 3,000 scientists and engineers to realize the atomic bomb. He was nevertheless a controversial character. During the war, he claimed to the Secret Service that several work colleagues were Russian agents, resulting in their dismissal; no evidence was subsequently found to substantiate the claims. After the war he held senior positions on American atomic development.

The Atomic Bombings

At 0815hrs on August 6, 1945, the atomic bomb "Little Boy" exploded over the city of Hiroshima, killing up to 80,000 people either through the immediate blast and fireball, or through the subsequent conflagration. Nagasaki received the same treatment on August 9, the city of Kokura, the primary target, spared because of smoke obscuration following a nearby conventional bombing raid.

Sidney Lawrence was a British leading aircraftsman with the 36th Torpedo Bomber Squadron, Royal Air Force Volunteer Reserve. He was also at this time a POW in Nagasaki, and witnessed the new era of warfare at horrifying close distance:

"On August 9 I was working at the camp, near the Mitsubishi Works—it was actually about 11 o'clock in the morning when they dropped the bomb, and I actually saw it coming down. It came down on a parachute. I was working in the open, and I was fortunate to get away with not being rubbed out with the bomb or being badly burned. The amazing thing is the effects on me afterwards. I came out in all sorts of strange boils with green pus. I had various skin complaints. I still suffer from some problems . . .

"I saw the plane fly over, then the bomb dropping. Then a blinding flash. There were other people around me who were burned to a

Left: A clock from Nagasaki records the time at which the city was virtually obliterated in the atomic blast of August 9, 1945.

cinder—and I was saved by a pile of rubble. Prior to their dropping the bomb, the Americans came over and just bombed us and there was a lot of devastation caused. Of course we were the ones who had to clear it up. We used to hope they wouldn't come over as we were still trying to clear the place up.

"The horrifying thing was to see that people were just shadows. You didn't find the body, but you found their shadow, emblazoned on the concrete. The person wasn't there—they had done up in smoke. That was alright. They were dead, gone. The horrible part was to see the torn limbs and flesh hanging off so many of the Japanese. I ended up helping the Japanese, and trying to do everything we could, those of us who were still alive and able to. They couldn't understand that we were trying to treat them. the Americans came over and dropped food to us on parachutes—and it was food galore, like we hadn't seen in years. It was K rations, and we shared them with the Japanese. They couldn't understand why the few of us that were left didn't turn on the Japanese and kill them. We were British. We couldn't. We helped them and they were grateful—but it was a horrifying sight to see the horrible burns and the way the flesh hung off them.

"Buildings were actually destroyed altogether. Things were on fire and justwent up in flames. There was one building with its steel girders all twisted, and it looked as if it was still intact. You hit a girder with a stick, and the stick went right through it. It was like brick dust. The girder just twisted. It was frightening. It was quite a while before I came to my senses after the blast. I was with one particular guard, who also escaped being killed. He was in such a state that he just put his rifle down and ran for it. The biggest horror in the after-effects was the utter silence. I had been used to bombing of all kinds and after it you hear the cries for help and noise—things happening. The eerie thing was the silence."

American troops would also become acquainted with the devastation and silence of Hiroshima and Nagasaki, when they moved in as occupation troops. Buckner Fanning was serving with the 6th Regiment, 2nd Marine Division, at the end of war, and moved into Nagasaki just days after the blast:

Left: The mushroom cloud from the atomic detonation at Hiroshima towers up over the city on August 6, 1945. The initial blast and the resulting firestorm killed an estimated 80,000 people.

day I can smell Nagasaki. One hundred twenty thousand people killed instantly. We saw people with burns all the time. It really began to eat on me. The thing that really began to get under my skin . . . we didn't see any men. All the men that were at least fifteen or sixteen years of age were off in the Japanese military. Everyone that we saw, were women, children, and the elderly. They were just in total dismay. They probably knew less about that atomic bomb than my daughter knew about Vietnam when she was five years old. . . . We started giving food and clothing to them. We had kids coming up and scrounging for food out of the trash cans where we were. We were living in a Mitsubishi warehouse that wasn't completely destroyed. It had no roof on it and it would rain on us. We would have to put those ponchos over us and tie our shoes on our cot so they would be dry when we put them on in the morning. You know, all the stuff you go through in times like that."

Above: Survivors of the Hiroshima bombing leave the city. Many thousands subsequently suffered from the crippling short- and long-term effects of radiation poisoning.

"We landed in Nagasaki and we expected resistance because we knew the kamikaze mentality. If they were coming to Dallas, I would be out there fighting so I thought they would be out there fighting too. But there was nothing, we didn't even see anybody for a day or two. They were just totally devastated. Not only physically but stunned emotionally. To this

Left: The city of Nagasaki was left derelict and unnervingly quiet by the atomic bombing, the surviving residents wandering around like ghosts.
Right: Temperatures of 7,050°F (3,900°C) were generated by the atomic explosions. The material effects of this heat can be seen in these melted coins.

Final Surrender

The twin atomic bombings on Hiroshima and Nagasaki compelled, in decisive fashion, both the Japanese government and military to issue their final surrender, made effective on August 14, 1945. The move to surrender had been given additional force by the Soviet invasion of Manchuria on August 8, an invasion that the war-depleted Japanese Army was in no fit position to resist.

Defeat was now inevitable, a concept that had seemed truly unthinkable just three years earlier, when much of East Asia lay under Japanese occupation. Yet on August 14 Emperor Hirohito and the

Prime Minister, Kantaro Suzuki, finally accepted the "unconditional surrender" terms established in the Potsdam Declaration. An attempted military coup on August 15 momentarily threatened the peace, the coup forces occupying the imperial palace and destroying the Prime Minister's residence before they were finally crushed in the late afternoon. Later that day, the Emperor announced to his people: "we have resolved to pave the way for a grand peace for all the generations to come by enduring the unendurable and suffering what is insufferable."

War in the Pacific was over, but it was not until September 2 that the official surrender ceremony took place, on board the battleship USS

Missouri, docked in Tokyo Bay. Frank Tremaine was a reporter for United Press, and he observed this solemn event at close hand:

"Of course, it took place on the battleship *Missouri* in Tokyo Harbor, anchored about 35 miles [56km] south of Tokyo and surrounded by all the ships of the 3rd Fleet, except the aircraft carriers and their escorts. They were at sea, but their planes were patrolling overhead, taking no chances. It was a semi-sunny, semi-cloudy day. Clouds were hanging over the Miura Peninsula to the west, and you couldn't see Mount Fujiyama through them. I'm sitting on the forward 16in gun turret looking down on the veranda deck, which is a small deck forward of amidships on the starboard side, about 40ft [12m] wide at the aft end of it, and it tapers down to a short flight of stairs going down to the main deck forward. I'm sitting up here on this gun turret, and there are about a hundred American and some Allied officers down here on this veranda deck below me. They're milling around. This is sometime between 7:30 and 8:00 in the morning. Right below my feet, Halsey and Vice-Admiral 'Jock' McCain, who was commander of Task Force 33, the fast carrier task force, were standing there. They're chatting, and all of

Left: *Japanese soldiers on the shoreline of their homeland surrender to Royal Navy personnel, one of whom has the former enemy clearly in the sights of his rifle.*
Below: *In northern Honshu, Japanese ground crews turn over their surviving fighter aircraft to American military authorities.*

Below: *Japanese pilots make the act of surrender in the late summer of 1945. Given the overwhelming US air superiority at this stage of the war, their surrender almost certainly saved their lives.*

a sudden McCain grabbed Halsey by the arm, and he did a little dance step. I couldn't hear what they were saying, but they're grinning like a couple of kids just out of school. McCain died four days later of a heart attack. Anyway, at 8:00 the ship's band plays the 'Star Spangled Banner,' and they run up the flag that flew over the capitol in Washington on December 7, 1941. Then about 8:05 Nimitz arrived in his barge and came up the stairway along the side and comes aboard. Then the foreign delegations come, and they're all in full uniform, except the British. The others are in full uniform with decorations and everything. Anyway, Nimitz comes on and then the foreign delegations. Then—I don't know—about 8:30 or 8:45 MacArthur arrives. He was on the *Buchanan*. He comes up the stairway with his staff, including General [Richard K.] Sutherland, his chief of staff. Nimitz and Halsey greet him at the head of the stairway. At 8:59 a.m. MacArthur reappears followed by Nimitz, Halsey, and Sutherland. MacArthur steps to a small nest of microphones near the table. It is hooked up to the Missouri's loudspeaker system and to a worldwide radio network. His face is grim. His voice deep and intense. His hands

Above: *An astonishing pile of Japanese swords are melted down, impotent symbols of defeat.*
Left: *In the defining culmination of his wartime career, General Douglas MacArthur countersigns the Japanese surrender documents.*

tremble visibly as he reads a brief statement.
He tells the Japanese that he will discharge his responsibilities as Supreme Commander in charge of the occupation of Japan with justice and tolerance, but will ensure that the terms of the surrender are fully, promptly, and faithfully complied with. 'It is my earnest hope,' he says, 'and indeed the hope of all mankind, that from this solemn occasion a better world shall emerge out of the blood and the carnage of the past. A world dedicated to the dignity of man and the fulfillment of his most cherished wish for freedom, tolerance, and justice.' MacArthur invites the Japanese to sign the documents, two large, bound books, both in English. [Foreign Minister Mamoru] Shigemitsu limps forward, removing his top hat as he seats himself with some difficulty, and begins the distasteful job of signing away his country's sovereignty."

PART 3
R&R and the Home Front

Rest and Recuperation

"I was sent home on thirty-days leave. By this time I had been overseas two-and-a-half years. I had a twenty-six-month-old son I had never seen, and I was anxious to get home. My home was in Texas, and my wife and little boy were down in Austin. While I was home on leave—we traveled around Texas seeing family and friends."

—US Marine Gordon Gayle

All military personnel on active service need if not frequent, at least predictable and regular periods of rest and recuperation (R&R) to retain efficiency and morale. In the Pacific during World War II, that situation was complicated by one factor above all others—the sheer scale of the theater. Covering 46 percent of the earth's surface, the Pacific Ocean has a total area of 63.8 million square miles (165.25 million square kilometers). Once deployed into its depths, a soldier or sailor in the Pacific would find that opportunities for distant leave, especially home leave, could be restricted. Some might not see home for two or three years.

The most common form of R&R was a two- or three-day pass, applied on a rotation basis among the unit personnel. Opportunities for travel on such a short pass were naturally limited, so the soldier (here I use the term "soldier" as a blanket term for all service personnel) would generally divide it between relaxation on base or at a dedicated rest camp, plus hedonistic trips to any nearby town or city. On base, core activities were reading, sleeping, and gambling, the latter centered around cards and dice, but with additional innovations like racing tropical insects. Alcohol actually formed little part of the entertainment, principally because it was so scarce in the Pacific. The military gave alcohol a variable importation priority—the best services for alcohol supplies were the USAAF and the US Navy, while the Army was officially "dry"—sometimes driving up prices to unaffordable levels (a bottle of beer on a remote island, for example, could cost $3). Furthermore, local Pacific

Left: *Simple possessions became highly meaningful thousands of miles from home. Here we see the classic "Zippo" lighter, decorated with the image of a half-track armored vehicle.*

Below: *The booklet "What about girls?" was published by the Public Affairs Committee as an educational booklet designed to warn of the dangers of consorting with prostitutes.*

Right: *A bunk and chest of drawers could be home from home.*

peoples would often have little in the way of a drinking culture and bar life. In response, many more enterprising soldiers distilled their own alcohol, fermenting substances like coconut milk or tins of fruit to make unusual but potent varieties of "jungle juice."

Food was also a major preoccupation of the soldier on R&R, but again opportunities for indulgence could be scant. Rations in the Pacific were notoriously poor and monotonous. The stodgy and uninspiring "C" and "K" rations might form the bulk of the soldier's sustenance, especially if operational conditions prevented the prompt establishment of a unit field kitchen. Local products could add some variety to the menu, although the tropical heat and humidity meant that storing such foods for any period was problematic.

The service life of a soldier in the Pacific tended to alternate between periods of frenzied activity, usually anchored around a specific operation, and then several months of more sedate activity as the forces built up for the next onslaught. During the periods of relative quiet, a soldier might be given the opportunity for a more significant period of leave, of several weeks. As long as the troopship transportation was available, and depending on where the soldier was located in the Pacific, such leave

provided the soldier with a broader choice of destinations. Popular lures included Hawaii, Fiji, New Zealand, and Australia, the latter particularly desirable on account of its hard-drinking culture and the reputed beauty and open-mindedness of its female population. US Navy submariner Joseph Base was sent for a period of R&R in Fremantle, western Australia. His leave priorities would be instantly recognizable to many soldiers today, but the leave also gave a gentler way in which to experience a foreign culture:

"They put us up in a hotel in Perth, which is not that far away from Fremantle. It's a little further south. They put us up in a hotel and we could order meals off the menu. You had time to yourself to do whatever you wanted to do. We had a nice decent room. Australia wasn't quite as far along as we were, hotels and stuff. Most of the homes down there didn't have indoor plumbing, but the hotels had indoor plumbing. You didn't have your bathroom in your room like you do now. We would go down the hall but it was a nice hotel. It strikes me that it was called the Wentworth but I don't remember what street it was on. It was interesting. They [the Australians] had a few different words than we had.

"We had stopped at a beer distributor. We were going to get some beer to put up in our rooms and we were talking to him. The guy with me said that we would take a case. He asked, 'You want a whole case?' 'Yes,' He said, 'Where do you want us to deliver it to?' He said, 'Drag it out here and we will take it with us.' When they dragged it out, it was a big wooden case that was all quart bottles. There was no way that you could carry that, so we ended up just buying some bottles. We asked him where we could get some playing cards. He said, 'Go three streets up to I Street and make a right and you will see a store right there.' So we went up three streets and we were looking around and we didn't see an I Street. We were on Hays Street. I asked a policeman, 'Could you tell me where I Street is,' he said, 'You are standing on it.'

So it was a little different at first but we got used to it. All the cars down there, the cabs particularly, had the charcoal burners in the back of the car and that is what they were using for gas. They would get out and stoke that thing and take off in it. It would work okay but it was pretty hard on the engines; they carbonned up a lot. If you went up a hill you might get halfway up the hill and it wouldn't go any further and you would have to get out and stoke that engine a little bit to make it the rest of the way up the hill. But the people were very nice. There were an awful lot of women but not too many men. Most of the men were up in New Guinea fighting. It wasn't too bad that way."

Another US Navy serviceman, Melvin Bice, also appreciated the hospitality he found on leave in Australia: "Down there it was a lot like

Above: *Card games helped millions of servicemen and women while away their recreational hours. Here we see off-shift crewmen aboard the battleship USS* New Mexico *engaged in a game of poker during a lull in operations in mid 1944.*
Left: *Members of a PBY squadron set about collecting the ingredients for a nutritious tropical fruit salad, on Samarai Island, 1944.*

it was here in the United States. They had a lot of these doors that you had to push and they would rotate and you would go in. . . . Down there they treated you real good. It wasn't bad at all. We found out that; you smarten up after a while. We found that those Australian cowboys who wore those flat hats up on the side; we would go in and there would be four or five of us and we would get a pitcher of beer or whatever. I think it was 10 or 15 cents . . . . We saw all these Australian guys sitting around there together and it didn't look like they were

"I was sent home on thirty days leave. By this time I had been overseas two-and-a-half years. I had a twenty-six-month-old son I had never seen, and I was anxious to get home. My home was in Texas, and my wife and little boy were down in Austin. While I was home on leave—we traveled around Texas seeing family and friends—I got PCS [permanent change of station or transfer] orders to go to Quantico. I didn't know what I was going to do, but I suspected what I was going to do, and that's what I did. I was assigned to teach in the schools there because the war ended eight months after I arrived at Quantico. I stayed there for about two-and-a-half years. My tour would otherwise have ended much sooner—except for the atomic bomb ending the war—because until the war ended, I was in that category which was shortly due to return overseas after just a few months stateside."

While Gayle's experience of home leave was a positive one, for many other soldiers from the Pacific such visits could bring mixed emotions. Often the leave served to underline just how much the war had changed them.

Above: *Even while on R&R, a soldier might feel more secure with an M1911 pistol on his hip.*

Right: *Nurses of the Women's Army Corps take a break outside their quarters on Saipan island. Female military personnel had to take firm management of the expectations of male soldiers.*

paying the same price that we were. So we went and asked them. They said, 'Yes, you can come and sit with us. Pitchers of beer are only 6 cents or whatever it was.' And we were paying about double. We smartened up and we sat with those guys. I'm telling you those Australian jungle fighters as they called them, those guys that wore those flat hats, they were tough hombres and they were good soldiers."

While a break in somewhere like Australia was obviously welcome, the ultimate R&R for a Pacific soldier was home leave. After participating in the horrific battle for Peleliu in 1944, Marine Gordon Gayle received some much-appreciated leave back home in Texas:

The USO in the Pacific

The great distances involved in the Pacific Theater, both from Europe and the United States and within the theater itself, meant that Pacific servicemen and women were frequently starved of quality organized entertainment. The USO attempted to prevent that.

The largest of the military entertainment bodies was the United Service Organizations (USO), founded in 1941 to bring together the efforts of six civilian groups: Salvation Army, Young Men's Christian Association (YMCA), Young Women's Christian Association (YWCA), National Catholic Community Service, National Travelers Aid Association, and the National Jewish Welfare Board. The remit of the USO was to provide both entertainment and R&R facilities for US military personnel on active service abroad. This they accomplished in abundance, establishing tens of thousands of recreational clubs and laying on dances, film

USO

Until they're home

NATIONAL WAR FUND

Above left: This poster focuses on the connection between National War Fund investments and the ability of the USO to deliver its entertainment services abroad..

Above right: The great entertainer Bob Hope, who worked for the USO across all theaters of war in which US troops were deployed.

Left: US Navy sailors check out the list of activities offered at a Fleet Recreational Center in Purvis Bay, Florida Island, near Guadalcanal in April 1944. Most of the activities are sport related.

showings, theatrical performances, comedy events, musical concerts, and other entertainments from the United States to the South Pacific.

The Pacific Theater was, by dint of its very geography, a poorer relation to the European Theater of Operations (ETO) when it came to USO activities. Yet some famous faces did grace Pacific USO stages, especially from late 1943 when the United States began to establish more forward bases. Comedian and entertainer Bob Hope was a star act, delivering his own form of comedic "island hopping" during the summer of 1944, clocking up

Above: *In this profoundly sentimentalized and staged image, a US Navy sailor waits expectantly for a slice of cake, served to him by a girl working in a USO hospitality house in Astoria, Oregon, before deployment overseas.*

more than 30,000 miles (48,279km) of traveling and performing in locations such as Eniwetok, Tarawa, Kwajalein, Saipan, and Majuro. Hope even went to perform shows in the Aleutian Islands, reminding those up there that they were not forgotten. Male comedians aside, the service community particularly appreciated visits by female performers; a glimpse of a USO performer might be the only female a US soldier in the Pacific would see for several months. More respectfully, the USO also facilitated visits by Eleanor Roosevelt, who traveled widely through the South Pacific.

Big-name performers should not distract us from the fact that the majority of the USO personnel were far more humble musicians, actors, dancers, and simple assistants, doing their best in difficult circumstances, and for tough audiences. A USO performing tour would typically last about six months, and during that time the troupe could be exposed to real dangers, especially during air transfers between isolated points of land and also from the diseases of the region, which made no discrimination between combat and entertainments personnel. The famous singer and actor Al Jolson, for example, contracted malaria while on tour of the Pacific. Such was the severity of his illness that he had to have his left lung removed surgically.

The activities of the USO continued even after the the final surrender of the Japanese in August 1945. Tens of thousands of American troops remained on occupation duties in the theater, and still needed relief from the boredom of their postings. In total, the USO established ninety-one entertainment units throughout the Pacific after VJ day. In 1947 the USO was disbanded, but came to life again in 1950 for the Korean War and remains active to this day.

Conditions Back Home

"There was a great deal of money around. The people who were working there were people who had been in the workforce in the late 1930s—for whom jobs were risky. And here were secure jobs with quite good pay. So I don't know that they had to think too much of the advantages of there being a war on—it was a great relief to have a steady income."

—Burton Stein, writing about conditions in the United States in 1943

World War II was, in many regards, the event that truly created the modern United States. To apply the label "revolutionary" to US social and economic transformations wrought by the conflict is not hyperbole. Not only did the war reshape America's entire economic structure, in many ways it laid the foundations for the subsequent postwar prosperity, and the entrepreneurial optimism that created the world's greatest superpower.

Prior to its entry into the war in December 1941, the United States was, like many other nations, still suffering from the economic black mood of the 1920s and 1930s. In 1939 unemployment ran at more than 17 percent, dropping to just under 15 percent in 1940. The percentage fell in 1941, as the American government began to increase military investment in response to the German victories in Europe and troubling developments in the Pacific, but still remained at 9.9 per cent. Although the United States was comparatively a wealthy country, for large sectors of its society that wealth was passing them by. Union dissent was common, and much of manufacturing cried out for investment.

The attack on Pearl Harbor was the infamous starting gun that transformed the United States into an industrial powerhouse of immense scale. At dizzying pace, the President, government, federal agencies, and private business had to gear themselves up as a war

A Gas Mask requires 1.11 pounds of rubber

A Life Raft requires 17 to 100 pounds of rubber

A Scout Car requires 306 pounds of rubber

A Heavy Bomber requires 1,825 pounds of rubber

America needs your SCRAP RUBBER

economy, not only for themselves but also as the major external providers of war products for the beleaguered allies in Europe. In the first months, businesses in particular seemed to experience a high degree of concern, tempered by patriotic optimism. Ted Vernasco provided one of the government-collected "Man-on-the-Street" interviews conducted in January 1942, and he expressed typical anxieties:

"I am Ted Vernasco, an employee of a rubber company in Mishawaka, Indiana. Since the outbreak of the war, our factory has been forced to curtail production on many of its products, thus causing many workers to be laid off at least until the reconstruction of national defense work is set up. However, the spirit of cooperation prevails among all the workers for we realize how important a task lies ahead.

"There is no bitter feeling between the workers and the rubber company because of the layoff, for we realize the necessity of national defense work. Cooperation between the union and the rubber company has become stronger and the union has laid aside all controversial issues in order to speed up production. Those of us who have been laid off are hoping to be called to work in some kind of defense industry and we feel sure that the government will be on hand to help us. In the meantime we're all pulling hand in hand for Uncle Sam and ultimate victory."

Vernasco's reference to curtailed production of company products was something that affected all Americans. The government prohibited production of costly consumer items such as private automobiles, houses, and even domestic appliances, channeling the skills and factories behind these products into essential war outputs. Furthermore, rationing of food and certain luxury goods placed a cap on what the American public could buy.

Yet Vernasco needn't have worried in the long term. The demand for war materiel led to a volcanic expansion in both employment and productivity, unparalleled in the history of the United States. Millions of men and women were brought into essential war industries, which grew to such a scale that unemployment fell to under 5 percent in 1942, then dropped to 1.9 percent in 1943, nearly disappearing at 1.2

Right: Bell P-39 Airacobras are being produced here, one of the dozens of aircraft types manufactured in the United States during the war. In total, 9,588 of this type went into service between 1940 and 1944.

Above left: Some 100,000 Japanese-Americans were interned in the United States for the duration of the war. Here we see internees planting cucumbers at the Tule Lake Relocation Center.

Above right: A male and female riveting team works cooperatively on the cockpit shell of a C-47 transport aircraft at the North American Aviation Inc. plant located in Inglewood, California.

percent in 1944. Some of the surge in employment was accounted for by workers moving into manufacture of "durable goods," a broad term covering everything from airplanes to munitions. In May 1940, some 4.7 million people had been employed in this sector; by December 1943 there were 10.7 million workers. Areas of the country previously deeply mired in financial depression, especially in poor southern regions, were transformed into upward-moving economic zones, often by the galvanizing presence of new factories or military bases. African Americans, immigrants, and young people also found more opportunities for skilled labor work, rather than the deadening low-paid unskilled jobs that had previously been the lot for many of them.

Productivity was transformed as much as employment. Every aspect of technology and manpower was adjusted for maximum output, particularly in the development of production-line machinery, the federal authorities and business leaders also benefiting from patriotic unions that were suddenly more receptive to change. Working hours

Above: Liberty cargo ships, on which this women is working as a scaler, were one of the great productivity success stories of the war. A total of 2,710 were produced between 1941 and 1945.

increased to an average of around forty-seven hours in 1943 (up from thirty-eight hours in 1939), and shift-working patterns meant that some critical production plants could keep their engines whirring twenty-four hours a day. In return for the hard slog, workers enjoyed significant pay increases, especially through the addition of overtime bonuses, although these increases were partially offset by a heavier wartime taxation burden.

Women were also brought into the workforce in significant numbers, to help cope with the sudden loss of manpower to the armed services, plus to fill the sheer volume of new jobs created by war industries that previously hadn't existed. The image of the hard-working woman was popularized by the "Rosie the Riveter" poster, but some myths need to be dispelled. Even before the war, there were 16 million women in employment in the United States. Specific war work swelled the numbers by 3 million, but it was still evident that a large female workforce predated the war.

Also, the majority of the women employed in the war went into administrative or non-heavy manual work (partly as an attempt by the unions to protect the jobs of men), although many women did perform long and grueling hours in munitions factories, manning cranes, or welding ship plates. One bonus the war years did provide for many women was a genuine taste of independence from the menfolk, although more than 4 million women left their jobs when the men returned at the end of the war, grateful that they no longer had to bear alone the double burden of raising a family and working full-time.

American historian Burton Stein remembers the largely positive atmosphere in the United States in 1943, as he entered the workforce as a young man: "I started working in 1943 on a swing shift at the Wisconsin Steel Works in South Chicago as a laborer. The steel mills were working three shifts. There was about a dozen of us who would just go out to the steel mills every day after school. It was mostly laboring. There was a great deal of money around. The people who

Do with less— so they'll have enough!

RATIONING GIVES YOU YOUR FAIR SHARE

Left: A US public information poster explains the virtues of rationing, and its impact on the frontline soldier. Althought rationing did not bite as hard in the USA as in Europe, there were definite restrictions.

were working there were people who had been in the workforce in the late 1930s—for whom jobs were risky. And here were secure jobs with quite good pay. So I don't know that they had to think too much of the advantages of there being a war on—it was a great relief to have a steady income. People did wonder why it was necessary to feel some security in their employment only because there was a war on. And it was all war work. It brought women into the work force. At the steel mills, less so, because steel workers, open-hearth men, and crane operators, were exempted. [There were many specific vocations, either technical or heavy manual, that might exempt a man from military service.] But at the gear factory the women ran a great many of the machines. For women it was terrific being able to work—the enormous liberation from being at home, for not just young women, but middle-aged women who found this an extraodinarily exciting time, a time when they were really sort of important and independent, and loving it."

Some dry statistics illustrate the immensity of the US economic transformation. In 1940 the United States produced 331 tanks and self-propelled (SP) guns; 32,064 military trucks (figure includes production from 1939); 12,804 military aircraft, no aircraft carriers, and 528,697 gross tons of merchant shipping. Jump forward a few years and the contrast is marked. In 1943 the total output of these war products was 29,497 tanks and SP guns; 621,902 trucks; 85,898 military aircraft (the peak year was 1944, at 96,318 units); sixty-five aircraft carriers; and 11,448,360 gross tons of merchant ships. Out of a total of 497 million metric tons of crude steel made by all the Allies during the war, the United States account for 334.5 million metric tons.

Of course, the United States also benefited from the fact that the physical destruction of the war was largely a long way from hearth and home, unlike Europe. The American people did experience hardship, loss, separation, and many of the other anxieties of war, but it emerged from the conflict far stronger than it entered it.

Left: A line of citizens snakes out from a shop, in the hope of acquiring some rationed sugar. Sugar rationing was introduced in the United States on April 27, 1942, and affected both consumers and producers of confectionary.

Glossary

.45 Refers to the .45-cal. ACP cartridge, often used as a shorthand for the Colt M1911 pistol

.50 Refers to the .50-cal. Browning Machine Gun (BMG) round used in the Browning M2 machine gun

AA Antiaircraft (fire); also known as AAA, or antiaircraft artillery

ABDA/ABDACOM An abbreviation of American-British-Dutch-Australian Command, a command structure for all Allied forces in the Pacific in 1942.

Amtrac A popular name for the Landing Vehicle Tracked (LVT).

banzai A "banzai charge" referred to an suicidal frontal assault by Japanese troops, usually accompanied by shouts of "banzai" (lit. "10,000 years").

BAR Browning Automatic Rifle, a light 20-round automatic support machine gun

Betty The Allied reporting name for the twin-engine Mitsubishi G4M bomber.

C ration The Field Ration, Type C, consisting of canned and pre-packaged rations.

CAS Close Air Support; ground-attack missions delivered by aircraft in support of land forces objectives.

CBI China-Burma-India Theater

Corpsman An enlisted medical specialist in the US Navy, who can also work within the US Marine Corps

dive-bomber An aircraft that delivers a precision bombing attack via a near-vertical dive.

ETO European Theater of Operations

Garand The M1 Garand rifle, the standard semi-automatic rifle of the US armed forces in World War II.

Higgins Boat The familiar name for the Landing Craft, Vehicle, Personnel (LCVP).

Howitzer A relatively short-barreled artillery piece firing projectiles on high, arcing trajectories.

IJA Imperial Japanese Army

IJN Imperial Japanese Navy

Incendiaries Bombs designed to ignite fires rather than cause damage through explosive power.

JCS Joint Chiefs of Staff

K ration An individual daily combat ration introduced into the US armed forces during World War II

Kamikaze Refers to the suicide aircraft attacks in the Pacific against Allied shipping. The word literally means "divine wind."

Kate The Allied reporting name for the Nakajima B5N torpedo bomber

LCVP Landing Craft, Vehicle, Personnel, a troop-landing craft used in amphibious assaults.

Lend-Lease The provision of military materiel by the United States to the Allies during World War II.

Long Lance The nickname given to the highly effective Type 93 Japanese torpedo.

LSD Landing Ship, Dock; an amphibious vessel used to transport other landing craft.

LSO Landing Signal Officer; an aircraft carrier crew member trained in guiding aircraft down to landing.

LST Landing Ship, Tank; an amphibious vessel used to transport vehicles, cargo, or troops.

LVT Landing Vehicle, Tracked; a tracked amphibious assault vehicle, also known as the "Amtrac."

Mae West An affectionate name for a life preserver jacket, as worn by sailors and naval airmen

MG A common abbreviation for a machine gun.

MTO Mediterranean Theater of Operations

NCB Naval Construction Battalion; the personnel of these battalions were also known as the "Seabees."

Nick The Allied reporting name for the Kawasaki Ki-45 Toryu, twin-engine fighter.

OWI Office of War Information

PBY Common shorthand for the Consolidated PBY Catalina flying boat.

PTO Pacific Theater of Operations

RAF Royal Air Force

RAAF Royal Australian Air Force

RAP Regimental Aid Post

SBD A typical shorthand for the Douglas SBD Dauntless dive-bomber

Semi-automatic Denotes a firearm that fires a single round with each pull of the trigger, and automatically reloads between shots.

SIGINT Signals Intelligence; intelligence derived from intercepting the enemy's electronic communications.

TF Task Force; a major Allied naval unit, created for a specific operation.

torpedo bomber An aircraft designed to attack enemy shipping via air-launched torpedoes.

Tracer A bullet featuring a pyotechnic compound that shows the bullet's trajectory.

USAAC US Army Air Corps

USAAF US Army Air Forces

USMC US Marine Corps

Zeke Allied reporting name for the Mitsubishi A6M "Zero"

Further Reading

The majority of the first-person accounts are taken from the digital archives of the National Museum of the Pacific War. Other key sources of first-person accounts are included below:

BBC, WW2 People's History:

– Baynes, Len (Snowie), "Soldier's View of the Fall of Singapore 1941–2": http://www.bbc.co.uk/history/ww2peopleswar/stories/88/a2110988shtml

– Curtis, Stan, "The Sinking of HMS Hermes": http://www.bbc.co.uk/history/ww2peopleswar/stories/26/a4667826.shtml

– Reid, Neil Millar, "POW in Nagasaki": http://www.bbc.co.uk/history/ww2peopleswar/stories/73/a2715473.shtml

– Ward, R.V. (Commander), "The Sinking of HMS Prince of Wales and HMS Repulse": http://www.bbc.co.uk/history/ww2peopleswar/stories/79/a4217979.shtml

– Weedman, Sergeant Frederick J., "Kohima – The Battle of Naga Village and Church Knoll": http://www.bbc.co.uk/history/ww2peopleswar/stories/98/a5034098.shtml; also at www.worcestershireregiment.com

Costello, John, *The Pacific War* (New York, William Morrow, 1982)

Dear, I.C.B. (ed.), *The Oxford Companion to the Second World War* (Oxford: Oxford University Press, 1995)

Department of Veterans' Affairs (Australia): Eric Williams and Paul Cullen, Kokoda Veterans Video Interviews:

– http://kokoda.commemoration.gov.au/australian-veterans-accounts/veterans-accounts_eric-williams.php and:

– http://kokoda.commemoration.gov.au/australian-veterans-accounts/veterans-accounts_paul-cullen.php

Ellis, John, *The Sharp End: The Fighting Man in World War II* (London, Aurum, 1980)

Garrett, J.R., *A Marine Diary: My Experiences on Guadalcanal*: http://www.nettally.com/jrube/

Groves. General Leslie R., "General Leslie Groves's Interview–Part 1."

By Stephane Groueff. Atomic Heritage Foundation's "Voices of the Manhattan Project." January 5, 1965: http://manhattanprojectvoices.org/oral-histories/general-leslie-grovess-interview-part-1

Hammel, Eric, *War in the Western Pacific: The US Marines in the Marianas, Peleliu, Iwo Jima, and Okinawa, 1944–45* (Minneapolis, MN: Zenith Press, 2014)

Hastings, Max, *Nemesis: The Battle for Japan, 1944–45* (London: HarperCollins, 2007

Hiroyuki, Agawa, *The Reluctant Admiral: Yamamoto and the Imperial Navy* (Annapolis, MD: Naval Institute Press, 1979)

Lorelli, John, To Foreign Shores: U.S.Amphibious Operations in World War II (Annapolis, MD: Naval Institute Press, 1994)

McNeely, Gina, and Jon Guttman, *War in the Pacific* (London, Elephant, 2011)

Nalty, Bernard C. (ed.) *The Pacific War: The Story of the Bitted Struggle in the Pacific Theatre of World War II* (London: Salamander, 1999)

O'Neill, Robert, *The Pacific War: From Pearl Harbor to Okinawa* (Oxford: Osprey Publishing, 2015)

Prange, Gordon W., *At Dawn We Slept: The Untold Story of Pearl Harbor* (London: Penguin, 1991)

Rottman, Gordon, World War II Pacific Island Guide: A Geo-Military Study (Westport, CT: Greenwood, 2001)

Stille, Mark, *The Imperial Japanese Navy in the Pacific War* (Oxford: Osprey Publishing, 2014)

Toll, Ian W., *Pacific Crucible: War at Sea in the Pacific, 1941–42* (New York: W.W. Norton, 2012)

n.a. *The War Years 1939–45: Eyewitness Accounts* (London: Marshall Cavendish, 1994)

Winton, John, The Forgotten Fleet: The Story of the British Pacific Fleet, 1944-45 (Wadhurst: M.Joseph, 1970)

Wright, M.A., *The World at Arms* (London: Reader's Digest, 1989)

Picture Credits and Acknowledgments

Memorabilia photographs, unless indicated below, were taken at the National Museum of the Pacific War by Patrick Bunce or from the author's archives, and remain the copyright of Elephant Books

Page number and position are indicated as follows: L = left; TL = top left; TR = top right; C = center; CL = center left; B = bottom; BL = bottom left

AirSeaLand Photos Ltd: 23: TR, BL; 26: C; 27: TL; 32: BL; 33: TL, BR; 34: TL; 35 TL; 38: all; 40: all; 41: all; 42: all; 43 TL; 44: CL, CR; 45: TL, CR; 48: all; 49: all; 50: all; 51: TL, CR; 52: B; 53: all; 54: all; 55: BL; 58: all; 59: C, BR; 60: all; 61: TL, TR; 62: all; 63: TL; 66: TR; 67: BL; 68: BL, TR; 69: L; 70; 72: BL; 75: C, CR; 76: all; 77: CL, CR; 78: all; 79: all; 80: T; 81: BL; 84: all; 85: TL, TR; 86: all; 87: C, CR; 88: CR, BR; 90: all; 91: all; 92: all; 93: all; 94: all; 95: L, BR; 96: TR, BL, BR; 97: all; 98: all; 99: TL; 100: BL, TR; 101: BL, TR; 102: BL CR; 104: TC; 105: CL; 106: all; 107: TL, TR; 108–09: all; 110: TR, BR; 111: BL, BR; 114–15: all; 116: all; 117: BR; 120–21: all; 122: BL, BR; 123: TL, CR; 124–25: all; 126: all; 127: TL, BR; 128: all; 129: CTC, TR, BR; 130: CR; 132–33: all; 134: TL; 135: TC; 138: BL, BR; 139: TL, BR; 140: TC, BR; 141: TL, CR, BL; 142: BL, BR; 143: TR, CR, BL, BR; 144: all; 145: CL, CR; 146: BL; 147: all; 148–49: all; 151: TL; 152: CL, CR; 153: TR, CR; 154: all; 155: CL, CR; 158–59: all; 160: CL, CR; 161: all; 162; 163: CR, B; 164–65: all; 166: TL, CR; 167: R; 168: all; 170: CL, CR; 171: all; 172: all; 173: TL, TR; 174: all; 175: BL, BR; 178–79: all; 180: CR; 182: all; 183: BL, CR; 184: BL, BR; 185: all; 186: all; 187: TL, BL; 188–89: all

Anagoria CC licence: 187: BR

Corbis: 10: BL; 17: CR; 29: TL; 88: CL; 196: TR

Daderot CC0 1.0: 46: BL

Getty: 9: B; 131: B; 143: TL; 197

Government of Japan: 14: C; 16: TC; 19: C, BR; 22: BL; 32: BR; 56: TR; 57: all

Jeff Ethell Collection: 195: B

Library of Congress: 18: TR, TC; 46: CR; 46: CR; 131: TL; 199: all; 200

NARA: 15: TR, B; 17: CR; 20 C; 146–47; 30–31; 35: BL; 36: BL, TR; 37: all; 39: TL, BR; 67;71: TL, CL; 74: all; 75: T; 82; 89: TL; 89: BR; 104: B; 105: CR; 112; 119: BR; 136; 151: BR; 152: TR; 156; 169; 190–91; 192: BR; 193; 194: all; 196: BL; 201: BL

Naval History and Heritage Command CC-BY-2.0: 150: TC

pow.larkin.net: 46: TC; 47: TL

Stan Piet: 63: BR; 176; 180: BL, BR

The Picture Desk: 12–13

UK government (Crown Copyright expired): 17: TL; 43: BR; 150: BL, CR

US Government: 15: TL; 21: TL; 24: BL, TR; 25: B; 27: CR; 55: TR; 63: C; 146: BR

USMC Archives: 47: BL; 103: TL

US Navy: 61: BR; 64; 66: BR; 72: BR; 80: B; 110: BL; 118: TR; 130: BL; 134: BR; 181: BR

NATIONAL MUSEUM OF THE PACIFIC WAR

Home of Admiral Nimitz Museum | Fredericksburg, Texas

National Museum of the Pacific War

The National Museum of the Pacific War, located in Fredericksburg, Texas, is dedicated to telling the complete story of World War II in the Pacific Theater. Within the 6-acre museum complex, feature areas include the George H.W. Bush Gallery, Admiral Nimitz Museum, the Plaza of the Presidents, Japanese Garden of Peace, Memorial Courtyard, and the Pacific Combat Zone. Contact details for the museum are:

The National Museum of The Pacific War
340 East Main Street
Fredericksburg, Texas 78624
United States

Tel: +1 830-997-8600
Website: http://www.pacificwarmuseum.org